CNN互动英语系列

STEP BY STEP 听懂

CNN Learning English With Celebrities

全球巨星专访

LiveABC 编著

科学出版社

北京

图字：01-2012-8846

本书原名《CNN 全球巨星专访——名人教你说英语》，原出版者 LiveABC
Interactive Corporation，经授权由科学出版社在中国大陆地区独家出版发行。

图书在版编目（CIP）数据

Step by Step 听懂 CNN 全球巨星专访/LiveABC 编著.—北京：科学出版社，
2013.1
　（CNN互动英语系列）
　ISBN 978-7-03-036285-8

I.①S⋯　Ⅱ.①L⋯　Ⅲ.①英语—听说教学—自学参考资料　Ⅳ.①H319.9

中国版本图书馆CIP数据核字（2012）第305405号

责任编辑：张　培 / 责任校对：李　影
责任印制：赵德静 / 封面设计：无极书装
联系电话：010-6401 9074 / 电子邮箱：zhangpei@mail. sciencep. com

科 学 出 版 社 出版
北京东黄城根北街16号
邮政编码：100717
http://www.sciencep.com
北京佳信达欣艺术印刷有限公司 印刷
科学出版社发行　各地新华书店经销
＊
2013年1月第 一 版　开本：B5 (720×1000)
2013年1月第一次印刷　印张：17
字数：480 000
定价：68.00元

（含DVD互动光盘1张）
（如有印装质量问题，我社负责调换）

当红名人教你说英语！

当全耳边响起艾薇儿《展翅高飞》的歌声的时候，您是否也想进一步了解这个摇滚精灵的魅力？但是否一旦看到艾薇儿的个人专访视频，却发现自己听不懂她说些什么？

想要不通过翻译，就能在访谈中获得第一手的信息，英语绝对是您不可或缺的能力。而通过当红名人的专访视频来学习，想必能够激发您学好英语的兴趣！本书精选 29 篇 CNN 名人访谈，按照受访对象的专业领域分为四大类："影视娱乐"、"时尚生活"、"政治财经"、"体坛文艺"。多元化的选材使您不但能了解自己感兴趣的名人，也能多方接触各领域的焦点人物，拓展视野并吸收新知识。

通过自己感兴趣的事物来学习英语，是最没有压力的学习方式！跟着本书所收录的专访报道——流行乐界的当红明星（Lady Gaga、艾薇儿等）、时尚界的领军人物（彩妆女王、新锐设计师吴季刚）、政坛的焦点人物（美国第一夫人米歇尔·奥巴马）、耀眼的体坛明星（中国篮球明星姚明）、古典乐界的天才奇葩（郎朗）等人都会助您一臂之力，让您通过轻松有趣的对话，学好英语。

或许很多读者在收看英文新闻报道时，曾有过"听了却没懂"的经历。主要原因多半是因为主播、记者或受访对象说话的速度太快，或您认识的英文单词、短语或惯用语太少，导致您无法理解访谈的重点。

本书的专访报道采用中英文对照体例，除了列出单词与重要短语的解析，还适时补充了近义词并比较易混淆的用法，同时针对受访对象与主题内容补充各种相关信息。随书附赠互动光盘，运用多媒体科技，将文字（text）、影像（image）、声音（sound）结合在一起，如此一来将能够加深读者的学习印象，进而提高学习效率。针对苦于跟不上英语一般语速的读者，互动光盘中除了有正常速度的原音报道 MP3 之外，还附有慢速的朗读 MP3。慢速语音由专业外籍人士所录制，提供清晰的发音，方便让您循序渐进，由慢至快理解访谈内容。

中文标题

正常及慢速 MP3

新闻标题

新闻副标题

短语、惯用语及
重要词汇补充

课文单词

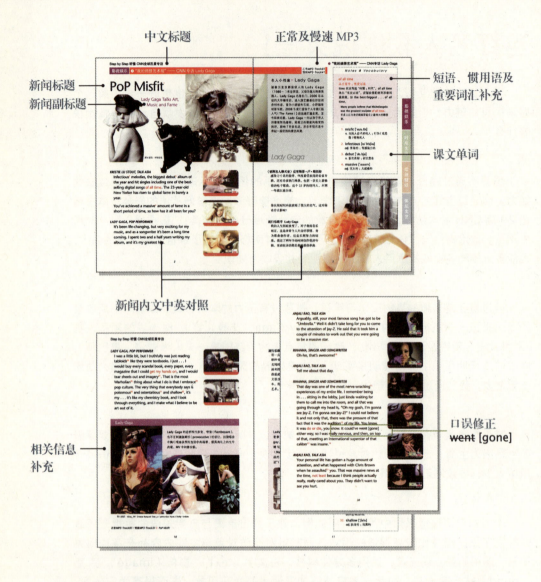

新闻内文中英对照

口误修正
went [gone]

相关信息
补充

跟随当红名人学英语，在兴趣中吸收最常用的词汇、短语用法及口语表达，锻炼
听力，培养语感，这就是精通英文的最佳途径！

光盘使用方法

系统需求建议

[硬件]

* 处理器 Pentium 4 以上（或同等 AMD、Celeron 处理器）

* 512 MB 内存

* 全彩显卡 800×600 dpi（16K 色以上）

* 硬盘需求空间 200 MB

* 16 倍速以上 DVD 光驱

* 声卡、扬声器及麦克风（内置或外接）

[软件]

* Microsoft Windows XP 、Vista 、Windows 7 简体中文版系统

* Microsoft Windows Media Player 9

* Adobe Flash Player 10

请注意！

出于对版权的保护，本光盘只能在电脑上带盘运行，将光盘内容复制到电脑硬盘上再进行安装则无法运行，请读者予以谅解。

如果您的电脑装有 360 软件，请在安装光盘之前先关闭**所有**与 360 相关的软件，包括 360 杀毒软件、360 安全卫士、360 浏览器等。

在 Vista 系统中，如果安装互动光盘时遇到以下问题：

1. 出现【安装字体错误】的信息。

2. 出现【无法安装语音识别】的信息。

请依照下列步骤操作：

1. 卸载本产品。

2. 进入控制面板。

3. 点击"用户账户"选项。

4. 点击"开启或关闭用户账户控制"。

5. 将"使用（用户账户控制）UAC 来协助保护您的电脑"选项取消勾选。

6. 再次运行安装光盘。

在 Windows 7 系统中，安装互动光盘若遇上述问题请按以下步骤操作：

1. 进入控制面板，开启程序栏，进入程序和功能，卸载本产品。

2. 进入控制面板，点击"用户账户和家庭安全"选项。

3. 再点击"用户账户"。

4. 点击"更改用户账户控制设置"。

5. 将滑动条拖至最底端（"从不通知"的位置）。

6. 按确定后，需重新启动电脑。

7. 再次运行安装光盘。

光盘安装程序

步骤一：进入中文操作系统。

步骤二：将光盘放进光驱。

步骤三：本产品带有 Auto Run 运行功能，如果您的电脑支持 Auto Run 光盘程序自动播放功能，则将自动出现【Step by Step 听懂 CNN 全球巨星专访】的安装画面。

主画面

说明：

1. 如果您的电脑已安装过本系列任一产品，您可以直接点击"快速安装"图标，进行快速安装；否则，请点击"安装"图标，进行完整安装。

2. 如果您的电脑无法支持 Auto Run 光盘程序自动播放功能，请打开 Windows "我的电脑"，点击光驱，并运行光盘根目录下的 autorun.exe 程序。

3. 如果运行 autorun.exe 仍然无法安装本光碟，请进入本光盘的 setup 文件夹，并运行 setup.exe 程序，即可进行安装。

4. 如果您要删除【Step by Step 听懂 CNN 全球巨星专访】，请点击"开始"，选择"设置"，选择"控制面板"，选择"添加／删除程序"，并在菜单中点击"Step by Step 听懂 CNN 全球巨星专访"，并运行"更改／删除"即可。

5. 当语音识别系统或录音功能无法使用时，请检查声卡驱动程序是否正常，并确认硬盘空间是否足够且 Windows 录音程序可以使用。

说明：

1. 主画面右下角共有六个图标，分别为：影视娱乐、时尚生活、政治财经、体坛文艺、听力测验、索引。画面左下角另有说明、科学出版社网站及退出三个图标。

2. 点击四大类主题中任一类别，将在屏幕中列出该类课程内容，点击后可进入该则新闻的影片学习画面。

课程学习画面

影片学习

操作说明

点击"运行"，即进入本光盘的学习内容。按顺序说明如下：

说明：
在主画面中点击任一单元，即进入本学习画面。

工具栏说明：

1. 画面右侧由上至下依次为：自动播放、播放／暂停、停止、播下一句、播上一句、反复播放本句、全屏幕播放、设置。

2. 点击"设置"图标，即可设置"反复朗读"的播放次数及间隔的秒数；若您想恢复为一直播放的模式，只要将次数调回 0 即可。

3. 画面左侧由上至下依次为：目录、上一篇、下一篇、单词解释、文字学习、主画面、退出。

4. 画面下方的英文及中文字幕，通过选取字幕前的图标，可选择出现或隐藏字幕，以便做听力练习。

5. 字幕下方有一个影片播放点控制栏，可决定影片播放的起点。

文字学习

说明：

1. 在影片学习中，点击"文字学习"图标，即进入本画面。

2. 在画面的右上方有一个影片视窗，在播放

原声的同时，您可以在此视窗看到该段声音的影片。

工具栏说明：

听力练习

点击"听力练习"图标，屏幕中的学习内容将会消失，读者只能通过右上角的影片画面进行听力练习。

全文朗读

点击"全文朗读"图标，电脑将自动朗读本段新闻的内容。

角色扮演

点击"角色扮演"图标，则会在图标左侧列出该段新闻的角色人名。此时，您可选择想扮演的角色，程序将关闭该角色的声音，由您和电脑进行对话练习。如果您的发音不正确，则会出现一个窗口，您可以选择"再读一次"、"略过"或"读给我听"来完成或略过该对话；也可以调整语音识别的灵敏度。若您的发音正确，则对话会一直进行下去。

快慢朗读

当您觉得对话速度太快时，可以点击"快慢朗读"图标，再点击"全文朗读"图标或任一句子，朗读速度将变慢，让您听得更清楚。慢速朗读时，为了让您更容易学习，我们将一句话断成几小段，逐段录音。若您觉得速度太慢，想恢复为一般速度时，只要再次点击"快慢朗读"图标，即可恢复成一般速度。

反复朗读

点击"反复朗读"图标后，再选取任一句子，电脑将反复播放该句。您可以点击"设置"自行设置"反复朗读"的播放次数，若您想恢复为一直播放的模式，只要将次数调回 0 即可。

中文翻译

点击"中文翻译"图标后，画面下方将出现中文翻译框，您可在中文翻译框内看到本段新闻内容时，听到对应的英文句子；同样，点

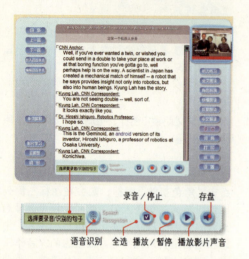

击文中的任一句子，也会朗读该句英文，并显示其中文翻译。

录音

1. 点击"录音"图标后，开启录音功能控制栏。

2. 按键功能由左至右为：全选、录音／停止、播放／暂停、播放影片声音以及存盘。按左方的"全选"图标，会出现全部句子录音；若您只想选择某段内文，只要在该段前方的方框（□）点击一下即可。若您点击右边的"播放影片声音"图标，则在您进行录音或播放录音前，都将会播放该段影片原声。

3. 录音步骤如下：

   (1) 先点击您要进行录音的句子，并选择是否要在录音前播放原声。

   (2) 点击"录音"键。

   (3) 请在电脑"播放原声"后，对着麦克风读出您所选取的句子。

   (4) 当您完成该句录音后，请按键盘上的"空

格键"（space bar），结束录音。

   (5) 点击"播放"键，即可听到您所录的声音。

4. 点击左边的"Speech Recognition"图标，将启动"语音识别"功能，请依照以下步骤进行语音识别：

   (1) 先选择要进行语音识别的句子，并选择是否要在语音识别前播放原声。

   (2) 点击"Speech Recognition"图标。

   (3) 当画面出现"请录音"时，您必须对麦克风读出您所选取的句子，如果您的发音正确，则将继续进行下一句；如果发音不正确，则会出现一窗口，您可选择"再读一次"、"略过"或"读给我听"来完成或略过该对话；也可在此调整语音识别的灵敏度。

5. 若您要在中途结束录音或语音识别，请在任意处点击一下即可。

词典

当您点击"词典"图标后，在画面下方将出现词典框，此时点击文中的任意一个单词，词典框内会出现该单词的音标及中文翻译，并读出该词发音。

打印

当您点击"打印"图标后，在画面下方将出现打印控制键。您可选择"全部打印"或"部分打印"；打印内容可选择是否包括中文翻译。

说明

当您点击"说明"图标后，将开启辅助说明页。您可借此了解本光盘内容的各项操作说明及用法。

学习重点

当您在点击文中蓝色文字的学习重点，画面下方会出现说明框，并配有发音；若在开启"中文翻译"功能时点击，则朗读您点击的句子。

段落朗读

当您点击文中的人名时，程序将自动朗读此人该段会话。若您是处于"慢速朗读"模式，则播放该段话时，声音及反白文字将以小段方式出现。

加入及编辑自选单词

点击"加入自选单词"图标后，可以点击您要记录的单词。在此，您可以进行单词学习，也可以删除或打印任意一个单词。

单词解释

列出本课的重点单词（词性、音标、中文解释），点击该单词会发音。

听力测验画面说明

1. 点击"听力测验"后，可看到"听力填空"及"听力理解"两类测验题型。

2. 在"听力填空"中，请点击影片右下方的"Play"图标，你会看到一段 CNN 报道，段落中有几处空格，请在空格处填入你听到的词。

3. 在"听力理解"中，请点击影片右下方的"Play"图标播放影片并作答，完成该题后，点击"下一题"图标进行下一题，完成该测验题型后，可继续进行其他测验，或点击"退出"退出测验界面。

题型界面如下

(1) 听力填空：

(2) 听力理解：

索引

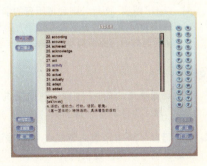

说明：

1. 在主画面点击"索引"图标，进入索引画面，内含单词检索及学习重点索引。

2. 单词检索：

   (1) 在此将所有的单词依字母分类，点击单词会出现该单词的音标、中文翻译及发音。

   (2) 连续点击单词两次或选取某一单词后点击"显示例句"图标，即会显现该单词的课文例句。

   (3) 连续点击例句两次或选取任一例句后点击"连接课文"图标，即跳至该例句的"文字学习"画面。

   (4) 点击"自选单词"图标，即可在此看到您在学习过程中加入的自选单词。

   (5) 点击"朗读"图标，则会将所选字母开头的单词从头到尾读一次；点击"打印"图标，则将以该字母开头的所有单词打印出来。

   (6) 点击任一单词后，再点击"打印"图标，则可打印该单词的内容。

3. 学习重点：

   (1) 在此列出本光盘内容的学习重点。用鼠标点击任一学习重点，会自动朗读。

   (2) 连续点击两次或选取任一学习重点后点击"连接课文"图标，即跳至该学习重点的"文字学习"画面。

   (3) 点击"返回"图标，则回到单词检索画面。

   (4) 点击"朗读"图标，则会将所有的学习重点从头到尾读一次；点击"打印"图标，则将所有的学习重点打印出来。

说明

1. 在主画面点击"说明"图标，在此提供"操作说明"及"语音识别设置说明"。

2. 您可借此了解本光盘内容的各项操作说明、用法及语音识别设置说明。

网站

点击"网站"图标，将连接至科学出版社官方网站。

原文朗读 MP3

互动光盘中含有新闻原声及慢速朗读 MP3 内容，您可以放在 MP3 播放器中收听，也可以将光盘放在电脑中，从"我的电脑"中点击您的光驱，再从中选择光盘文件里的 MP3 的文件夹，使用播放软件将文件打开收听 MP3 的内容。

目　录

前言　　　　　　　　　　　　　　　　　　　　　　　　　*i*

光盘使用方法　　　　　　　　　　　　　　　　　　　　*iii*

影视娱乐 Entertainment　　　　　　　　　　　　　　1

1 Pop Misfit

Lady Gaga Talks Art, Music and Fame

"我的搞怪艺术观" ——CNN 专访 Lady Gaga　　　　　　**2**

2 Skater Girl Grows Up

Avril Lavigne Discusses Music, Fashion and Charity Work with Talk Asia

CNN 专访摇滚朋克精灵艾薇儿　　　　　　　　　　　**12**

3 Sting Sings in the Holidays

Veteran Musician Celebrates the Winter Season

摇滚诗人斯汀的冬季狂想曲　　　　　　　　　　　　**18**

4 Diana Krall's Brazilian Odyssey

The Jazz Musician Takes a Tropical Turn on Her Latest Recording

CNN 专访新生代爵士天后戴安娜·克瑞儿　　　　　　**24**

5 Unusual Suspect

Talk Asia Interviews Acclaimed Stage and Screen Actor Kevin Spacey

"电影与我" ——CNN 专访凯文·斯贝西　　　　　　　**30**

6 Robert Redford Talks Tech

Legendary Actor and Director Discusses the Intersection of
Art and Technology

现代科技与电影艺术的对话——CNN 专访罗伯特·雷德福　　**38**

7 Celluloid Prophet

Talk Asia Looks through the Lens of Filmmaker Oliver Stone

大导演奥利佛·斯通镜头下的世界观　　　　　　　　**44**

8 Vintage Coppola

Fine Wine and Iconic Films Flow through Legendary Director's Career

大导演的另一片天——CNN 专访弗朗西斯·科波拉　　**56**

9 A Man of Action
A Talk Asia Exclusive Interview with Influential Hong Kong Director John Woo
CNN 专访吴宇森——华人导演的好莱坞经验 　　　　64

10 Taking Hollywood by Storm
Talk Asia Interview with South Korean Actor Lee Byung-hun
成名的滋味——CNN 专访李秉宪 　　　　72

11 Chasing a Dream
Talk Asia Exclusive Interview with Korean Film Star Jang Dong-Gun
CNN 专访韩国个性巨星张东健 　　　　84

12 Butt-Kicking Beauty
A Talk Asia Exclusive Interview with Action Star Michelle Yeoh
智慧、美丽与身手——CNN 专访华人邦德女郎杨紫琼 　　　　92

13 Zhou Xun
Talk Asia Interview with the Quirky Queen of Chinese Cinema
CNN 专访中国最具影响力的女演员周迅 　　　　100

14 Transplanted Talent
Talk Asia Sits Down with Actor-Director Daniel Wu
无心插柳的星路奇缘——CNN 专访吴彦祖 　　　　108

15 Ballad of John and Yoko
Rock Legend's Widow Remembers Lennon on His 70th Birthday
约翰·列侬与我——CNN 专访小野洋子 　　　　118

时尚生活 Fashion & Life 　　　　133

16 A Partnership in Fashion
Love and Business Intertwine for Style Icons Dolce and Gabbana
永远的时尚伙伴——CNN 专访 D&G 创始人 　　　　134

17 Putting Your Best Face Forward
Behind the Scenes with Makeup Artist Bobbi Brown
从彩妆师到彩妆王国——CNN 专访波比·布朗 　　　　142

18 Dressing for Success
Fashion Upstart Jason Wu's Star Continues to Rise
台湾设计师吴季刚——打造自己的时尚舞台   150

19 Wok on the Wild Side
Talk Asia Goes into the Kitchen with Celebrity Chef Bobby Chinn
创造另类的美食风格——CNN 专访名人主厨鲍比·秦   158

20 Architect for the Ages
Norman Foster Looks to the Past, Present and Future of Building Design
当代建筑大师诺曼·福斯特谈本于人性的建筑观   166

政治财经 Politics & Finance   173

21 When Michelle Met Barack
First Lady Describes Her Initial Impressions of the Future U.S. President
第一夫人眼中的奥巴马   174

22 The World Is Flat . . . so What Next?
Talk Asia Interview with Thomas Friedman
为什么世界是"平"的？——CNN 专访作者托马斯·弗里德曼   182

体坛文艺 Athletics & Art   193

23 Going the Distance
Ultra-marathoner Scott Jurek Pushes Mind and Body to the Edge of Endurance
超越身心的极限——CNN 专访超级马拉松名将斯科特·尤雷克   194

24 King of the Mound
Talk Asia Interview with Japanese Pitching Sensation Yu Darvish
CNN 专访日本职业棒球投手——达比修有   202

25 Battered but Not Broken
Yao Ming Battles Back from Injury to Resurrect His NBA Career
CNN 专访姚明——"职业生涯终有结束的一天"   212

㉖ Courting Victory
Dreams Come True at the French Open for Chinese Champ Li Na
史上首位网球大满贯赛事中国冠军——李娜 **220**

㉗ Her Toughest Opponent
How Tennis Champ Martina Navratilova Battled and Beat Cancer
女性不可忽视的防癌常识——网球女将娜拉提诺娃细说抗癌之路 **228**

㉘ Unconventional Maestro
CNN Interview with the Remarkable Chinese Pianist Lang Lang
飞跃在琴键上的一双手——CNN 专访华裔钢琴家郎朗 **236**

㉙ Piano Prodigy
Young Virtuoso Marc Yu Wrestles with "Little Mozart" Label and
Promising Future
CNN 专访钢琴神童"小莫扎特"余峻承 **248**

附录：美式英语与英式英语和澳大利亚英语的发音区别 *252*

影视娱乐
Entertainment

PoP Misfit[1]

Lady Gaga Talks Art, Music and Fame

图片提供：环球音乐

KRISTIE LU STOUT, TALK ASIA

Infectious[2] melodies, the biggest debut[3] album of the year and hit singles including one of the best-selling digital songs of all time. The 23-year-old New Yorker has risen to global fame in barely a year.

You've achieved a massive[4] amount of fame in a short period of time, so how has it all been for you?

LADY GAGA, POP PERFORMER

It's been life-changing, but very exciting for my music, and as a songwriter it's been a long time coming. I spent two and a half years writing my album, and it's my greatest hits.

① "我的搞怪艺术观" —— CNN 专访 Lady Gaga

正常MP3-Track01
慢速MP3-Track31

名人小档案 ▼ Lady Gaga

被誉为麦当娜接班人的 Lady Gaga
（1986— ）来自美国，父母为意大利裔美
国人。Lady Gaga 出身名门，2006 年从
纽约大学辍学后，进入演艺圈幕后担任词
曲创作者，曾为小甜甜布兰妮、小野猫等
明星写歌。2008 年发行首张个人专辑《超
人气（The Fame）》后迅速红遍全美，至
今获奖无数。Lady Gaga 一向以异于常人
的着装特色著称，她前卫的着装风格受到
热评，影响了许多名流，并在年轻乐迷中
带起一股狂热的模仿风潮。

Lady Gaga

Notes & Vocabulary

of all time
从古至今；有史以来

time 在这里指"时期；时代"，of all time
表示"有史以来"，前面会搭配使用形容词
最高级，如 the best/biggest . . . of all
time。

Many people believe that Michelangelo
was the greatest sculptor of all time.
许多人认为米开朗基罗是史上最伟大的雕塑
家。

1. misfit ['mɪsˌfɪt]
   n. 与别人合不来的人；行为（或思
   想）怪异的人

2. infectious [ɪnˈfɛkʃəs]
   adj. 传染的；有感染力的

3. debut [ˈdeˌbju]
   n. 首次亮相；初次登台

4. massive [ˈmæsɪv]
   adj. 巨大的；大规模的

《亚洲名人聊天室》克里斯蒂·卢·斯托特
感染力十足的旋律、年度最受欢迎的首张专
辑，还有许多热门单曲，包括一首史上最畅
销的电子歌曲。这个 23 岁的纽约人，不到
一年就红遍全球。

你在短时间内就获得了很大的名气，这对你
有什么影响？

流行乐歌手 Lady Gaga
我的人生因此改变了，对于我的音乐
而言，这是非常令人兴奋的事情。身
为歌曲创作者，这是长期努力的结
果。我花了两年半的时间创作我的专
辑，里面收录的都是我的最佳单曲。

影视娱乐
时尚生活
政治财经
体坛文艺

3

KRISTIE LU STOUT, TALK ASIA

You're also a songwriter; you write your own stuff. So, how does that creative process take place?

LADY GAGA, POP PERFORMER

In all sorts of ways. Inspiration comes to me all day long, every day. Sometimes when I'm falling asleep, I have these visions[5]. But it's not just music—it's music, it's the clothing, it's the stage performance.

KRISTIE LU STOUT, TALK ASIA

Do you feel that you're more of a performance artist than a pop star?

LADY GAGA, POP PERFORMER

I certainly am a performance artist, yes.

KRISTIE LU STOUT, TALK ASIA

Yeah. And do you ever fear that what you got goin' today with your costume, your per[sona][6]—no, I shouldn't say persona, because you are Gaga—your music, the entire package[7] . . . will it be able to stay there? I'm trying to ask about the longevity[8], 'cause pop careers, sometimes they last like this (snaps fingers). How are you gonna stick around?

LADY GAGA, POP PERFORMER

How am I going to stick around? Well, the truth is that careers are either (snaps fingers), like you said, lightning fast, or they're forever, and they're historical[9]. They are made up of a select[10] group of women that changed the way that society views what a lady is supposed to be. And I just must remain prolific[11] and relevant, as equally irrelevant[12], and continue to make great music. Longevity has a

《亚洲名人聊天室》克里斯蒂·卢·斯托特
你也是歌曲创作者，你会写自己的歌。这样的创作过程是怎样开始的？

流行乐歌手 Lady Gaga
各种各样的方式都有。我在每天的任何时刻都会获得灵感。有时候，在我的睡眠中也会出现一些画面。不只是音乐，有音乐、服装，也有舞台表演。

《亚洲名人聊天室》克里斯蒂·卢·斯托特
你会不会觉得与其说你是流行歌星，不如说你更像行为艺术家？

流行乐歌手 Lady Gaga
我的确是行为艺术家，没错。

《亚洲名人聊天室》克里斯蒂·卢·斯托特
的确。你会不会担心你今天深受欢迎的服装和你所扮演的角色——不对，我不该说角色，因为你是 Lady Gaga——还有你的音乐，这整套的呈现……是不是能够持续下去？我问的是演艺寿命，因为流行音乐事业，有时候弹指之间就结束了。你要怎么继续下去？

流行乐歌手 Lady Gaga
我要怎么继续下去？事实上，每个人的事业要不是像你说的那样稍纵即逝，就是恒久持续，并在历史上占有重要地位。这部分是由一群优秀的女性组成，她们改变了社会对于女性该扮演什么角色的观点。而我就是必须不断推出大量作品，跟上时代潮流，同时又不理会时代潮流，持续创作好听的音乐。事

Notes & Vocabulary

more of A than B
与其说是 B，不如说是 A
more of A than B 是用来比较两个名词的句型，字面意思是"比较像 A 而非 B"，即表示"与其说是 B，不如说是 A"，主要目的是强调 A。

No matter what the title is, the film is more of a comedy than a horror film.
不管片名是什么，这部影片都更像是喜剧片，而非恐怖片。

stick around
留下来；逗留
stick 在此有"粘住"的意思，stick around 为不及物动词，表示"留在原地；逗留"，在本文中即比喻能存留在瞬息万变的演艺圈。

Maggie stuck around until the end of the party.
麦琪一直待到聚会结束。

5. vision [ˈvɪʒən]
   n. 想象；画面；幻象

6. persona [pəˈsonə] n. 人物角色；形象

7. package [ˈpækɪdʒ]
   n. 包装；整套节目

8. longevity [lɔnˈdʒɛvətɪ]
   n. 持久；长寿

9. historical [hɪˈstɔrɪkəl]
   adj. 历史性的

10. select [səˈlɛkt]
    adj. 精选的；严格挑选的

11. prolific [prəˈlɪfɪk]
    adj. 多产的；创作丰富的

12. irrelevant [ɪˈrɛləvənt]
    adj. 不相关的；无关紧要的

影视娱乐 时尚生活 政治财经 体坛文艺

5

lot to do with discipline[13] and ambition[14], which are two things that are certainly in my blood.

KRISTIE LU STOUT, TALK ASIA

Now, you've cited[15] Andy Warhol as a major influence. I mean, he's someone who did have a lot of longevity in his work, of course—it still resonates[16] today—but why is he in particular an influential[17] person to you?

LADY GAGA, POP PERFORMER

He made commercial art that was taken seriously as fine art. And I'm starting to notice a change in the tides[18] as well. When I first came out it was, "Who is this crazy girl?" And then it's, "Who's this crazy girl with all the hit records?" And now I find that I'm being probed[19] a bit more.

KRISTIE LU STOUT, TALK ASIA

What do you mean being probed?

LADY GAGA, POP PERFORMER

People want to know more about my musical background as a musician. They want to understand more about my songwriting process. They're interested in the inspirations behind the shows. It's not just about trying to put me in a category anymore. People are starting to realize that I don't belong in a category, and they're alright with that. Change bothers people, but I'm sort of a pop musical misfit.

业寿命的长短与自制力及野心息息相关，而我绝对天生具备这两项特质。

《亚洲名人聊天室》克里斯蒂·卢·斯托特

你曾说安迪·沃霍尔对你的影响非常大。我是说，他是一个作品流传相当久远的人——至今仍能引起共鸣——可是为什么他对你的影响特别大？

流行乐歌手 Lady Gaga

他创作的商业艺术作品获得了正视，被当做艺术品看待。我也开始注意到流行潮流中的一个变化。我刚出道的时候，大家的反应是"这个疯狂的女孩是谁？"接着是"这个每张唱片都这么畅销的疯狂女孩是谁？"现在，我则发现自己受到的刺探多了一点。

《亚洲名人聊天室》克里斯蒂·卢·斯托特

你说受到刺探是什么意思？

流行乐歌手 Lady Gaga

大家想要知道更多我身为音乐人的音乐背景。他们想要进一步了解我创作歌曲的过程。他们对于我表演背后的灵感感兴趣，不再只想把我归入一个类别，人们开始意识到我不属于一个特定的类别，而且也能接受这一点。改变总是让人不安，但我就像个与其他人格格不入的流行乐艺人。

Notes & Vocabulary

in one's blood
天生的；与生俱来的
字面意思是"在（某人的）血液中"，延伸比喻特质或天分是"天生的；与生俱来的"。

- Though Jim never formerly trained as an actor, performing is **in his blood**.
吉姆以前从未接受表演训练，他的表演才能是与生俱来的。

近义词

- **in the genes** 与生俱来
- **innate** [ɪˈnet] 先天的；固有的
- **inherent** [ɪnˈhɪrənt] 遗传的；先天的
- **congenital** [kənˈdʒɛnətl]
先天疾病的；生性就有的
- **inborn** [ˈɪnˈbɔrn] 天生的；先天的

13. **discipline** [ˈdɪsəplən]
n. 纪律；自制力

14. **ambition** [æmˈbɪʃən]
n. 野心；抱负

15. **cite** [saɪt] *v.* 提及；列举
Jim cited many examples during his speech.

16. **resonate** [ˈrɛzə.net] *v.* 引起共鸣
The speech resonated with conservative voters.

17. **influential** [.ɪnfluˈɛnʃəl]
adj. 影响很大的

18. **tide** [taɪd] *n.* 潮流；趋势

19. **probe** [prob] *v.* 追问；探究；调查
The committee probed allegations that one of the senators from Texas committed fraud.

影视娱乐
时尚生活
政治财经
体坛文艺

KRISTIE LU STOUT, TALK ASIA
Now let's get back to your background and I want to ask you what it was like being Gaga as a kid, and I can gather[20] that you weren't a shy kid.

LADY GAGA, POP PERFORMER
No.

KRISTIE LU STOUT, TALK ASIA
Did you like showing off?

LADY GAGA, POP PERFORMER
I was a real pain in the ass.

KRISTIE LU STOUT, TALK ASIA
Yeah? How so? What did you do?

LADY GAGA, POP PERFORMER
I just was very loud. I was always singing and dancing, and my father was always laughing with me, and . . . I had a great childhood. I just was a very dramatic[21] young woman. During free time, I was in the chapel[22] playing some classical piece that I was learning or writing music. I just was [a] very creative young woman. And I'm just a very secluded[23] person. I mean, just in all honesty, I only associate now even with the people that I work with. I don't really have many friends and it's the life that I choose.

KRISTIE LU STOUT, TALK ASIA
And when you were writing the song *Paparazzi*[24] at the time, were you already conceiving[25] the stage performance at the same time?

Notes & Vocabulary

《亚洲名人聊天室》克里斯蒂·卢·斯托特
接下来再谈谈你的背景。我想要问小时候的 Gaga 是什么模样，而且我猜应该不是个害羞的孩子。

a pain in the ass
烦人的事物
a pain in the ass/butt 比喻"讨厌的人或事；（常制造麻烦而）令人头痛的人或事"，是不雅的美语俚语，英式英语的说法则是 a pain in the arse/backside。

· Lester liked his younger cousins, but they could be a pain in the ass at times.
雷斯特喜欢他的表兄弟，但他们有时也是很烦人的。

流行乐歌手 Lady Gaga
不是。

《亚洲名人聊天室》克里斯蒂·卢·斯托特
你小时候喜欢出风头吗？

近义词
a pain in the neck
极讨厌的人（或事物）
· Marcy enjoyed the freedom of having her own business, but bookkeeping was a pain in the neck.
玛西很享受自己开店的自由，不过记账实在很讨厌。

流行乐歌手 Lady Gaga
我是个让人很头痛的小孩。

《亚洲名人聊天室》克里斯蒂·卢·斯托特
真的吗？怎么会？你做了什么事？

associate with sb.
与某人来往
associate 当动词时常见意思是"联想；联系"，这里则表示"与某人来往"。

流行乐歌手 Lady Gaga
我很爱吵闹，我随时都在唱歌跳舞，我爸爸总是和我一起大笑……我的童年过得很精彩。我是个很爱表现的小女孩。空闲时间，我不是在教堂里弹奏我正在学习的古典乐曲，就是在写歌。我就是个充满创作力的小女孩。不过，我也是个很封闭的人。我是说，老实说，我现在甚至只和共事的人来往。我的朋友不多，这是我自己选择的生活。

20. gather [ˈgæðə]
    v. 认为；猜想；推断

21. dramatic [drəˈmætɪk]
    adj. 戏剧性的；夸张的

22. chapel [ˈtʃæpəl] n. 教堂

23. seclude [sɪˈklud]
    v. 使隔离；使孤立

《亚洲名人聊天室》克里斯蒂·卢·斯托特
你在写《Paparazzi》这首歌的时候，就已经同时在构思舞台表演方式了吗？

24. paparazzi [ˌpɑpəˈrɑzi]
    n. 专门追逐名人的摄影记者（单数形式为 paparazzo）

25. conceive [kənˈsiv] v. 想出；构想

影视娱乐

时尚生活

政治财经

体坛文艺

LADY GAGA, POP PERFORMER

I was a little bit, but I truthfully was just reading tabloids[26] like they were textbooks. I just . . . I would buy every scandal book, every paper, every magazine that I could get my hands on, and I would tear sheets out and imagery[27]. That is the most Warholian[28] thing about what I do is that I embrace[29] pop culture. The very thing that everybody says is poisonous[30] and ostentatious[31] and shallow[32], it's my . . . it's like my chemistry book, and I look through everything, and I make what I believe to be art out of it.

Lady Gaga

Lady Gaga 的造型相当多变、夸张 (flamboyant)，也不乏刺激挑衅的 (provocative) 的设计，如演唱会中胸口喷血及倒在血泊中的场景、颁奖典礼上的生牛肉装、MV 中的修女装。

图片提供：Hilary_JW / Domain Barnyard / kate_xo / petercruise / Ryan J. Reilly / Joshiku

正常 *MP3-Track01* / 慢速 *MP3-Track31* ▌ *PoP Misfit*

Notes & Vocabulary

流行乐歌手 Lady Gaga

有一点，但其实我当时只是把八卦小报当成教科书来读。我会买每一本我找得到的有关丑闻的书籍、报纸和杂志，然后把里面的页面和图片撕下来。我最厉害的一点，就是我热爱流行文化，就是大家都说是有害、做作又肤浅的东西。流行文化就像我的化学课本，我什么都看，然后从中得出我所认为的艺术。

Lady Gaga 一直都公开支持同性恋，曾参加保护同志（LGBT，lesbian、gay、bisexual 与 transgender 的缩写）的全国性呼吁平等的游行（National Equality March），以及缅因州一场支持废除（repeal）"不问不说"（Don't ask, don't tell）的活动。

get one's hands on sth.

取得；得到

字面上指"将手放在某物上"，引申指"取得、得到某物"，get 可以用 lay 代替。

- Thousands of shoppers lined up to **get their hands on** the new video game system.
  数千名消费者为了得到这款新的电子游戏主机排起长队。

延伸用法

get one's hands on sb.

抓到、逮到某人（尤指为了惩罚对方）

- If I ever **get my hands on** that kid, he'll be sorry!
  要是让我逮到那个小孩，他会后悔的。

26. **tabloid** [ˈtæˌblɔɪd]
    n. 小报；通俗小报

27. **imagery** [ˈɪmɪdʒrɪ] *n.* 画像；照片

28. **Warholian** [ˌwɔrˈhoʊliən]
    adj. 沃霍尔风格的

29. **embrace** [ɪmˈbres]
    v. 欣然接受；乐意采纳
    The public embraced the young candidate.

30. **poisonous** [ˈpɔɪznəs]
    adj. 有毒的；邪恶的
    Poisonous household chemicals should be kept away from small children.

31. **ostentatious** [ˌɔstɛnˈteʃəs]
    adj. 夸张的；招摇的
    The ostentatious professor often referenced his personal achievements during lectures.

32. **shallow** [ˈʃælo]
    adj. 肤浅的；浅薄的

影视娱乐 时尚生活 政治财经 体坛文艺

Skater Girl
Grows Up

Avril Lavigne Discusses
Music, Fashion and
Charity Work with
Talk Asia

图片提供：新力音乐

ANJALI RAO, TALK ASIA

She stormed onto the international stage with this anthem of teenage angst[1]. Nine years later and with this, her latest single, Canadian singer-songwriter Avril Lavigne still proves to be a firm favorite.

One of the things that's really interesting about you is that when you look at songs that are, you know, the more upbeat[2] ones like *Girlfriend*, they're really sort of bratty[3] happy, but then the more slow tempo[4] ones like *When You're Gone*, they're a lot more thoughtful[5] and kind of anguished[6] in a way. Does that contradiction[7] tell us something about you as a person?

AVRIL LAVIGNE, SINGER-SONGWRITER

Yeah. As a human being I have different emotions

正常MP3-Track02
慢速MP3-Track32

名人小档案 ▼ 艾薇儿

常常带着一脸叛逆表情的艾薇儿（1984— ）来自加拿大，5岁时就在地方教堂的唱诗班里唱歌，小学就无师自通学会弹吉他。2002 年以《展翅高飞（Let Go）》专辑初试啼声，可谓一夜走红，并在 2006 年入选《加拿大商业杂志》选出的"好莱坞最有影响力的加拿大人"。这几年，除了音乐事业之外，艾薇儿更参与配音、表演等工作，极力延伸事业范围。

Avril Lavigne

《亚洲名人聊天室》安姿丽

她以一首描写青少年忧虑的经典名曲在国际舞台走红。9 年后，加拿大歌手兼词曲创作者艾薇儿推出这首最新单曲，证明她仍然深受歌迷喜爱。

你很有趣的一点就是，你创作的比较轻快的歌曲，例如《女朋友》，都带有有些调皮的欢快气息；可是比较慢拍的作品，例如《当你离去》，则深沉得多，而且在某种程度上也带着苦涩味道。这样的矛盾是不是能够让我们看出你的真实性格呢？

词曲创作歌手 艾薇儿

是啊。我是一个人，我有各种不同情绪，也有一面……我是个非常深沉的人。有时候我会很严肃，很内向，很安静，而且我常常思

Notes & Vocabulary

anthem
经典名曲

anthem [`ænθəm] 原本指"国歌；圣歌"，引申指特定音乐类别中众所皆知、广为流传的代表性歌曲，例如某个年代或某位歌手的"经典名曲"。

• Bruce Springsteen recorded several popular rock anthems in the 1980s.
布鲁斯·斯普林斯廷录了好几首 20 世纪 80 年代流行摇滚经典歌曲。

1. **angst** [æŋst]
   n. 忧虑；焦虑

2. **upbeat** [ˈʌpˌbit]
   adj. 乐观的；快乐的
   Tom made an upbeat presentation about the company's future.

3. **bratty** [ˈbrætɪ]
   adj. 淘气的；不乖的；不礼貌的
   The bratty kid refused to share his toys.

4. **tempo** [ˈtɛmpo]
   n. 速度；节奏

5. **thoughtful** [ˈθɔtfəl]
   adj. 关心别人的；关切的

6. **anguished** [ˈæŋgwɪʃt]
   adj. 痛苦的；苦恼的
   The poet was known for writing anguished verse about his troubled childhood.

7. **contradiction** [ˌkɑntrəˈdɪkʃən]
   n. 矛盾；对立

注
标题中的 Skater Girl 是由艾薇儿第一张专辑《展翅高飞（Let Go）》中的一首单曲《滑板男孩 (Skater Boy)》延伸而来。

影视娱乐

时尚生活

政治财经

体坛文艺

and there's a side . . . I'm a very deep person. Sometimes I can be very serious and introverted[8] and quiet and, you know, I think a lot and that's why I'm a songwriter, because I go to that place. And of course, then there's a side of me that, you know, [is] just a chick[9]. I like to have fun, I like to be spontaneous[10], I like to live on the edge a little. So, you know, I love ~~with~~ my music to have that diversity[11] and to go out on stage and to rock out[12] and to have my guitar and run around, but I also love the feeling of just sitting down at a piano and just singing alone to that.

So, that's why music's great. I get to express all the different sides, and different emotions ~~to~~ [of] me as a person.

ANJALI RAO, TALK ASIA

Let's talk about your fashion sense, because your look has been emulated[13] by fans, you know, right back since the days of *Complicated*. These days though, you're on the front cover of magazines. How has your style changed over the years?

AVRIL LAVIGNE, SINGER-SONGWRITER

Well, definitely I would say since my first album my style is . . . it's a little more feminine[14] than before. On my first album I was wearing a lot of, like, guys' pants, baggy[15] clothes and stuff like that. I mean I was 17 and I was kind of a little tomboy[16], and that you would never see me wearing a dress or heels on my first record.

Now, I'm a lot more into fashion and I have a clothing line, and it's called Abbey Dawn, and I started that a couple years ago. And fashion really

考，这就是为什么我会创作歌曲，因为我会进入那样的境界。当然，我也有只是个小女孩的一面，喜欢玩乐，喜欢随性，也喜欢追求一点刺激。所以，我很高兴自己的音乐能够表现出这种多样性，我喜欢能够在舞台上尽情享受摇滚，抱着吉他跑来跑去，但我也很喜欢简单地坐在钢琴前面，独自对着钢琴的伴奏唱歌。

这就是为什么音乐很棒的原因。我可以表达自己作为普通人的不同面和不同的情绪。

《亚洲名人聊天室》安姿丽

我们来谈谈你的时尚观，因为自从你发行《复杂》这首单曲以来，歌迷就一再模仿你的装扮。近来，你更是成为杂志封面的常客。你的装扮风格在这些年来有什么变化？

词曲创作歌手 艾薇儿

嗯，确实，自从我的第一张专辑发行以来……我会说我的风格比以往变得更女性化了。在我发行第一张专辑的时候，我穿了很多类似男生的长裤、松垮垮的衣服和那类的东西。我是说，我当时 17 岁，有点像有男孩子气的女生，所以你在我的第一张唱片里绝对看不到我穿女装或高跟鞋。

现在我比较注重时尚，也有自己的服饰品牌，叫做 Abbey Dawn，几年前我创立了这个品牌。时尚也和我的音乐密不可分。比如说，我需要拍很多照片和影片，也要在舞台上表演，所以我总是不断地想自己要穿什

Notes & Vocabulary

live on the edge
过着癫狂的生活

on the edge 字面意思是"处于边缘"，live on the edge 则是喜欢追求刺激、紧张、疯狂的生活。

- Irene became a Hollywood stunt coordinator because she likes to live on the edge.
艾琳成为好莱坞武术指导，因为她喜欢紧张刺激的生活。

be into sth.
对……有兴趣；热衷于……

口语中 into sb./sth. 可以指对某人或某事感兴趣，2009 年由詹妮弗·安妮斯顿等人主演的电影《他其实没那么喜欢你（He's Just Not That Into You）》中的 into 即为此意。

- Sue is really into professional wrestling.
苏真的很喜欢职业摔跤比赛。

8. introverted [ˈɪntrəˌvɜtəd]
   adj. 内向的

9. chick [tʃɪk] n. 【口】小姐

10. spontaneous [spɑnˈteniəs]
    adj. 自发的；即兴的

11. diversity [daɪˈvɜsəti]
    n. 多样性；多元化

12. rock out 享受歌曲（尤指摇滚乐）

13. emulate [ˈɛmjəˌlet]
    v. 仿真；模仿

14. feminine [ˈfɛmənən]
    adj. 女性的；女性化的

15. baggy [ˈbægɪ]
    adj. 宽松的；不紧绷的

16. tomboy [ˈtɑmˌbɔɪ]
    n. 男孩子气的女生

ties into my music. Like, I have so many photo shoots and video shoots and I'm up on stage so, you know, I'm constantly thinking about what I'm gonna wear and what I want to wear and how I want to express myself.

So, it's been really fun to kind of see with each album when I change, to see the fans at the show kind of emulate ~~and,~~ my style, and the first record . . . a lot of the kids in the crowd were wearing neckties like I was. Now you'll see a lot of girls with pink hair, and it's cool.

ANJALI RAO, TALK ASIA

Early last year, Avril Lavigne created a foundation[17] in her name. Its aim is to work with other charitable[18] organizations to raise awareness and support children and teenagers living with an illness or a disability[19].

Recently, you've definitely been giving back through your Avril Lavigne Foundation. Tell me about it and also what it means to you to be in a position to do something like that, something that's truly good.

AVRIL LAVIGNE, SINGER-SONGWRITER

I've had a lot of opportunities to give back and to do charity, charity events, and get involved with different programs and stuff, and basically I just wanted to take it to the next level to really be able to give back as much as I possibly can.

I wanted to have my own foundation for a while and now that I'm just starting it, I'm so excited because it's gonna be a huge learning process and I can't wait to get my fans involved so they can contribute[20]. And I'm developing programs right now.

正常*MP3-Track02* / 慢速*MP3-Track32* ▌ *Skater Girl Grows Up*

么、想穿什么，要怎么表达自我。

所以，人们能够随着我的每一张专辑看到我的变化，看到来看表演的歌迷模仿我的风格，确实很有趣。我出第一张专辑的时候……人群里有很多小朋友像我一样系着领带。现在你会看到很多女孩子染了粉红色的头发，确实很酷。

《亚洲名人聊天室》安姿丽

去年年初，艾薇儿以自己的名字命名成立了一个基金会，目的在于和其他慈善机构合作，呼唤大家关注并扶助患病或有残疾的儿童与青少年。

你近来确实通过你的艾薇儿基金会对社会回馈很多。跟我谈谈这一点，还有能够做这样的事情，做些很棒的善事，对你有什么意义。

词曲创作歌手 艾薇儿

我有很多机会可以回馈社会，从事慈善工作、出席慈善活动、参与各种不同的慈善项目之类的。基本上，我只是想要再进一步，尽一己之力来回馈社会。

我想要成立自己的基金会已经有好长一段时间了。现在我才刚起步，我很兴奋，因为这一定会是一段内容很丰富的学习过程。我已等不及要让我的歌迷参与其中，让他们一起奉献爱心。我现在正在做一些计划。

Notes & Vocabulary

get/be involved with . . .
投入于……
involve 是"参与；涉及"的意思，所以 get/be involved with 是指"投入；涉及；有关"，有时也有"被迫卷入；被牵扯进"的含意。

· Tanya keeps busy by being involved with several local charities.
塔尼娅通过参与几个当地的慈善机构让自己忙碌起来。

17. **foundation** [faʊnˋdeʃən]
n. 基金会

18. **charitable** [ˋtʃɛrətəbl]
adj. 慈善的；行善的
Dan gave generously to a charitable organization.

19. **disability** [͵dɪsəˋbɪlətɪ]
n. 缺陷；障碍

20. **contribute** [kənˋtrɪbjut]
v. 捐献；捐赠
Alex contributed ten dollars to the party fund.

影视娱乐

时尚生活

政治财经

体坛文艺

Sting Sings in the Holidays

Veteran[1] Musician Celebrates the Winter Season

图片提供：Deutsche Grammophon / © Tony Molina

ASIEH NAMDAR, CNN ANCHOR

He is one of the world's most renowned[2] singers and his career has spanned three decades. Sting recently spoke with our Shannon Cook about his winter-themed[3] album.

SHANNON COOK, CNN CORRESPONDENT

Winter, it's a time that you revel in, isn't it.

STING, SINGER AND MUSICIAN

I would say it's an undervalued[4] season by most people because it's cold and uncomfortable. I think it's an important season for us because it's a time of reflection[5]. It's the season of the imagination, of spirits and ghosts in the chimney[6] and ghost stories and firesides and wanting to feel warm. And it's

18

正常MP3-Track03
慢速MP3-Track33

名人小档案 ▼ 斯汀

斯汀（1951—）是英国知名摇滚歌手，曾任警察乐队（Police）主唱。斯汀的名字源于他在 1971 至 1974 年间在爵士乐队表演时，经常穿着如黄蜂般黄黑色相间的毛衣，因而得到 Sting（"刺针"的意思）的绰号。斯汀于 1984 年从警察乐队单飞，独闯乐坛成绩斐然，而除了专注于音乐事业，近年来他也常参与环保、生态保护、人权保护等相关活动。

Sting

Notes & Vocabulary

revel in

陶醉；沉迷于

revel [ˈrɛvl] 是 "陶醉；着迷；沉湎" 和 "狂欢作乐；纵情" 的意思，后面用 in 加上让人沉醉的事物。

· Jack reveled in his victory over his father in the chess match.
杰克沉浸在下棋时赢了父亲的胜利中。

1. **veteran** [ˈvɛtərən]
   adj. 经验丰富的
   The director is a veteran filmmaker with a large body of work.

2. **renowned** [rɪˈnaʊnd]
   adj. 有名的；有声望的

3. **–themed** [θimd]
   sfx. 以……为主题的

4. **undervalued** [ˌʌndəˈvæljud]
   adj. （能力、价值）被低估的
   Deana felt undervalued in her office.

5. **reflection** [rɪˈflɛkʃən]
   n. 思考；沉思

6. **chimney** [ˈtʃɪmnɪ]
   n. 烟囱；烟囱管道

CNN 主播 艾谢·南达尔

他是全球最知名的歌手，他的事业长达 30 年之久。斯汀日前接受了夏侬·库克的采访，谈论关于他的一张以冬天为主题的唱片。

CNN 特派员 夏侬·库克

冬天，那是最让你感到陶醉的季节，对吧？

歌手兼音乐人 斯汀

我认为冬天的价值被大多数人低估了，因为冬天寒冷且不舒服。我认为冬天对我们而言是个重要的季节，因为那是我们反思的时候。冬天是个充满想象的季节，想象烟囱里的神灵、鬼魂，在壁炉边听鬼故事，并且希望能感受到温暖。冬天在心理上也非常重要，因为我们必须要反省过去，好让我们能

影视娱乐

时尚生活

政治财经

体坛文艺

19

also very important psychologically because we need to reflect on the past so that we can move into the spring. Unless we reflect, we can't really go forwards.

SHANNON COOK, CNN CORRESPONDENT
Is your beard part of the wintry[7] theme?

STING, SINGER AND MUSICIAN
I had to grow a beard last November because I was in an opera with Elvis Costello, and I had to play a Greek. I had to play Dionysus[8], so I grew the beard and they made my hair dark. And I sort of kept it, and I kind of enjoy it, and then we started to record this album, and it seemed appropriate[9], and I've still got it and Trudie hasn't complained yet. I remind her of one of her dogs, she says, but, you know, she likes dogs, fortunately.

SHANNON COOK, CNN CORRESPONDENT
What kind of a dog?

STING, SINGER AND MUSICIAN
She has Irish wolfhounds[10]. They have the same kind of texture[11].

We began recording last January in Tuscany. I have a home in Tuscany. I've lived there for years now. When you say Tuscany, most people think, oh it's warm and it's hot and they grow grapes and everything, but in the winter, it's freezing. It's really very cold. And the album cover is photographed on my estate[12] there, with all that snow and walking my dog. And so it was a very appropriate place to begin a winter album. And we all huddled[13] around a kitchen table with the fire on and our coats and

走向春天。除非我们反省，否则就不能真的向前迈进。

CNN 特派员　夏侬·库克
您的胡子是否是冬天这个主题的一部分？

歌手兼音乐人　斯汀
我去年 11 月开始就得开始留胡子，因为我要和埃尔维斯·卡斯提洛共同出演一部歌剧，我饰演一个希腊人。我要扮演狄俄尼索斯，于是我留起了胡子，然后他们把我的头发染黑。后来我就继续留着胡子，而且还挺喜欢这样的。接着我们就开始录制这张唱片，感觉挺搭的，所以到现在还留着胡子，特鲁迪（编注：Sting 的妻子）到现在还没抱怨过。她说，我让她想起她的一只狗。不过幸好，她喜欢狗。

CNN 特派员　夏侬·库克
什么样的狗？

歌手兼音乐人　斯汀
她有一只爱尔兰猎狼犬。那种狗的毛和我的胡子质感一样。

我们去年 1 月在托斯卡尼开始录音。我在托斯卡尼有个家，我在那儿已经住了 12 年。每当提到托斯卡尼时，大部分人都会以为那里很暖和、很热，那里都在种葡萄等等，但是冬天时，那里却是天寒地冻，真的很冷。唱片的封面就是在我的庄园拍摄的，有很多雪，而我在遛狗。所以那里是个非常适合开始制作冬天专辑的地方。我们所有人都围着厨房的餐桌，屋里生着火，桌上还放着我们的大衣和围巾，然后大家一起开始研究这些

Notes & Vocabulary

kind of
有点儿
kind of 在口语中表示"有一点；几分；稍微"的意思，与 sort of 同义，当副词用。要注意的是不要与 a kind of 搞混了，a kind of 是"……的一种"的意思。

> The song was **kind of** popular in Central Europe during the holidays.
> 那首歌在中欧逢年过节时还挺受欢迎的。

7. **wintry** ['wɪntrɪ]
adj. 冬天的；寒冷的（=wintery）
Even though it was April, the cold front brought wintry weather to the town.

8. **Dionysus** [ˌdaɪə'naɪsəs]
n. 狄俄尼索斯（希腊神话中的酒神，罗马神话中名为 Bacchus）

9. **appropriate** [ə'proʊprɪˌet]
adj. 适合的；恰当的
Mike's bicycle is not appropriate for riding on mountain trails.

10. **wolfhound** ['wʊlfˌhaʊnd]
n. 猎狼犬

11. **texture** ['tɛkstʃə]
n. 质地；质感；材质

12. **estate** [ɪ'stet]
n. （大面积）私有土地；（乡间）庄园

13. **huddle** ['hʌdl]
v. 挤在一起；依偎
The dogs huddled together to keep warm.

影视娱乐

时尚生活

政治财经

体坛文艺

our scarves, and we started to explore these songs together. In that kind of weather, it kind of helps. It's that kind of method recording.

SHANNON COOK, CNN CORRESPONDENT

In two years, time, you'll be 60. How do you feel about that?

STING, SINGER AND MUSICIAN

Well, I was, you know, 58 a week ago. I feel like I'm 14-and-a-half inside, and yet I have the memories of a 58-year-old man, and so I've the best of both worlds, you know. I have a certain sagacity[14], a certain wisdom that comes with reaching this, you know, very august[15] age, but also I feel very useful in myself, my physical self. Also mentally, I feel quite young but not immature[16], but just have a lot of energy. So it's good.

SHANNON COOK, CNN CORRESPONDENT

Over the years as your musical style has evolved[17], we've seen you in The Police, we've seen you with pop, with jazz, a lute[18] album. Do you see how your audience changes?

STING, SINGER AND MUSICIAN

I don't think my audience changes. I think the audience has come to expect the unexpected. I think I never want them to second-guess what I'm going to do next. I have no idea what I'm . . . even I don't know. I think they appreciate[19] that sense of, you know, "Well, what's he got this time?"

歌。那种天气状况其实还挺有帮助的。有点像是体验式录音。

CNN 特派员 夏侬·库克
两年后您就要 60 岁了。对此您有何感想？

歌手兼音乐人 斯汀
我一星期前刚满 58 岁，我感觉自己才 14 岁半，但我却拥有一个 58 岁的人的回忆，所以我拥有这两个世界里的精华。我拥有某种程度的睿智，某种到了这个年纪而拥有的智慧，这个岁数让人敬畏，但我觉得自己身体还很好。心理方面，我觉得我还很年轻，但并非不成熟，而是精力充沛。所以这样很好。

CNN 特派员 夏侬·库克
过去这些年来您的音乐风格有所改变，我们见过您在警察乐队时的表现，听过您演唱流行歌曲、爵士乐和一张鲁特琴专辑。您认为您的听众变了吗？

歌手兼音乐人 斯汀
我不认为我的听众变了。我认为听众已经预期到一些意料之外的事。我从未让他们去猜我接下来要做什么。我不知道我接下来要……连我自己都不知道。我认为他们会喜欢那种"他这次要拿什么东西出来？"的那种感觉。

Notes & Vocabulary

second-guess
事后批评；猜忌
second-guess 是动词，表示怀疑或犹豫而"猜忌；多想"，或是事后才加以评论、劝告，类似中文"事后诸葛；放马后炮"的意思。

- Darla second-guesses every task her supervisor gives her.
  达拉每次对主管交给她的任务都要事后批评一下。

14. **sagacity** [sə`gæsətɪ]
    n. 睿智；聪慧

15. **august** [ɔ`gʌst]
    adj. 威严的；令人敬畏的

16. **immature** [ˌɪmə`tʃʊr]
    adj. 幼稚的；不成熟的

17. **evolve** [ɪ`vɑlv]
    v. 演进；逐渐进展

18. **lute** [lut]
    n. 鲁特琴；诗琴（拨弦乐器）

19. **appreciate** [ə`priʃɪˌet]
    v. 喜爱；赏识；感谢

STING
IF ON A WINTER'S NIGHT...

Diana Krall's Brazilian Odyssey

The Jazz Musician Takes a Tropical Turn on Her Latest Recording

图片提供：Reuters

CNN ANCHOR

Now, singer Diana Krall is far from an overnight sensation. She's been a platinum-selling artist for years, and she's found success all over the world, but as Shannon Cook reports, there's one place in particular[1] where the musician recently found inspiration.

DIANA KRALL, MUSICIAN

I was in Brazil the year before last doing some concerts, and I've always loved the music, but when you go there, and you go to the botanical[2] gardens in Rio and different . . . other places in Brazil, you really see where this music originated[3] and the ties to American popular song, like Stan Getz and João Gilberto. So I felt like it was the right time to do this album.

24

④ CNN专访新生代爵士天后戴安娜·克瑞儿

正常MP3-Track04
慢速MP3-Track34

名人小档案 ▼ 戴安娜·克瑞儿

来自加拿大的戴安娜·克瑞儿（1964—）4 岁时开始学习钢琴，15 岁的时候已经在一些餐厅里定期弹奏。她擅长爵士乐，她以低沉慵懒的嗓音配上轻快的爵士钢琴，在乐坛上大放异彩。她的歌曲曾被许多电影选为配乐，例如 HBO 的自制电影《欲望都市》、由陈冲执导的文艺片《纽约的秋天》以及哈里森·福特主演的《疑云密布》，都间接使克瑞儿的歌曲获得非常高的知名度，克瑞儿也因此被视为是囊括流行与爵士音乐的典型。

Diana Krall

CNN 主播

戴安娜·克瑞儿绝不是那种一夜成名的歌手。她多年来出过许多张白金唱片（注 1），在世界各地都大受欢迎。不过，夏侬·库克带来的报道指出，这位音乐家近来从一个地方获得了许多灵感。

音乐家 戴安娜·克瑞儿

我前年在巴西举办了几场演唱会。我一向都很喜欢巴西的音乐，可是你一旦到那里去，到里约热内卢的植物园及巴西的其他地方，就会真正看到这种音乐究竟源自何处，还有这种音乐和美国流行歌曲的关联，例如斯坦·盖茨与乔安·吉巴托。所以，我当时就觉得正是制作这张专辑合适的时候。

Notes & Vocabulary

标题扫描

Brazilian Odyssey

《奥德赛（Odyssey）》是古希腊吟游诗人荷马（Homer）的史诗巨著，描述伊萨卡（Ithaca）国王奥德修斯（Odysseus 或 Ulysses）在特洛伊战争后经过漫长的 10 年旅程才最终回到故乡。后人便常用 Odyssey 比喻一段波折又壮丽的旅程。另外也用来形容抽象的心灵或艺术探索，好比戴安娜·克瑞儿来到巴西展开音乐交流之旅。

标题扫描

take a . . . turn
转折

take a turn 字面指"转了一个弯"，意思是说从原来既有的行为模式，换了另一个新的方向。副标题 take a tropical turn 也就是说戴安娜·克瑞儿在新专辑里呈现了热带风情的曲风。

· The lecture took a strange turn when the professor began referencing his private life.
这场演说突然出现了一个奇怪的转折，因为教授开始讲述自己的私生活。

1. in particular 特别地；尤其

2. botanical [bo`tænɪk]
   adj. 植物的；植物学的

3. originate [ə`rɪdʒə͵net]
   v. 发源；来自

注1

根据美国唱片业协会 RIAA（Recording Industry Association of America）的标准，唱片销量分级定为 50 万张的"金唱片 Gold"、100 万张的"白金唱片 Platinum"、200 万张的"双白金唱片 Multi-Platinum"及 1000 万张的"钻石唱片 Diamond"。

影视娱乐

时尚生活

政治财经

体坛文艺

One of the best parts of making a record is the dinner after where you all go to a restaurant, you decompress[4], have some great wine and just tell stories and listen to Claus and Tommy and Al Schmidt and all these people telling amazing stories about [those] ~~that~~ times.

SHANNON COOK, CNN CORRESPONDENT
And there's only one dinner? Shouldn't there be a series of dinners?

DIANA KRALL, MUSICIAN
Uh, no, there's a lot of dinners.

SHANNON COOK, CNN CORRESPONDENT
(laughing) I bet!

You have been producing Barbara Streisand's new album. What's that been like?

DIANA KRALL, MUSICIAN
Incredible[5], incredible. I mean, I just am so thrilled[6] with her performance on this album. It's been great work ng artist to artist, and we had a lot of fun. We play d cards. When there's little moments in the studio where there's something technical that has to be fixed, then we'll deal[7] the cards, and we'll play gin rummy, which I'm lousy[8] at. Thank goodness.

SHANNON COOK, CNN CORRESPONDENT
Oh, OK. So she normally wins?

DIANA KRALL, MUSICIAN
Yeah, no, I would let her win. (laughing)

SHANNON COOK, CNN CORRESPONDENT
And this is the first album you've produced for another artist.

DIANA KRALL, MUSICIAN
For another artist, yes.

26

在制作唱片的过程中，最棒的部分就是工作结束后，大家一起到餐厅吃晚餐，你可以放松下来，喝点美酒，说说故事，听着克劳斯、汤米、艾尔·施密特及其他那些人讲述那些年代的各种传奇故事。

CNN 特派员 夏侬·库克

只有一次聚餐？不是应该有一连串的聚餐吗？

音乐家 戴安娜·克瑞儿

嗯，没错，有很多次的聚餐。

CNN 特派员 夏侬·库克

（笑）我就说呀！

你最近制作了芭芭拉·史翠珊的新专辑。感觉怎么样？

音乐家 戴安娜·克瑞儿

难以置信，难以置信。我是说，她在这张专辑上的表现让我兴奋不已。同是音乐人在一起合作实在很棒，而且我们相处得很开心。我们会一起玩牌。有时候，录音室如果出了点技术问题，要等人修好，我们就会玩牌，玩金罗美（注2），可是我打得很差劲，感谢老天爷。

CNN 特派员 夏侬·库克

哦，所以通常都是她赢？

音乐家 戴安娜·克瑞儿

是啊，我都会让她赢。（笑）

CNN 特派员 夏侬·库克

这是你第一次帮其他艺人制作专辑。

音乐家 戴安娜·克瑞儿

帮其他艺人，没错。

Notes & Vocabulary

I bet

我相信；我确定

bet 是指"打赌"，而 I'll bet 或 I bet 是口语用法，在这里是指"相信、确定某事一定是真的"。另外，you bet 用于回答对方的问题，表示"当然；一定"，语气比 yes 强烈。

- I bet that Mary is here already.
  我相信玛丽已经到这里了。

4. **decompress** [ˋdikəmˌprɛs]
   v. 减压
   Judy took time off to decompress after completing her book.

5. **incredible** [ɪnˋkrɛdəbl]
   adj. 惊人的；美妙的
   The class did an incredible job with its production of The Music Man.

6. **thrilled** [θrɪld]
   adj. 非常激动、兴奋的
   The children were thrilled to meet their sports hero.

7. **deal** [dil]
   v. 发（纸牌）；经营
   The shop deals in imported handcrafts.

8. **lousy** [ˋlauzɪ]
   adj.【口】不好的；讨厌的
   The wine Fred brought to the party tasted lousy.

注2

金罗美是一种两人玩的扑克牌游戏，共有 52 张牌，最后得分最多的人获胜，牌面大小由低到高为 Ace 到 K。此游戏是 1909 年由贝克父子（Elwood T. Baker & Graham Baker）发明的。

影视娱乐

时尚生活

政治财经

体坛文艺

27

SHANNON COOK, CNN CORRESPONDENT

Way to choose somebody really small to start off with!

DIANA KRALL, MUSICIAN

I didn't choose. She chose me! I had a few phone calls and I was . . . you know, it was a little daunting[9], and, but it was a great experience and really, really intense[10], as you would expect it to be, and challenging[11], but in a . . . you know, in a way that I think we ended up with a really beautiful record that she's really happy with. And that's the most important thing, that she loves the record.

SHANNON COOK, CNN CORRESPONDENT

You and your husband, Elvis Costello, two very creative people, and two very intense people living under the one roof, it must get zany[12] at times under this one roof.

DIANA KRALL, MUSICIAN

Yeah, it's pretty great. It's really, really fun, and we have this amazing home in Vancouver now. And I finally have a home, because I've always lived out of a suitcase on the road, and just, you know, sort of a tiny little flat[13] that I can come drop things off. But now we have this home with kids running around, and I love to cook, so we're always cooking, and we always have people over. It's zany in the most wonderful way, and you know, it's great. I mean, you have two little boys leaping off the furniture who think they're Buzz Lightyear—"infinity and beyond"—while we're practicing and playing. It's just a happy house, and they're really funny and really fun. And it's just, my life is just tremendous[14] right now. It couldn't be better.

正常 *MP3·Track04* / 慢速 *MP3·Track34* ▮ *Diana Krall's Brazilian Odyssey*

CNN 特派员 夏侬·库克

你第一次挑选的对象还真"小牌"啊！

音乐家 戴安娜·克瑞儿

不是我挑上她，是她挑中我的！我接了几个电话，然后就……是有点吓人，但也是很棒的经验，而且绝无冷场，就像预期的一样，充满挑战性。不过，我认为我们最后完成的专辑非常优美，她也很满意。她喜欢这张专辑，这才是最重要的。

CNN 特派员 夏侬·库克

你和你先生艾维斯·卡斯提洛都是非常有创意的人。两个这么有活力的人住在同一个屋檐下，家里一定常常有很疯狂的时刻吧。

音乐家 戴安娜·克瑞儿

是啊，确实很棒。我们的生活充满了乐趣，而且我们现在在温哥华有了一个很漂亮的家。我总算有了了个家。我过去总是带着一个皮箱到处奔波，只有一间小公寓让我放东西。但现在我们有了这个家，有小孩跑来跑去。我很爱做饭，所以我们随时都在做饭，随时都有客人过来。我们的生活疯狂得很美妙，很棒。我们练琴弹奏的时候，两个小男孩就在家具上跳上跳下，以为自己是巴斯光年，喊着"宇宙无限，浩瀚无垠！"我们家充满欢乐，孩子真的很好玩也很有趣。这实在……我现在的生活实在太棒了，不可能再比这样更好了。

Notes & Vocabulary

start off with

从……开始

start off with 是"从……开始"的意思，加上介词 with，表示开始的事物，此短语可放在句中或句尾。choose somebody really small to start off with 可以改成 to start off with somebody really small。

· Larry ordered a bowl of pumpkin soup to start off with before choosing an entrée.
拉里在点主菜之前，先点了一碗南瓜汤。

end up with

最后变成……

end up with 是很常见的英文惯用语，表示"最后成为；最后落得、获得"，可以用在好的或坏的情况下。

· After months of hard work, Jenny ended up with a beautiful backyard garden.
经过几个月辛勤的努力后，珍妮终于有了一个美丽的花园。

9. daunting [ˈdɔntɪŋ]
   adj. 令人却步的
   Bobby faced the daunting task of completing a book in four weeks.

10. intense [ɪnˈtɛns]
    adj. 强烈的；极度的
    The suspenseful movie was too intense for some viewers.

11. challenging [ˈtʃæləndʒɪŋ]
    adj. 具有挑战性的

12. zany [ˈzenɪ] *adj.* 稀奇古怪的

13. flat [flæt] *n.*【英】公寓

14. tremendous [trɪˈmɛndəs]
    adj. 极好的；很棒的

影视娱乐

时尚生活

政治财经

体坛文艺

Unusual Suspect

Talk Asia Interviews Acclaimed[1] Stage and Screen Actor Kevin Spacey

图片提供：AP

ANJALI RAO, TALK ASIA

Kevin, welcome to Talk Asia. Great to have you on the show today.

KEVIN SPACEY, ACTOR

Thanks.

ANJALI RAO, TALK ASIA

The world does know you for your movie roles, and you just sort of burst onto the scene, really, with *Usual Suspects*, and you got a Best Supporting Actor Oscar for it. Just take me back to that time where you went from sort of relatively[2] unknown actor to suddenly ridiculously[3] famous.

30

正常MP3-Track05
慢速MP3-Track35

Notes & Vocabulary

名人小档案 ▼ 凯文·斯贝西

凯文·斯贝西（1959—）是一位美国演员及导演。他在20世纪90年代早期开始得到赞赏，凭借在《非常嫌疑犯（The Usual Suspects）》中的演技夺得奥斯卡最佳男配角奖，又在2000年凭借在《美国丽人（American Beauty）》中的出色表现夺得奥斯卡最佳男主角奖。

Kevin Spacey

burst onto the scene
突然蹿红

burst 本身就有"突然出现；突然发生"之意，burst onto the scene 除了表示"突然出现"，也常用来形容"突然蹿红"。

· The singer burst onto the scene in a Broadway musical.
那名歌手因一部百老汇音乐剧突然蹿红。

1. acclaimed [əˈklemd]
   adj. 受到赞扬的
   The acclaimed actor will star in a sequel to his summer hit.

2. relatively [ˈrɛlətɪvlɪ]
   adv. 相当地；相对地
   The restaurant was relatively easy to find, so I was able to arrive on time.

3. ridiculously [rəˈdɪkjələslɪ]
   adv. 荒谬地；可笑地
   The jewelry on display is ridiculously expensive, so there is no way we are going to buy it.

《亚洲名人聊天室》安姿丽
凯文，欢迎来到《亚洲名人聊天室》，很高兴你今天能够到节目中来。

演员 凯文·斯贝西
谢谢。

《亚洲名人聊天室》安姿丽
全世界都因为你在电影中饰演的角色而认识你。你当初可以说是以《非常嫌疑犯》突然蹿红的，也因此赢得了奥斯卡最佳男配角奖。请带我回顾一下当初那个时刻，你原本是个没有多少人知道的演员，却突然间名气大得不得了。

影视娱乐

时尚生活

政治财经

体坛文艺

KEVIN SPACEY, ACTOR

It was a very gradual[4] transition[5] for me. It may not have felt that way if you were on the outside, but on the inside of it I had been working very successfully as a theater actor for a long time and had made a name for myself in New York theater. Then I started to work in television and began to make a name for myself in television. Now, what I mean by that is that people started to recognize[6] me. What happened after *Usual Suspects* and a number of other films I did, sort of that all came out in a span[7] of about six months, was that I think suddenly people started to connect the dots. Oh, that was that guy from . . . Oh, he was in that . . . Oh . . . And then people start to actually learn your name.

ANJALI RAO, TALK ASIA

But winning a best supporting actor must have been, you know, a great time, but I imagine that winning a Best Actor Oscar would have been amazing. And you did that for *American Beauty*, where you played a depressed[8] suburban[9] dad and husband. Help me revisit that time in your life.

KEVIN SPACEY, ACTOR

You know, it was a . . . it's a remarkable acknowledgement[10] from your peers[11]. I love the industry[12] so much, I have so much respect for so many people that both I've had a chance to work with and have yet to have a chance to work with, so that for the members of the Academy to have given me such a recognition was beyond my wildest dreams.

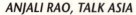

演员 凯文·斯贝西

对我来说，那是一段缓慢渐进的转变过程。在外人看来也许不是这样，但我作为成功的舞台剧演员其实已经有很长一段时间了，也在纽约的舞台剧界颇有名气。后来，我开始出演电视剧，也开始在电视圈闯出名声。我的意思是说观众开始认得我了。后来我演了《非常嫌疑犯》和其他几部电影，大约都在6个月的时间内推出，所以我想观众就开始突然联想起这些形象了。哦，他就是某部片里面的那个人……；哦，他演过那一部……；哦……于是大家就知道我的名字了。

《亚洲名人聊天室》安姿丽

不过，赢得最佳男配角奖一定很棒吧。后来又赢得奥斯卡最佳男主角奖，我想一定更是痛快。你因为出演《美国丽人》里那个抑郁消沉的无趣老爸和丈夫而赢得了这个奖项。请谈谈你人生中的那段经历。

演员 凯文·斯贝西

奥斯卡奖是同行对你的一大肯定。我深爱这个行业，我很敬重合作过及还没有机会合作的许多人，所以电影学院评委愿意给我这么大的肯定，实在远远超越我的梦想。

Notes & Vocabulary

make a name for oneself
打响名声；出名
name 在这里指的是 "名声；名气"，make a name for oneself 则解释为 "某人打响名声"，也可以写成 make one's name。

Jack's father made a name for himself as a famous defense lawyer.
杰克的爸爸打响了名声，成为一位著名的辩护律师。

connect the dots
联想
connect/join the dots 的用法源自一种连连看游戏，把纸上的所有黑点画线连起来后，就可看出图形全貌，所以 connect/join the dots 就引申出 "把信息串联起来而明白；联想" 的意思。

· Police connected the dots to solve the mysterious series of murders.
· 警方把所有证据串联起来解开了一连串谋杀疑案。

4. gradual [ˈgrædʒwəl]
   adj. 渐进式的；逐渐的

5. transition [træˈzɪʃən]
   n. 转换过程；过渡期

6. recognize [ˈrɛkɪɡˌnaɪz]
   v. 认同；认出

7. span [spæn] n. 一段时间

8. depressed [dɪˈprɛst] adj. 忧郁的

9. suburban [səˈbɜbən]
   adj. 平淡无趣的；郊区的

10. acknowledgement
    [ɪkˈnɑlɪdʒmənt] n. 认同

11. peer [pɪr] n. 同仁；同辈

12. industry [ˈɪndʌstrɪ] n. 产业；企业

影视娱乐

时尚生活

政治财经

体坛文艺

ANJALI RAO, TALK ASIA

Not all of your movies though have been so well received. *Pay it Forward* and *Life of David Gale* were not, you know, hits at the box office. How do you handle[13] it when a movie that you've worked on flops[14]? Does it particularly affect you?

KEVIN SPACEY, ACTOR

At the end of the day, the only thing that I can really say about movies is that movies aren't an actor's medium[15], and so if people are disappointed in a film, actors are just a color in someone else's painting. I mean, I can tell you quite honestly, and I think there's almost any actor who's been around for a while who could say this with absolute[16] conviction[17], that sometimes you go and see a movie that you've made and you know in your heart you made a better movie than they cut. But you have no authority[18] with which to make that change, no matter how much you might jump up and down and say, "You just missed it!" So, it's sometimes hard when movies don't turn out the way you hope, but you always go into them with the best of intentions[19].

ANJALI RAO, TALK ASIA

What does a role have to have, theatrical[20] or cinematic[21], for you to take it on?

KEVIN SPACEY, ACTOR

Nine times out of ten, I have to really like the story, and I mean the story beyond what the particular part might offer. Sometimes, and this is certainly true, I'll read a play or a screenplay[22] that will have a fantastic part in a really, really lousy movie. And I

《亚洲名人聊天室》 安姿丽

不过，你也不是每部影片都卖座。《让爱传出去》和《大卫·戈尔的一生》的票房就不太好。你自己参与其中的电影一旦表现不佳，你怎么面对这样的结果？你会受到很大的影响吗？

演员 凯文·斯贝西

归根究底，我真正能够说的就是电影其实不是演员的媒体。观众如果对一部电影感到失望，演员其实只能算是别人画作中的一种颜色而已。我是说，我可以坦白告诉你，而且我认为只要是在业界待过一段时间的演员，肯定都会这么说，"有时候你去看自己拍的电影，内心会知道自己当初拍的片子，比他们剪出来的成品好多了。"可是演员没有权力改变这样的结果，就算暴跳如雷大吼，"你们根本没抓到重点！"也无济于事。所以，有时候电影拍出来的结果也许不如你的期望，可是你总还是会尽心尽力把片子拍好。

《亚洲名人聊天室》 安姿丽

不论是舞台剧还是电影，一个角色必须有什么样的特质，你才会愿意接演？

演员 凯文·斯贝西

十有八九，我必须真的很喜欢其中的故事，而且不只是这个角色本身，而是整部戏的故事。我确实看过有些剧本，里面有个角色很棒，但整部电影却很差劲。我想参与的是能够禁得起时间考验的电影。你的选择当然不

Notes & Vocabulary

turn out

结果是……；出现

这个短语常用来表示事情水落石出或有某种结果，意思类似于中文的"原来是；结果是"。

- Few people's lives **turn out** the way they expect.
  很少有人的生活能万事如意。

13. **handle** [ˈhændl]
    v. 处理；处置
    Not everyone can handle the pressure of holding down a job and taking care of a family.

14. **flop** [flɑp]
    v.（作品；表演）表现不佳；失败
    The play flopped, but the movie version was a hit.

15. **medium** [ˈmidiəm] n. 媒介；媒体

16. **absolute** [ˈæbsəˌlut] adj. 绝对的
    Susan could not say with absolute certainty who phoned her in the middle of the night.

17. **conviction** [kənˈvɪkʃən]
    n. 确信；信念

18. **authority** [ɔˈθɔrətɪ]
    n. 权威；权力；当局

19. **intention** [ɪnˈtɛnʃən]
    n. 企图；目的

20. **theatrical** [θɪˈætrɪkəl]
    adj. 戏剧的
    The writer made his theatrical debut with an off-Broadway play.

21. **cinematic** [ˌsɪnəˈmætɪk]
    adj. 电影的

22. **screenplay** [ˈskrinˌple]
    n. 电影剧本

影视娱乐

时尚生活

政治财经

体坛文艺

think that I want to do movies that are gonna stand the test of time. You can't always, you know, in the end, to choose right, and you can't always . . . every movie you do won't necessarily ignite[23] the public. But I also don't think that every movie that makes money is necessarily a good film, you know. So the barometer[24] of what is good, the barometer of what does last, I think only history can tell us.

Kevin Spacey 演出作品

2009　《以服杀人（The Men Who Stare
　　　　at Goats）》

2008　《玩转 21 点（21）》《选票风波（Recount）》

2007　《北极的圣诞老人兄弟（Fred Claus）》

2006　《超人归来（Superman Returns）》

2005　《"爱迪生"（Edison）》

2004　《飞越情海（Beyond the Sea）》，身兼编剧、导演及制作人

2003　《大卫·戈尔的一生（The Life of David Gale）》

2001　《航运新闻（The Shipping News）》

2000　《让爱传出去（Pay It Forward）》

可能永远正确，你拍的每部影片也不一定都能够激发大家的热情。但我也不认为卖座的电影就是好电影。所以，什么样的电影是好电影，什么样的电影能够流传后世，我想只有历史能够告诉我们答案。

1999　《大骗局 / 征服钱海（The Big Kahuna）》

　　　《美国丽人（American Beauty）》，获奥斯卡最佳男主角等大奖

1998　《王牌对王牌（The Negotiator）》

1997　《洛城机密 / 铁面特警队（L.A. Confidential）》，获波士顿影评人协会奖最佳男配角

1995　《危机总动员（Outbreak）》，获纽约影评人协会奖最佳男配角

　　　《七宗罪（Seven）》，获纽约影评人协会奖最佳男配角、MTV 电影奖最佳银幕反派

　　　《非常嫌疑犯（The Usual Suspects）》，获纽约影评人协会奖最佳男配角、奥斯卡最佳男配角等大奖

影视娱乐　时尚生活　政治财经　体坛文艺

Robert Redford Talks Tech

Legendary[1] Actor and Director Discusses the Intersection[2] of Art and Technology

图片提供：Reuters

CNN ANCHOR

One of the ways mobile technology is adapting[3] is by getting closer to the film industry, and one of Hollywood's best known names, Robert Redford, is joining the revolution. The movie star and filmmaker spoke with Adrian Finighan, I have to say, in a tux[4]—check that out, too—at those mobile awards in Barcelona.

ROBERT REDFORD, ACTOR AND DIRECTOR

What interests[5] me about modern technology, I'm more interested . . . I'm not so much interested in it except as a phenomenon in and of itself. What interests me is how new technology can interact[6] with entertainment, which is art, and so that's where my interest comes in—how can . . . what new

38

正常MP3-Track06
慢速MP3-Track36

名人小档案 ▼ 罗伯特·雷德福

20世纪50年代，罗伯特·雷德福（1936—）与许多大明星一样，在纽约因舞台剧和电视剧开始发迹，曾以《The Voice of Charlie Pont》获艾美奖最佳男配角奖提名。此后，罗伯特·雷德福在1981年以《普通人（Ordinary People）》一片获得奥斯卡最佳导演奖及其他大奖多项提名。他在电影界的功劳莫过于1978年在犹他州盐湖城创立圣丹斯影展（Sundance Film Festival）。这个专门鼓励美国独立制片的影展，让许多有才华的新锐导演和演员有机会崭露头角。

Robert Redford

Notes & Vocabulary

1. **legendary** [ˈlɛdʒənˌdɛrɪ]
   adj. 传奇的；传说的

2. **intersection** [ˌɪntəˈsɛkʃən]
   n. 道路交叉口；交叉点

3. **adapt** [əˈdæpt] *v.* 适应
   After several months, Susan adapted to living overseas.

4. **tux** [tʌks]
   n.（男士无尾半正式）晚礼服
   （= tuxedo）

5. **interest** [ˈɪnt(ə)rəst]
   v. 使产生兴趣
   Mystery novels interest Janine more than horror stories.

6. **interact** [ˌɪntəˈrækt]
   v. 互相作用；互动
   He seldom interacts with his colleagues.

CNN 主播

与移动科技相适应的方式之一就是走近电影业，好莱坞名声最为响亮的一位人物——罗伯特·雷德福，正投入这场革命。这位电影明星和制片人在巴塞罗那举行的移动业颁奖典礼中，穿着燕尾服——这点也请大家看仔细了——接受了亚德里安·费尼根的采访。

圣丹斯影展

圣丹斯影展（Sundance Film Festival）为独立制片电影节之一。由导演罗伯特·雷德福所创办，专为独立电影而设。每年1月18日至28日在美国犹他州的帕克市（Park City）举行，为期11天。"圣丹斯"名称的由来，是根据雷德福和保罗·纽曼一起出演的一部经典电影《虎豹小霸王（Butch Cassidy and the Sundance Kid）》而来。

演员兼导演 罗伯特·雷德福

现代科技吸引我的地方，我比较喜欢……除了对于现代科技本身引起的现象以外，我对它其实并不那么感兴趣。我感兴趣的是新科技如何与娱乐业这门艺术互动，我对新科技的兴趣是从这里来的。怎么做……要创造出

影视娱乐 时尚生活 政治财经 体坛文艺

39

platforms[7] can be created to increase opportunities for artists to tell their stories. And what sits at the bottom of it, no matter what's going on, no matter what the size of the screen is, or how short the film is, is I just don't believe that you can ever keep going forward without story. So, as long as you're able to tell a story on this new platform, then I think it's going to be successful.

ADRIAN FINIGHAN, CNN CORRESPONDENT
Does modern technology help or hinder[8] as far as the medium of film, of storytelling, is concerned?

ROBERT REDFORD, ACTOR AND DIRECTOR
Yes, in other words, again it's storytelling. You have to have a good story. I mean I'm thinking, when I was a kid, you know, I grew up with funny papers. Main headlines didn't interest me when I was four, five, six years old, but the funny papers did, and one of the things I realized later on when I became a filmmaker, in looking to refine[9] the work of filmmaking as a director, was that these . . . there were stories told in four panels[10], maybe five.

That's it. You had to tell a story with a beginning, middle and an end, and it had to have an emotional grabbing[11] point, it had to satisfy you, it had to entertain you. And that was just four panels. So if you can do it with a comic, you can do it with film. To me, it's a discipline that can be put on the filmmaker that I think is pretty healthy. I love the idea.

什么样的新平台才能增加艺术家述说他们故事的机会。最重要的一点是，无论科技有多进步，无论屏幕的尺寸有多大，无论影片有多短，我不相信你能在没有故事的情况下一直往下走。所以，只要你能在这个新平台上说故事，我认为就会成功。

CNN 特派员 亚德里安·费尼根

就作为说故事和电影媒介而言，新科技究竟是一项推动力还是阻力？

演员兼导演 罗伯特·雷德福

是的，换言之，这又牵涉到了说故事。你必须要有一个好的故事。我的意思是，我小时候是伴着报纸中有趣的漫画专栏长大的。我四五六岁的时候，报纸的标题并不会吸引我，但是那些有趣的漫画却会，后来我当上制片人以后领悟到的其中一点就是，在我以导演的身份尝试要去改进拍电影这件事的时候，是这些……有些故事在四格或五格画面里就说完了。

就是这样。你说故事必须要有个开始、转折和结尾，必须要有个触动人心的点，必须要让你感到满足并有娱乐性。而那不过就是四格画面而已。所以如果你在漫画上做得到，在电影上就做得到。对我而言，这是可以对电影导演的一种要求，而我认为这么做是健康的。我喜欢这种想法。

Notes & Vocabulary

what sits at the bottom of it . . .

这是口语的用法，意思等于 the bottom line，表示"根本的原因；最重要的一点"，放在句首，后面引出要讲的论点，有强调的作用。

- The company is instituting a hiring freeze. The bottom line is that they can't afford to grow the staff in this economy.
这家公司开始停止招聘人员，主要是因为在目前的经济状况下，他们无法给更多的员工发薪水了。

7. platform [ˈplætˌfɔrm]
   n. 平台；台

8. hinder [ˈhɪndə] v. 妨碍；阻碍

9. refine [rɪˈfaɪn] v. 使升华；使完善

10. panel [ˈpænl]
    n. 画板上的一格

11. grabbing [ˈgræbɪŋ]
    adj. 掳获……的

影视娱乐 时尚生活 政治财经 体坛文艺

ADRIAN FINIGHAN, CNN CORRESPONDENT

Among the current generation of filmmakers, who interests you most? Who do you most admire[12]?

ROBERT REDFORD, ACTOR AND DIRECTOR

What I really like are new filmmakers. I mean at the [Sundance film] festival this year, which we just finished, what was really . . . there were a lot of exciting things about it. One of them was the crossover, the amount of crossover[13] that's occurring[14], that has a lot to do with this new technology.

The new technology is sponsoring[15] new ways of seeing things and new ways of doing things. And so suddenly in our festival this year we had more new filmmakers than we've ever had since we started. Secondly we had crossovers. We had . . . you had Bono and U2 coming with their 3D experimental[16] film for IMAX. You had Martin McDonald, the playwright[17], with a first directing piece. You had poets, you had musicians, you had artists from different, other disciplines crossing over into film, and the work to be seen was really exciting. To me that's . . . anything new that comes along that still enables[18] an artist to work and tell a story is exciting.

正常 *MP3 - Track06* / 慢速 *MP3 - Track36* ❙ *Robert Redford Talks Tech*

CNN 特派员 亚德里安·费尼根

在现代的电影导演中，谁最让你感兴趣？你最仰慕哪一位？

演员兼导演 罗伯特·雷德福

我最喜欢的是新锐导演。今年在我们刚办完的圣丹斯影展中……有很多让人感到兴奋的东西，其中一项是跨媒体电影，影展中有大量的跨媒体电影，这和这项新科技有很大关系。

这种新科技造就了看事情和做事情的新方式。所以忽然间在今年我们的影展中参展的新导演数量居影展开办以来之冠。其次，我们有跨媒体电影，有 Bono（编注：U2 乐队的主唱）和 U2 乐团带着他们的 3D IMAX 实验电影来。剧作家马丁·麦克唐带来他执导的第一部片子。有诗人，有音乐家，有从其他不同专业领域跨界来拍电影的艺术家，其所呈现的作品真让人感到兴奋。对我而言，那是……任何朝这个新方向发展，让一名艺术家可以据此创作和说故事的全新事物都令人感到兴奋。

Notes & Vocabulary

cross over (into) . . .

横跨……领域

cross over 在这里是指"交错；交叉"，后面接 into 表示"跨入某领域"的意思。

- The jazz band crossed over into rock and R&B music.
  那个爵士乐团包涵了摇滚与节奏蓝调的曲风。

其他与 cross 连用的词组

cross one's mind

闪过某人的脑海的念头

- The possibility that Joan's boyfriend might be cheating on her did cross her mind.
  琼曾认为她男友可能与别人交往。

cross swords

交锋；针锋相对

- The two candidates crossed swords in the presidential debate.
  那两位候选人在总统辩论会中交锋。

12. admire [əd`maɪr] v. 钦佩；欣赏
13. crossover [`krɔs͵ovə] n. 跨媒体电影
14. occur [ə`kɜ] v. 发生
    Many changes have occurred in the entertainment industry over the last decade.
15. sponsor [`spɑnsə] v. 资助；赞助
16. experimental [ɪk͵spɛrə`mɛntl] adj. 实验性的
17. playwright [`ple͵raɪt] n. 剧作家
18. enable [ɪ`nebl] v. 使能够
    Mandy's GPS enables her to find her way around to the city to meet clients.

影视娱乐　时尚生活　政治财经　体坛文艺

Celluloid[1]
Prophet[2]

Talk Asia Looks through the Lens of Filmmaker Oliver Stone

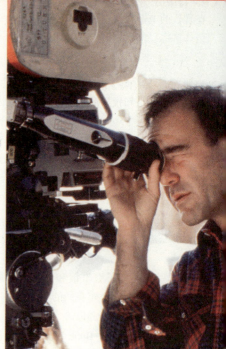

图片提供：Reuters

ANJALI RAO, CNN CORRESPONDENT
He's one of the most acclaimed and most controversial[3] directors of his time, tackling[4] everything from war to world leaders to the excess on Wall Street.

MICHAEL DOUGLAS AS GORDON GEKKO IN "WALL STREET"
Greed—for lack of a better word—is good.

ANJALI RAO, CNN CORRESPONDENT
He's Oliver Stone. This is Talk Asia.

ANJALI RAO, CNN CORRESPONDENT
So, this is the premiere[5] of *W*. How do you feel going into premieres? Do you get nervous?

名人小档案 ▼ 奥利佛·斯通

美国电影导演和编剧奥利佛·斯通（1946—），同时也是一名演员。其电影多围绕政治或战争等主题。其中《刺杀肯尼迪》、《天生杀人狂》等都是公认的佳作。他的《野战排》、《生于七月四日》、《天与地》三部越战题材的作品被誉为"越战三部曲"。由于曾经参加过越战并负伤，他常在电影中利用暴力对社会进行反思。

Oliver Stone

🔊 大导演奥利佛·斯通镜头下的世界观

Notes & Vocabulary

1. **celluloid** [ˈsɛljəˌlɔɪd]
   n. 赛璐珞片；胶片；电影

2. **prophet** [ˈprɑfət]
   n. 预言者；先知

3. **controversial** [ˌkɑntrəˈvɜʃəl]
   adj. 有争议的
   The artist is known for making controversial political statements with his work.

4. **tackle** [ˈtækl̩]
   v. 处理；对付
   Vincent tackled the problem of his leaking roof over the weekend.

5. **premiere** [prɪˈmjɛr]
   n. 初次上演；首映

影视娱乐
时尚生活
政治财经
体坛文艺

CNN 特派员 安姿丽
他是当代最受赞誉也最具争议性的导演之一，他探究过的议题形形色色，包括战争、世界领袖，乃至华尔街的奢华、贪婪。

《华尔街》戈登·盖科（迈克尔·道格拉斯饰演）
贪婪——我们缺乏更好的词汇——可是件好事。

CNN 特派员 安姿丽
他就是奥利佛·斯通。欢迎收看《亚洲名人聊天室》。

CNN 特派员 安姿丽
这是《小布什传》的首映式。你参加首映式有什么感觉？会紧张吗？

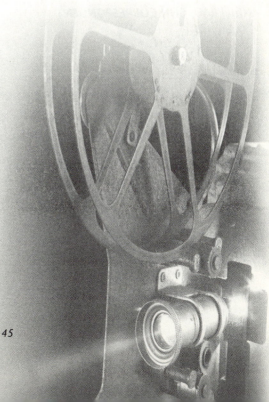

OLIVER STONE, FILM DIRECTOR

A little bit. You know, no matter how many times, you . . . it's always that frisson[6].

ANJALI RAO, CNN CORRESPONDENT

Have you ever had a really nightmare premiere where the reaction has just bombed[7]?

OLIVER STONE, FILM DIRECTOR

No, because people are generally polite, and if they . . . if . . . you know, they don't throw tomatoes.

ANJALI RAO, CNN CORRESPONDENT

That's good.

OLIVER STONE, FILM DIRECTOR

You sense it. You sense . . . you know, a lot of my films do end on a puzzle or they end up leaving you thinking.

ANJALI RAO, CNN CORRESPONDENT

Well, yeah.

OLIVER STONE, FILM DIRECTOR

So it's not necessarily the jump-to-your-feet big thing. And sometimes those can be very deceptive[8], too. You got some silly film that everybody likes, and they love it.

ANJALI RAO, CNN CORRESPONDENT

Right.

电影导演 奥利佛·斯通
有一点。不论参加过几次，还是会有兴奋的感觉。

CNN 特派员 安姿丽
你有没有遇到过噩梦般的首映式，得到的反应非常糟糕？

电影导演 奥利佛·斯通
没有，因为大家通常很客气，就算不喜欢，也不会扔西红柿。

CNN 特派员 安姿丽
那很好啊。

电影导演 奥利佛·斯通
可是你感觉得到。你也知道，我很多作品都是以谜团收场，或是结局发人深省。

CNN 特派员 安姿丽
的确。

电影导演 奥利佛·斯通
所以不是什么严重到让人跳脚的事。有时候观众的反应也可能造成误导。有些片子傻得很，偏偏大家都喜欢。

CNN 特派员 安姿丽
没错。

Notes & Vocabulary

6. **frisson** [friˋson]
   n.【法】（一时的）兴奋；悸动；震颤

7. **bomb** [bɑm]
   v.【美】【俚】惨败；完蛋；卖得差
   The play bombed with critics and audiences alike.

8. **deceptive** [dɪˋsɛptɪv]
   adj. 迷惑的；骗人的
   Maria's small size is deceptive, for she has a black belt in judo.

影视娱乐

时尚生活

政治财经

体坛文艺

OLIVER STONE, FILM DIRECTOR

They remember it, and they forget it fifteen minutes later. My films, sometimes you walk out, you know, you got to think about it a little bit.

ANJALI RAO, CNN CORRESPONDENT

You know, a lot of people were expecting this one— knowing your politics—to be [a] fierce criticism of George W. Bush, and you actually sort of end up portraying him in a rather sympathetic[9] light. How come you didn't want to go down the route where you just tear strips off him?

OLIVER STONE, FILM DIRECTOR

Because that was easy. That's like shooting fish in a barrel. Everybody was attacking him. His poll ratings were low. My . . . the idea with Stanley Weiser and his script was to walk the path of Bush—to be in his shoes[10], to feel what he's feeling. He thinks he's a wonderful man. He thinks he's doing the right thing. He doesn't have any doubt.

So, what can you do? You have to walk in their path. That's the way they . . . let the audience react to what they're seeing. Some people even sympathize with him because he's lost. He's lost his soul and he's lost his bearings[11]. But at the end of the day, you know, they'll think about it. I don't think "sympathize" is the right word; I think "empathize[12]. "And that's what I do—dramatists[13] empathize. In other words, you may not like the man—

ANJALI RAO, CNN CORRESPONDENT

Yeah.

电影导演 奥利佛·斯通

这样的片子他们刚看还记得，可是 15 分钟后就忘了。至于我的片子，有时候你走出戏院，还是需要稍微思考一下。

CNN 特派员 安姿丽

大家都知道你的政治倾向，所以都以为这部影片是对小布什的猛烈批判，可是你其实把他拍得颇令人同情。你为什么不把他鞭挞得体无完肤呢？

电影导演 奥利佛·斯通

因为那样太简单了，就像探囊取物一样。大家都骂他，他的民意调查支持率非常低。斯坦利·韦泽想在这个剧本中从小布什的角度出发，设身处地想象他的处境，体会他的感受。小布什认为自己是个很好的人，他认为自己的所作所为是正确的。他没有疑虑。

所以，你要怎么办呢？你必须站在他们的立场，这样才能让观众对所见的内容产生共鸣。有些人甚至会同情小布什，因为他迷失了。他迷失了自己的灵魂，迷失了方向。总之，他们会思考。我认为用"同情"这个词不太对，我觉得是"同感"。这就是我的工作——剧作家的工作就是感同身受。换句话说，你可能不喜欢这个人。

CNN 特派员 安姿丽

是啊。

Notes & Vocabulary

tear a strip off sb.
严厉斥责
tear [tɛr] 当动词有"(使)撕开；撕裂"之意，名词 strip 有"条；带；细长片"之意。此短语原指鞭打某人赤裸的上身使其皮开肉绽，后引申指"严厉斥责某人"。

- The teacher tore a strip off the student who was caught cheating on a test.
  老师严厉斥责了那个考试作弊的学生。

like shooting fish in a barrel
简单的不得了
字面上意思是"射击桶子里的鱼"，比喻事情"简单的不得了"，类似中文的"探囊取物"、"瓮中捉鳖"。

- Beating Nathan in an argument was like shooting fish in a barrel.
  和内森吵架要吵赢是再容易不过的了。

9. **sympathetic** [ˌsɪmpəˈθɛtɪk]
   adj. 同情的；有同情心的；支持的
   Rachel was sympathetic to her friend's misfortune.

10. **in one's shoes**
    易地而处；设身处地
    Robert didn't know how difficult his manager's job was until he spent a week in his shoes.

11. **bearings** [ˈbɛrɪŋz]
    n. 方向；方面（复数形式）

12. **empathize** [ˈɛmpəˌθaɪz]
    v. 同感；移情
    Daniel empathized with orphans because he also lost his parents at a young age.

13. **dramatist** [ˈdræmətɪst]
    n. 剧作家

影视娱乐

时尚生活

政治财经

体坛文艺

49

OLIVER STONE, FILM DIRECTOR

But you have to feel for him. You have to feel what he's like.

ANJALI RAO, CNN CORRESPONDENT

When this whole economic mess[14] first sparked, it was inevitable that people would start talking about your film again—your 1987 movie, *Wall Street*. Do you think that it was prophetic[15] in a way?

OLIVER STONE, FILM DIRECTOR

I think it's sad, you know? At the time we did it, it was bad enough. In 1987, you know, the greed factor[16] was enormous. But I was surprised that it went on for 20 more years, you see? I thought there'd be some turnaround. But what happened with the Clinton years was this Greenspan. He did keep this thing going; the bubble of the technological bubble became the housing bubble.

So there's a series of things that happened, that they pumped, they inflated[17]. They inflated. And it reached a place which I think Greenspan—these people—should have seen it coming. I mean, anybody who did their basic mathematics knew. And unfortunately now they . . . it's reached . . . the bubble burst. The bubble's burst.

MICHAEL DOUGLAS AS GORDON GEKKO IN "WALL STREET"

Greed, you mark my words, will not only save Teldar Paper, but that other malfunctioning[18] corporation called the U.S.A. Thank you very much.

电影导演 奥利佛·斯通

可是你必须为他设想，去感受他是什么感受。

CNN 特派员 安姿丽

这场经济乱象刚爆发的时候，大家不免又会开始讨论你的电影——你1987年的作品《华尔街》。你认为那部作品具有先见之明吗？

电影导演 奥利佛·斯通

我觉得很悲哀。我们拍那部影片的时候，情况就已经够糟了。在 1987 年，贪婪的情况已经很严重了。可是我很惊讶这种现象竟然又持续了 20 年，你知道吧？我以为情况会改善，可是克林顿当政期间却出了个格林斯潘。他延续了这种现象，科技泡沫变成了楼市泡沫。

结果发生一连串的状况，他们不断炒作，物价膨胀，一再膨胀，而且达到了一定程度，我认为格林斯潘那帮人应该能预见到当今的下场。我是说，任何会做基础数学的人，就知道结果会是这样。可惜……泡沫破灭了，就这么破灭了。

《华尔街》戈登·盖科（迈克尔·道格拉斯饰演）

贪婪——各位听好了——不但挽救了泰尔达造纸公司，也救了那家叫做美国的运作不良的公司。谢谢各位。

Notes & Vocabulary

turnaround
突然好转；彻底改变；回复时间

turnaround 一般指的是（运营、经济的）突然好转；彻底改变。在商业英语中也可指 turnaround time "回复时间"。指在订货流程中收到订单后（receiving），接着制造或加工产品（processing），再将产品运回订货者（returning）整个流程所需的时间。

- A new emphasis on quality and customer service helped the company's turnaround.
  重视质量与客户服务的新规定帮助公司的运营好转起来了。

- The standard turnaround for Prime Manufacturing orders is two months.
  普兰制造公司订单的标准回复时间是两个月。

14. **mess** [mɛs]
    n. 混乱；凌乱的状态
    His work station is a mess with a slew of papers all over his desk.

15. **prophetic** [prə`fɛtɪk]
    adj. 预言的；预示的
    The book's premise of an economic downtown starting in the real estate market turned out to be prophetic.

16. **factor** [`fæktɚ] *n.* 因素；要素

17. **inflate** [ɪn`flet]
    v.（通货）膨胀；充气；骄傲
    All of the praise she received inflated Terry's ego.

18. **malfunctioning** [ˌmælˋfʌŋkʃənɪŋ]
    adj. 故障的
    Victor took the malfunctioning part to a repair shop.

影视娱乐 时尚生活 政治财经 体坛文艺

OLIVER STONE, FILM DIRECTOR

Gekko is for profit. You must never forget. And I do believe there's profit in survivability[19]. If you can take our economy and say, "It can work," fair market can work. Not free market—fair market. And if you can keep it fair, you can make money on this market, and you can make money with survival. You can go green, and you can make money. In other words, I am for the private side, but the government has to lead.

ANJALI RAO, CNN CORRESPONDENT

Oliver, what do you think is the most important thing to impart[20] to budding[21] filmmakers about surviving the industry today?

OLIVER STONE, FILM DIRECTOR

It's emotional; it's your spirit. A spirit is something that comes from within. It's energy; it's wisdom. It's whatever you can . . . whatever is special to you. Find that thing. It takes time. Life is experiment.

ANJALI RAO, CNN CORRESPONDENT

You studied at the NYU film school under Martin Scorsese.

OLIVER STONE, FILM DIRECTOR

Among others, yes.

ANJALI RAO, CNN CORRESPONDENT

What did you learn from him?

电影导演 奥利佛·斯通

盖科追求的是利润。千万别忘了这一点。我确实认为生存能力可以带来利润。你如果能够针对我们的经济说，"这样行得通"，只有公平的市场才行得通。不是自由市场，是公平的市场。你只要能够保持市场的公平，就能够在这个市场上赚钱，也能够通过生存赚钱。你可以追求环保，也还是能够赚钱。换句话说，我支持私营，但是政府必须领导。

CNN 特派员 安姿丽

奥利佛，刚出道的电影人如果要在今天的电影业中生存下去，你给他们最重要的忠告会是什么？

电影导演 奥利佛·斯通

重点在于情感，在于你的精神。精神是种源自内心的东西，是活力，是智慧，就是任何对你具有特殊意义的东西。你必须找到那个东西。这要花时间。人生就是不断地实验。

CNN 特派员 安姿丽

你曾经在纽约大学电影学院跟随马丁·斯科赛斯学习。

电影导演 奥利佛·斯通

他是其中一位，没错。

CNN 特派员 安姿丽

你从他那里学到了什么？

奥利佛·斯通的代表作

1987《华尔街（Wall Street）》

1991《门（The Doors）》

越战三部曲：

1986《野战排（Platoon）》

1989《生于七月四日（Born on the Fourth of July）》

1993《天与地（Heaven & Earth）》

总统三部曲：

1991《刺杀肯尼迪（JFK）》

1995《白宫风暴（Nixon）》

2008《小布什传（W.）》

影视娱乐

时尚生活

政治财经

体坛文艺

OLIVER STONE, FILM DIRECTOR

Martin . . . Marty was one of the most energetic teachers: young, crazy, in his twenties with hair down to his shoulders. He would stay up all night watching crazy movies on TV because there was no video in those days. And he imparted to us that enthusiasm[22] he had for film, which I think was beautiful.

ANJALI RAO, CNN CORRESPONDENT

As far as your style, I mean, it's very flamboyant[23], whiz-bang, in your face. There's loads of stuff going on all at the same time. How has that developed over the years?

OLIVER STONE, FILM DIRECTOR

It's my nature. I mean, actually some of my later films are quiet. I mean, I have done quiet films, like *Heaven and Earth* is relatively quiet. Now it depends on the film. You know, ~~somebody~~ [something] like [the] Kennedy murder, you wanna fracture[24] it. You wanna make people rethink. You wanna re-juggle[25] the . . . re-juggle—take the same facts [and] re-juggle them. Make them see it a different way. That's the key.

电影导演 奥利佛·斯通

马丁是位精力非常充沛的老师：年轻、疯狂、二十几岁、发长披肩。他会为了观看电视播放的古怪电影而整夜不睡，因为那时候还没有录像带。他把他对电影的那股热情传递给了我们，我认为这是很美妙的。

CNN 特派员 安姿丽

至于你的风格，可说是非常眩目，节奏紧凑、让人目不暇接，一大堆事情同时在进行。这样的风格在这些年来有什么改变？

电影导演 奥利佛·斯通

这就是我的本性。我后期有些片子其实挺安静的。我是说，我也拍过步调平缓的片子，像《天与地》的步调就很平缓。关键其实在于片子本身。像肯尼迪的刺杀案，你会想打破窠臼来拍它，让人重新思考。你会想要重组——拿同样的事实重新组合，让观众从不同的角度看待事情。这才是关键所在。

Notes & Vocabulary

whiz-bang
精彩的；快速进行的
由 whiz "飕飕掠过" 和 bang "砰；爆炸" 两个词组成，原本是指快速射出，立即爆炸的炮弹或爆竹，口语中比喻 "惊人而成功的事物"。当形容词则是指 "精彩的；惊人而出色的"，还有 "快速进行的；紧凑的" 之意。

· A marching band and fireworks display provided a whiz-bang welcome to the victorious soldiers returning home.
乐队游行和燃放烟火让欢迎军人凯旋的盛会精彩万分。

22. **enthusiasm** [ɪn`θuzɪˌæzəm]
    n. 热忱；热心

23. **flamboyant** [flæm`bɔɪənt]
    adj. 浮夸的；炫耀的

24. **fracture** [`fræktʃə]
    v. 折断；违反；毁坏

25. **re-juggle** [rɪ`dʒʌgl]
    v. 重组；耍弄；篡改
    Could you re-juggled your schedule to make room for a meeting tomorrow?

影视娱乐 时尚生活 政治财经 体坛文艺

Vintage[1] Coppola

Fine Wine and Iconic[2] Films Flow through Legendary Director's Career

图片提供：Reuters

REVEALED

Master filmmaker Francis Ford Coppola relaxes in the grounds of his vineyard[3] in California. He appears to be a man very much *at peace with* himself. An Oscar winner who is responsible for a series of films that have consistently been voted as being among the best ever to be made, to describe him as a living legend is no exaggeration. Born in Detroit in the year the Second World War started, a childhood illness left him bedridden[4] for long periods.

FRANCIS FORD COPPOLA, DIRECTOR AND VINTNER[5]

I don't think I was a very extraordinary person, certainly a very extraordinary kid. I, if anything, I

名人小档案 ▼ 弗朗西斯·科波拉

弗朗西斯·科波拉（1939—）出身意大利移民音乐世家，祖父母自意大利南部贝纳尔达（Bernalda）移民到美国。科波拉小时因患小儿麻痹而长期卧病。科波拉学生时期曾制作过低成本独立电影，同时撰写剧本，1963年他执导处女作恐怖片《Dementia 13》。1971年他以《巴顿将军（Paton）》的剧本首次获得奥斯卡奖。而20世纪70年代的经典《教父》和《教父第二集》由他担任编剧和导演，两部影片都赢得了奥斯卡最佳影片奖，后者更成为首部获奖的续集电影。

Francis Ford Coppola

《揭秘》

电影大师弗朗西斯·科波拉在他位于加州的葡萄园里休憩。他看起来相当平静悠然。身为奥斯卡得主的他，所拍的许多电影都一再被票选为史上佳片。因此，称他为活生生的传奇一点都不为过。他在第二次世界大战爆发的那一年出生于底特律，儿时曾经因病卧床许久。

导演兼酿酒人 弗朗西斯·科波拉
我不认为自己非常特殊，小时候也一点都不特别。如果要说我有什么特点，就是丰富的

Notes & Vocabulary

at peace with
与……和谐相处

peace 是指"和平；平静"，at peace 是指"处于和平、和睦的状态"，后面用 with 加上人表示"与……相处和谐"，如果是 at peace with oneself 则是"某人自身感到平和、快乐"，有怡然自得的意思。

· Valerie is at peace with her choice to retire early.
瓦莱丽对自己提早退休的决定很满意。

1. vintage [ˈvɪntɪdʒ]
   adj.（葡萄酒）上等的；最典型的；古色古香的
   Randal collects vintage automobiles.

2. iconic [aɪˈkɑnɪk]
   adj. 象征性的；代表性的

3. vineyard [ˈvɪnjəd]
   n. 葡萄园

4. bedridden [ˈbɛdˌrɪdn]
   adj. 卧床不起的；长期卧床的

5. vintner [ˈvɪntnə]
   n. 葡萄酒商；酿酒人

The Making of 'Tetro'
Courtesy American Zoetrope

影视娱乐

时尚生活

政治财经

体坛文艺

57

had a good imagination, and I was just in love with science and girls. And that brought me to theater.

REVEALED

During the '60s, he teamed up with[6] a man who was going to have a long-lasting impact on his future plans. Alongside George Lucas, he set up film company American Zoetrope. *The Godfather* won three Oscars and is generally regarded as one of the greatest films ever. Coppola is quick to acknowledge[7] the impact the film had on the rest of his life.

FRANCIS FORD COPPOLA, DIRECTOR AND VINTNER

That project really changed my career to something very different than（美语表达方式，等同于 different from what）I would have imagined. I never would have thought of myself as, you know, kind of a more Hollywood or industry film director, or certainly not at that level of success.

REVEALED

The Godfather was the first film in a trilogy[8] completed over almost two decades. For a lot of directors, it would represent an unsurpassable[9] body of work, but Coppola had another masterpiece[10] up his sleeve.

想象力，而且我热爱科学和女孩子。我就是因此踏入了戏剧这一行。

《揭秘》

20世纪60年代期间，他与一个人合作，而且这个人对他未来的规划产生了深远的影响。这个人就是乔治·卢卡斯，他们两人共同成立了美国西洋镜这家电影公司。《教父》（注1）赢得三项奥斯卡奖，并且被公认为史上巨作之一。科波拉毫不讳言这部电影对他后续人生造成的冲击。

导演兼酿酒人　弗朗西斯·科波拉

拍摄那部电影对我事业的改变超乎我的想象。我从没想过自己会成为好莱坞或商业电影的导演，至少从没想过会达到这么成功的程度。

《揭秘》

《教父》是一套三部曲当中的第一集，整部影片历经将近二十年才完成。对于许多导演而言，这么一整部的作品想必已是无可超越的一大成就。不过，科波拉却还有另一部经典之作。

注1

改编自马里奥·普佐1969年同名小说，描述第二次世界大战后纽约的西西里黑手党柯里昂家族的历史，获得奥斯卡金像奖最佳影片、最佳改编剧本、最佳男主角（马龙·白兰度）。

Notes & Vocabulary

a body of 大量的；大批的

body 原指"身体；遗体"，还可当做"团体；机构；群体"，如 student body "学生团体"。a body of 则是指"一大群；大批的；大量的"，也就是 a large amount of 的意思。
- The writer was responsible for a large body of work.
  那位作家写了一大堆作品。

have sth. up one's sleeve
暗藏玄机；自有妙计
按照字面意思就是"袖子里藏了东西"，比喻暗地里有所准备，有中文中"暗藏玄机；袖里乾坤"的意思，sth. 也可以用 an ace 或 a card 替代，指赌徒在袖子里藏一张好牌作弊。
- Things may look bleak, but I still have a few tricks up my sleeve.
  事情也许看似无望，不过我还有几个妙招。

其他与 sleeve 连用的词组：

roll up one's sleeves
（卷起袖子）准备行动
- It's time to roll up our sleeves and get to work.
  该是大家卷起袖子开始工作的时候了。

wear one's heart on one's sleeve
表露心情、想法
- Julia tends to wear her heart on her sleeve when discussing her political beliefs.
  朱莉娅在谈论她的政治信念时态度鲜明。

6. **team up with** 与……合作
7. **acknowledge** [əkˈnɑlɪdʒ]
   v. 承认；认知
8. **trilogy** [ˈtrɪlədʒɪ] n. 三部剧；三部曲
9. **unsurpassable** [ˌʌnsəˈpæsəbl]
   adj. 不能超越的
10. **masterpiece** [ˈmæstərpis]
    n. 杰作；名著

影视娱乐　时尚生活　政治财经　体坛文艺

An iconic scene from one of the greatest films of all times, set to the music of Wagner's *Ride of the Valkyries*[11], *Apocalypse Now* was an epic[12] movie set during the Vietnam War. It was the film that nearly destroyed Francis Ford Coppola's fledgling[13] career. Filming, which started in 1976, took the better part of three years to complete and ran into immediate financial difficulties. Against all the odds, the movie was completed. It was hailed[14] as a masterpiece and went on to win numerous awards.

Alongside his first loves—family and film—Coppola has slowly been developing a new passion. In California's Napa Valley, he has his own vineyard, which has established quite a reputation[15].

FRANCIS FORD COPPOLA, DIRECTOR AND VINTNER
I realized then about, I don't know, 15 years ago, that the movie business wasn't really a business, that it was a crazy activity in which you might have a lot of success one year, but you couldn't bank on[16] it. And the wine business was really like every year you could do better than you had done the year before, and you could predict it.

And I said, jeez, you know, that's . . . this is like a job. This is like a real job, and maybe I could use that to subsidize[17] my own film, and I could be an artist, because how can you be an artist unless you have a day job? Oddly enough, the god of wine and the god of drama is the same god—Bacchus[18].

这幕经典的画面取自电影史上的一部伟大巨作，配乐是瓦格纳歌剧《女武神的飞行》，《现代启示录》（注2）是一部史诗电影，故事背景为越战。这部片几乎毁掉了科波拉才刚起步的电影事业。这部电影的拍摄工作始于1976年，花了将近3年才大功告成，并随即遭遇到财务困难。不过，尽管困难重重，这部电影终于还是制作完成，结果被赞誉为经典之作，并且获奖连连。

除了自始至终热爱的家庭与电影之外，科波拉也逐渐培养出一个新的爱好。在加利福尼亚州纳帕谷，他拥有自己的葡萄园，目前已颇有名气。

导演兼酿酒人 弗朗西斯·科波拉

我差不多在15年前了解到，拍电影其实算不上是真正的事业，而是一种疯狂的举动。你也许会有一年大获成功，但是你不能完全靠它。葡萄酒这个行业则是真正可以一年比一年进步，而且具有可预测性。

所以我说，哎呀，这……这才算是一份工作，一份真正的工作。说不定我可以利用这项事业资助我自己的电影，这样我就可以当个艺术家。毕竟，如果没有全职工作，怎么当得了艺术家呢？巧的是，酒神和戏剧之神同样都是巴克斯。

注2
改编自康拉德小说《黑暗的心（Heart of Darkness）》，以越南战争为背景，描述威拉德上尉奉命深入柬埔寨丛林，暗杀疯狂滥杀无辜的科茨上校。获得戛纳影展金棕榈奖、奥斯卡金像奖最佳摄影及最佳音效、金球奖最佳导演及最佳男配角（罗伯特·杜瓦尔）等诸多大奖。

Notes & Vocabulary

the better part of
大半的；一半以上的

better 在这里不是"较好的"的意思，而是解释为"大半的；超过一半的"，如 for the better part of an hour 就是"半小时以上"。因此，文中 took the better part of three years 是指"用掉了三年里大半的时间"。

· It took the better part of a week to finish the project.
那个计划耗费了大半周的时间才完成。

against all (the) odds
克服万难

odds 原指"可能性；机会"，但此处解释为"巨大的困难；不利的条件"，against all (the) odds 是"克服万难；尽管困难重重"的意思。

· Against all odds, Bill found his lost ring in the grass.
比尔克服万难，在草堆里找到了他遗失的戒指。

11. **Valkyrie** [ˈvælˌkiri]
    n. 女武神瓦尔基里（来自北欧神话，专司挑选及引导勇敢战死的灵魂）

12. **epic** [ˈɛpɪk]
    n. 史诗；史诗般的作品

13. **fledgling** [ˈflɛdʒlɪŋ]
    adj. 刚开始的；无经验的

14. **hail** [hel]
    v. 赞扬……是；誉为；拥立

15. **reputation** [ˌɹɛpjəˈteʃən]
    n. 名誉；声望

16. **bank on** 依靠……获利；指望

17. **subsidize** [ˈsʌbsəˌdaɪz]
    v. 资助；补贴

18. **Bacchus** [ˈbækəs]
    n. 巴克斯（罗马神话中专司酒、丰饶、戏剧的神祇，在希腊神话中称为 Dionysus）

REVEALED

The vineyard has helped Coppola finance[19] his latest film, *Tetro*, a saga[20] of family fortunes. He both wrote and directed it.

FRANCIS FORD COPPOLA, DIRECTOR AND VINTNER

Well, when I was young, I wanted to write and direct little personal films, or, you know, in those days, in the late '50s and '60s, we had the inspiration of all the great films coming from Europe and also from Japan. And that was the era that made us—many of my colleagues, myself—want to make films, you know, films like Fellini or Antonioni or Truffaut. And these usually were personal, written from the lives of the person making the film, rather than the project that was just made to, you know, be a successful mystery or a successful caper[21] film or whatever the genre[22].

REVEALED

Coppola is a man who is very happy in his own skin. He has achieved professional greatness and much personal happiness. Underpinning[23] all the success is a love of filmmaking.

弗朗西斯·科波拉 执导代表作

1972, 1974, 1990《教父（The Godfather）》三部曲

1979《现代启示录（Apocalypse Now）》

1983《斗鱼（Rumble Fish）》

1984《棉花俱乐部（The Cotton Club）》

1986《佩姬·苏要出嫁（Peggy Sue Got Married）》

正常 *MP3-Track08* / 慢速 *MP3-Track38* ▌ *Vintage Coppola*

Notes & Vocabulary

in one's own skin
做自己

skin 是指"皮肤；皮"，in one's own skin 从字面来说是"穿着自己的外皮"，引申指一个人对于自身的感觉，文中 is very happy in his own skin，就是表示自己"很悠然；怡然自得；泰然自若"的意思。

Philip's charisma comes from the fact that he feels comfortable in his own skin.
菲利普的魅力来自于他一直感到很自在。

19. **finance** [faɪˋnæns]
   v. 资助；提供资金
   Megan's father financed her first business venture.

20. **saga** [ˋsɑgə]
   n. 长篇故事；家世小说；英雄故事

21. **caper** [ˋkepə]
   n. 不法活动；犯罪行动、计划（抢劫等）

22. **genre** [ˋʒɑnrə]
   n.（文艺作品的）类型

23. **underpin** [͵ʌndəˋpɪn]
   v. 支撑；加固
   There was substantial scientific evidence underpinning the professor's controversial theories.

《揭秘》
这个葡萄园资助了科波拉的新作《泰特罗》，一部描写家族兴衰的电影。这是他自编自导的作品。

导演兼酿酒人 弗朗西斯·科波拉

我年轻的时候就想自编自导个人化的小型电影。你也知道，在 20 世纪 50 年代末期和 60 年代期间，欧洲和日本的许多杰作都为我们带来了大量的启发。就是因为生活在那个时代，我的许多同行和我自己才会开始想要拍电影，好比说费里尼、安东尼奥尼及特吕弗（注 3）这些导演的作品。那些电影都非常个人化，源自导演自己的人生经验，不像那些为了卖座而拍出来的悬疑片或犯罪片等类型片。

《揭秘》
现在的科波拉非常安然自得，他在专业方面已达成了崇高地位，个人生活也过得相当快乐。他一切成功的基础，就是对拍摄电影的热爱。

1992《吸血僵尸惊情四百年（Bram Stoker's Dracula）》

1997《造雨人（The Rainmaker）》

2009《泰特罗（Tetro）》

注 3
均为法国 20 世纪 50 年代末期到 60 年代中期新浪潮运动的代表人物，强调个人化的风格与主题。同时期日本重要导演有黑泽明、小津安二郎等。

影视娱乐 / 时尚生活 / 政治财经 / 体坛文艺

A Man of Action

A Talk Asia Exclusive Interview with Influential Hong Kong Director John Woo

图片提供：AP

ANJALI RAO, TALK ASIA

Hi, I'm Anjali Rao at the Hong Kong premiere of Asia's most expensive ever film, *Red Cliff*. My guest today is the director who worked his way up through Hong Kong cinema to direct some of Hollywood's biggest names. He's John Woo and this is Talk Asia.

John, it's fantastic to have you on Talk Asia today. Now, you've just finished *Red Cliff*, the most expensive Asian movie ever made. It's a huge blockbuster[1] with massive, elaborate[2] sets[3] and cast of thousands. Are you glad that it's finally over?

⑨ CNN专访吴宇森——华人导演的好莱坞经验

名人小档案 ▼ 吴宇森

吴宇森（1946—）出生于中国广州，成长于中国香港，是香港及好莱坞著名导演及编剧。吴宇森5岁时全家移居到香港，定居于治安很差的贫民区九龙石硖尾，小时候便喜欢躲到电影院偷看电影。27岁时他首次执导电影《铁汉柔情》，而他打入好莱坞的第一部影片是则由尚·克劳德·范·达美（Jean-Claude Van Damme）主演的《终极标靶》。2010年9月，吴宇森获第67届威尼斯影展颁发的终身成就金狮奖，成为该奖项的第一位华人得主。

John Woo

《亚洲名人聊天室》安姿丽

嗨，我是安姿丽，这里是香港一场电影首映式的现场，而这部电影正是亚洲有史以来造价最高昂的影片《赤壁》。我今天的来宾，是一位在香港电影界一路打拼，力争上游的导演，后来指导了不少好莱坞巨星。他就是吴宇森，您收看的节目是《亚洲名人聊天室》。

吴导，真高兴能够邀请你到今天的《亚洲名人聊天室》节目。你刚拍了《赤壁》，这是亚洲影史上造价最高的一部影片。这部卖座巨片有许多庞大繁复的场景，而且有好几千人参与演出。你是不是很高兴终于把这部影片拍完了呢？

Notes & Vocabulary

标题扫描

man of . . .
具有……特质或专长的人

man of 后面加上名词，是指"具有某种特质或专长的人"。本文标题 man of action 原意是"具有行动力的人；实践者"，而 action 又指"动作片"，同时也是拍电影时"开拍"的指令，指出吴宇森作为导演的身份特点。

· Julia is drawn to men of mystery.
朱莉娅总是被神秘的男子吸引。

英文谚语

Think like a man of action, act like a man of thought.
思考时要像行动家，行动时要像思想家。
（法国哲学家 柏格森 Henri-Louis Bergson）

work one's way up
努力向上

描述一个人靠着自己的努力，一步一步提升自己的社会地位、阶级等等，有中文的"力争上游"的意思。

· Nancy worked her way up from the company mail room.
南希努力工作，一路从公司的收发室升职上来。

1. **blockbuster** [ˈblɑkˌbʌstə]
   n. 大制作、高成本的巨片；轰动的事物

2. **elaborate** [ɪˈlæbərət]
   adj. 精心制作的；详尽的
   Jeff explained his elaborate plan for a new business.

3. **set** [sɛt] *n.* 布景；场景

影视娱乐

时尚生活

政治财经

体坛文艺

JOHN WOO, FILM DIRECTOR

I must say that is the hardest movie I have ever made. I mean it's spent a lot of money, I spent a lot of time, but it is one of my dream project[s]. I have been dreaming to make this movie for over 20 years. Now, at last, you know, I have such a good opportunity to make it, and when I ~~find~~ [found] out it got so much success in everywhere, that make[s] me feel very, very pleased.

ANJALI RAO, TALK ASIA

What were the most challenging parts of the film for you?

JOHN WOO, FILM DIRECTOR

The action scenes ~~was~~ [were] the most challenging part. You know, in part one we had the huge turtle formation[4]. I knew there's a lot of people [that] have read the *Chinese Art of War*, and especially for most American[s], they are so familiar with that book. So how to show it on the screen, that was a problem. We have used over thousands of people, and we have to use a lot of C.G.[5], which in fact, to make it happen. So ~~it~~ [we] spent one and a half month[s] to make it to make one scene.

ANJALI RAO, TALK ASIA

This was a return to Chinese cinema[6] for you after, you know, quite a long time of being in Hollywood. Of course, you had huge hits with *Mission: Impossible II* and *Face/Off*. How would you characterize[7] your time in Hollywood?

电影导演 吴宇森

我必须说这是我拍过的最辛苦的一部影片，花了很多钱，也花了很多时间，但这是我一直以来的梦想。我想拍这部影片已经有20年了。现在，我总算有这么好的机会可以拍，事后又发现这部作品在各地都大获成功，所以感到非常欣慰。

《亚洲名人聊天室》 安姿丽

你觉得拍这部影片，最困难的是哪个部分？

电影导演 吴宇森

动作场面是最难的部分。片中有个巨大的龟阵。我知道很多人都读过中国的《孙子兵法》，大多数美国人对这本书尤其熟悉。所以，该怎么把这个阵法搬上银幕，就是一大问题。我们动用了好几千人，使用了许多电脑动画，才总算完成。为了那一幕，我们就花了一个半月的时间。

《亚洲名人聊天室》 安姿丽

你在好莱坞待了好一段时间，现在才又回到中国电影界。当然，你在好莱坞也有《不可能的任务2》和《变脸》等卖座大片。你会怎么描述自己在好莱坞的这段日子？

Notes & Vocabulary

4. **formation** [fɔr`meʃən]
   n. 阵式；队形

5. **C.G.** [`si`dʒi] *n.* 计算机绘图
   (= computer graphics)

6. **cinema** [`sɪnəmə]
   n. 电影业；电影（总称）

7. **characterize** [`kɛrɪktəˌraɪz]
   v. 描绘……的特性
   The director characterized his new film as his masterpiece.

电影制作工作人员小词典

pre-production and production
前期制作

producer 制片

production manager 执行制片

production coordinator 制作执行

director 导演

assistant director 助理导演

casting director 选角指导

screenwriter 电影剧本编剧

location manager 场地经理

script clerk / continuity girl (boy) 场记员

JOHN WOO, FILM DIRECTOR

Well, I really enjoyed working in Hollywood. You know, that's even though I never ~~get~~ [got] used to their system. I didn't like much of the studio people, you know. Well, it's too politic[al], too politic[al], and there's so much going on, and there's so much going on that's nothing to do with the movie. It's all about power. It's all about . . .

ANJALI RAO, TALK ASIA

Egos[8]?

JOHN WOO, FILM DIRECTOR

Egos! You know, and the people, you know, they love meetings. You know, they can take six months just for a meeting. Meeting and always repeating the same, speaking the same thing, you know and then . . . and but, beside that, I really love the crew. I really love the film people there. I really love the actors. And also, I maybe learned so much. You know, I made a lot of good friends and I'm so much grateful[9] that I could have an opportunity to work with John Travolta, Nick Cage, you know, Christian Slater and Tom Cruise.

ANJALI RAO, TALK ASIA

There's a lot of Christian symbolism[10] in your movies, for instance, you know, the climatic scene in *The Killer* where it's the final church shootout[11] and there's all these white doves. What is the message that you're trying to send by including these, you know, religious references[12]?

电影导演 吴宇森

我很喜欢在好莱坞工作，虽然我一直都不习惯他们的制度，也不太喜欢制片人员。太政治化了，太多暗潮汹涌，太多与电影无关的尔虞我诈。这一切都是为了掌权，为了……

《亚洲名人聊天室》安姿丽

自我中心吗？

电影导演 吴宇森

就是自我中心！而且那些人非常爱开会。他们一场会可以开 6 个月，不断重复同样的东西，讲同样的事情。但尽管如此，我还是很喜欢那里的工作人员。我真的喜欢那里的电影从业人员，也真的喜欢那些演员。此外，我也可能学了很多东西，交了很多好朋友，我一直觉得很感激有机会和约翰·特拉沃尔塔、尼古拉斯·凯奇合作，还有克里斯蒂安·斯莱特、汤姆·克鲁斯等等。

《亚洲名人聊天室》安姿丽

你的电影里有许多基督教的象征，例如《喋血双雄》最后在教堂里的枪战，还有那些白鸽。你在影片中放入这些宗教元素，是希望传达什么信息呢？

Notes & Vocabulary

8. **ego** [ˈigo]
   n. 自我意识；自负；自我

9. **grateful** [ˈgretfəl]
   adj. 感恩的；感谢的

10. **symbolism** [ˈsɪmbəˌlɪzəm]
    n. 象征的使用；象征性

11. **shootout** [ˈʃutˌaut] *n.* 枪战

12. **reference** [ˈrɛfrəns]
    n. 提及；参考文献；引证

电影制作工作人员小词典

production design 制作设计

art director 艺术指导

set designer 场景设计

illustrator 绘图师

set decorator 布景师

make-up artist 化妆师

hairdresser 发型师

costume designer 服装设计

costume supervisor 服装管理

props master 道具管理

photography 摄影

cinematographer / director of photography 摄影指导

camera operator 摄影师

gaffer 灯光指导

lighting technician 灯光师

key grip / grip 场务领班／场务员

best boy 助手（照明、布景、台车等）

clapper boy 打板员

影视娱乐

时尚生活

政治财经

体坛文艺

JOHN WOO, FILM DIRECTOR

The church means a lot to me. You know, I feel safe, I feel happy, I feel comfort, you know, I feel peace in the church. You know, and I love the people in the church. And the church is a symbol of heaven. You know, you have all kind of building. You know, of course you could say I'm a dreamer, you know. OK, yeah, I'm a dreamer, you know, because I always believed in people, and of course, I also believe in Jesus, you know. Unfortunately, there's a . . . the evil's always there. They're out to ruin the building. The evil force usually turn[s] heaven into hell, and our heroes, they try to protect it. They try to fight for it, and they try to beat down the evil, you know. And they won, you know. So . . .

ANJALI RAO, TALK ASIA

I mean obviously people like Quentin Tarantino and the Wachowski brothers, Robert Rodriguez, they borrow very much from exactly what you've created, but if you had to name a director from any point in history whose work that you look at and go "I wish I could do that," who would it be?

JOHN WOO, FILM DIRECTOR

Francis Ford Coppola, you know I think he ~~make~~ [made] a great classic film, *The Godfather*. You know, the direction, the art design, the ~~cinematographer~~ [cinematography],[13] the performance, you know, and the style of the movie, it was so perfect, so beautiful. You know, so if I could make a movie like that, you know, that's enough. That's [what] a filmmaker should do.

正常*MP3-Track09* / 慢速*MP3-Track39* ▎ *A Man of Action*

电影导演 吴宇森

教堂对我而言有许多意义。我在教堂里总是觉得安心、快乐、欣慰、平静。我也喜欢教堂里的人，而且教堂是天堂的象征，有各式各样的建筑。当然，你可以说我喜欢梦想。没错，我确实喜欢梦想，因为我总是相信人，我也信仰耶稣。只可惜，会有……总是有邪恶存在。邪恶势力会摧毁建筑，把天堂变成地狱，而我们的主角则努力保护天堂，为天堂奋战，打败邪恶。最后他们也获得胜利，就这样……

《亚洲名人聊天室》安姿丽

我是说，像昆汀·塔伦蒂诺和沃卓斯基兄弟、罗伯特·罗德里格斯（注）这些人都从你的作品借用了许多元素，但如果说从古到今有哪位导演，会让你看了他的作品之后说，"真希望我也能拍成那样。"你会说是谁呢？

电影导演 吴宇森

弗朗西斯·福特·科波拉。我认为他拍了一部非常了不起的经典，就是《教父》。那部片的导演手法、美术设计、摄影美感、表演层次，还有电影的风格，都是这么完美，这么漂亮。我如果可以拍出这样一部电影，那就足够了。那就是电影人该做的事。

电影制作工作人员小词典

sound and music 音效配乐

sound designer 音响设计

production sound mixer 现场混音师

boom operator 收音人员

utility sound technician 录音技术员

dialogue editor 对白剪辑

sound editor 声音剪辑

foley artist 制音师

re-recording mixer / dubbing master 混音师

music supervisor 音乐监督

post-production 后期制作

film editor 影片剪辑

visual effects supervisor 视觉特效指导

compositor 影像合成师

matte painter 数字绘景师

注
昆汀·塔伦蒂诺（《黑色追缉令》、《杀死比尔》）在曼哈顿录像带出租店当店员时迷上二十世纪七八十年代的香港武侠片与警匪片，并在后来表现在作品中。罗伯特·罗德里格斯（《杀手悲歌》、《罪恶之城》）与他意气相投，曾多次合作。沃卓斯基兄弟的《黑客帝国》系列请来香港知名武术指导袁和平担任动作指导。三个人的电影在题材、动作与视觉效果上，都受到吴宇森风格的影响，如黑道兄弟情义、枪战慢动作特写等。

影视娱乐

时尚生活

政治财经

体坛文艺

Taking Hollywood by Storm

Talk Asia Interview with South Korean Actor Lee Byung-hun

电影资料照片

ANNA COREN, TALK ASIA

It's the opening night of the annual Puson Film Festival. Many of South Korea's finest are here for the event. And the man all of these people are waiting for is preparing to make an entrance—South Korean actor and heartthrob[1] Lee Byung-hun.

JOSH HARNETT, ACTOR

I became a big fan of his on set because of his sort of amazing work ethic,[2] his ability to be at once kind of a movie star and an incredibly gifted and kind of giving actor.

正常MP3-Track10
慢速MP3-Track40

名人小档案 ▼ 李秉宪

李秉宪（1970—）于 1991 年 KBS 电视台第 14 期演员班结业，刚出道不久就以《有太阳的日子》获得 KBS 演技大奖最佳新人奖。1995 年首次出演电影《是谁让我发疯》即获得韩国春史电影节新人演技奖，至今获奖无数，也多次被选为韩国最受欢迎演员、最具魅力男星。2006 年被法国政府授予法国文化艺术骑士勋章，这是第一位获得该荣誉的韩国艺人。2009 年被韩国舆论人联合会选为电影领域引以为傲的韩国人。在 2009 年的好莱坞电影《特种部队：眼镜蛇的崛起》中，李秉宪以片中"白幽灵"一角成功打入国际电影界，知名度大增。他在片中不仅秀出健美身材，还讲了一口流利英语。

Lee Byung-hun

《亚洲名人聊天室》安娜·科伦

这是一年一度釜山电影节的开幕之夜。许多韩国的杰出演员都为了这场盛事齐聚一堂。而这些人在等待的人正准备入场——韩国演员和大众情人李秉宪。

演员 乔什·哈奈特

我成为他的头号粉丝，因为他有了不起的敬业精神，他能做一位电影明星，也能做一位很有天赋又愿意付出的演员。

Notes & Vocabulary

标题扫描

take . . . by storm
完全征服；风靡

原本是指"强势攻占；袭击"某处，引申指"席卷；风靡；完全征服（观众、市场等）"，即大受欢迎、非常成功。

- The iPhone took the world by storm when it was released.
  iPhone 上市的时候风靡全球。

make an entrance
登场

entrance 一般指"进入；入场"，make an entrance 即表示"登场"，前面常加上 grand 表示"盛大登场"。

- Chelsea Clinton made a grand entrance into the world of high fashion at a fashion show in Paris.
  切尔西·克林顿在巴黎举行的一场时装秀中，隆重地进入时装界。

1. **heartthrob** [ˈhɑrtˌθrɑb]
   n. 万人迷；大众情人

2. **work ethic** [wɜk] [ˈɛθɪk]
   n. 职业道德；职业精神

影视娱乐

时尚生活

政治财经

体坛文艺

73

ANNA COREN, TALK ASIA

You made your Hollywood debut in the action film *G.I. Joe*. Why did you choose this vehicle to launch yourself in the United States?

LEE BYUNG-HUN, ACTOR

When I first heard about *G.I. Joe* from my agent[3], I didn't know what it was, so I refused it at first, but everybody told me to do it because it's going to be so huge, and it's going to be a huge opportunity to go there. So, one of my really good friend[s], Park Chan-wook, who made *Old Boy*, he advised me, "If you really want to go to Hollywood, then why don't you choose it? That would be [a] really good chance to do it." So . . . that advice was so helpful to me.

ANNA COREN, TALK ASIA

G.I. Joe was a huge success. [It] netted[4] 280 million plus at the box office[5]. I believe that you've signed on for the sequel[6] and also a third movie. Are you concerned at all that you may be typecast in Hollywood as the Asian bad guy?

LEE BYUNG-HUN, ACTOR

Yeah, of course I worry about that a little bit, but I'm trying to change it.

ANNA COREN, TALK ASIA

Is it your ultimate goal to crack Hollywood?

LEE BYUNG-HUN, ACTOR

No, I actually didn't think about it, to go [to] Hollywood. Even [a] few years ago, nobody thought it happens, because it's just a dream for Korean actors. Nowadays, it's not a dream anymore. It's

《亚洲名人聊天室》安娜・科伦

你以动作片《特种部队》在好莱坞初次登场。为什么选择这部电影打入美国？

演员 李秉宪

最初从经纪人那听到《特种部队：眼镜蛇的崛起》时，我并不知道那是什么，所以我开始拒绝了。但是每个人都告诉我放手去做，因为那会是部大片，也是进入美国的大好机会。所以，我一位相当好的朋友，执导《原罪犯》的朴赞郁，他建议我，"如果你真的想打进好莱坞，为什么不选择它呢？那真的是个绝佳机会。"那个建议对我有很大的帮助。

《亚洲名人聊天室》安娜・科伦

《特种部队》相当成功，它的票房净收入超过 2.8 亿美元。我相信你已经敲定拍摄续集和第三集。你究竟会不会担心在好莱坞被定型成亚洲恶徒呢？

演员 李秉宪

是的，当然我有点担心，但我正试着改变它。

《亚洲名人聊天室》安娜・科伦

你的最终目标是要打入好莱坞吗？

演员 李秉宪

不，我以前其实没想过进军好莱坞。即使仅仅几年前，没人想过这会发生，因为这对韩国演员来说是个梦想。现在，它不再是个梦想。它成真了。

Notes & Vocabulary

typecast
一再扮演同类型角色

有些演员在剧中总是被分配出演（cast）同一类型的角色，久而久之，观众看到这位演员就会产生固定的联想。例如一个总是演反派的人，若在某出戏中突然变成弱势受害者，难免令人感到突兀。中文中我们把这种情况称为"被定型了"，英文的说法则是 (someone) get/be typecast

(as . . .)。此语也引申出"形成刻板印象"的意思，类似 be typed/stereotyped。要注意 typecast 是不规则动词，其过去式和过去分词都是 typecast。

· The actor got typecast as an action hero after a successful summer blockbuster.
那名演员在拍了一部暑假卖座大片之后，就被定位成动作片英雄。

3. **agent** [ˈedʒənt]
   n. 经纪人；代理人

4. **net** [nɛt] *v.* 赚取；净收入
   The company netted over $12 million in sales during the last year.

5. **box office** [bɑks] [ˈɔfɪs]
   n. 票房（收入）；售票处
   The movie occupied the top spot at the box office for several weeks.

6. **sequel** [ˈsikwəl]
   n.（电影、书等）续集；续篇
   The author wrote the long-awaited sequel to his bestseller.

影视娱乐

时尚生活

政治财经

体坛文艺

reality.

ANNA COREN, TALK ASIA

Your career started in soap operas. I think you've starred in more than 20 soap operas here in South Korea. Tell us about the country's obsession with soap operas.

LEE BYUNG-HUN, ACTOR

I think Korean drama[s] tend to show the real life, even though it's just the small things, small emotions, small twist[7]. Still they really love it because the drama is like their life.

ANNA COREN, TALK ASIA

Why do you think Asia *is* so *obsessed with* South Korean pop culture?

LEE BYUNG-HUN, ACTOR

The Korean drama[s] [are] still talking about the family things—their love, their hate—they can feel the old emotions. That's why the Japanese people, Chinese people, like Korean dramas, and the songs normally include a lot of sadness in Korea.

ANNA COREN, TALK ASIA

Now there's not much information about your childhood. So, what was it like growing up as a kid?

LEE BYUNG-HUN, ACTOR

I think I was [a] silly trouble-maker. Not serious, but I was [a] kind of an out-going person, and I really

《亚洲名人聊天室》安娜·科伦

你的演员生涯从连续剧开始。我想你在韩国演过二十多部连续剧了吧。告诉我们这个国家对于连续剧着迷的程度。

演员 李秉宪

我想韩国的戏剧倾向表现真实生活，即使只是小事、细微的情绪、些微的转折。他们仍相当喜欢它，因为戏剧就像他们的生活。

《亚洲名人聊天室》安娜·科伦

你认为亚洲人为什么这么迷韩国流行文化？

演员 李秉宪

韩国戏剧还会探讨家庭琐事——他们的爱恨——他们可以感受到这些原始的情绪。这就是日本人、中国人喜爱韩剧的原因，而且韩国歌曲通常带着浓浓的伤感。

《亚洲名人聊天室》安娜·科伦

关于你的童年并没有太多的资料。你小时候的成长过程是什么样子？

演员 李秉宪

我想我是个傻傻的问题人物。不正经，但我是个有点外向的人，而且很喜爱电影。我读高中时，真的很想成为其中一员，但我不知

Notes & Vocabulary

be obsessed with
着迷于……；执著于……

obsess 当动词，指"使（某人）着迷、执著或惦记"，多用被动语态，介词则通常用with。

· Donald was obsessed with making his homework perfect.
唐纳德一心要把作业做得完美无瑕。

7. **twist** [twɪst]
n.（事情或状况）转折；突然变化
In a new twist, the mayor says he has changed his mind.

影视娱乐 时尚生活 政治财经 体坛文艺

liked the movies. When I was in high school, I really wanted to be a part of them, but I didn't know what to do. I've never learned acting or directing [in] my school. My major was French, and I've never said just one line in my life before that.

ANNA COREN, TALK ASIA

How would you describe yourself as an actor? Are you a serious actor? Are you a . . .?

LEE BYUNG-HUN, ACTOR

Yeah, I think I'm kind of serious. Yeah, I think I'm kind of [a] serious actor, but in my real life I'm so [such a] funny guy. And Sienna Miller said too . . .

ANNA COREN, TALK ASIA

She did. Sienna Miller said that.

LEE BYUNG-HUN, ACTOR

Yeah, she said I'm so [such a] funny guy.

ANNA COREN, TALK ASIA

And so did Stephen Sommers, the director. He said you've got a great . . . a bit of a wicked[8] sense of humor. I think you were playing practical jokes all the time.

LEE BYUNG-HUN, ACTOR

Yeah, that's [the] real me.

ANNA COREN, TALK ASIA

Following the success of *Joint Security Area*, Byung-

道怎么做。我在学校从没学过演戏或导演。我的专业是法语，我在高中之前从没说过一句台词。

《亚洲名人聊天室》安娜·科伦
你会如何形容自己是个什么样的演员？你是个认真的演员吗？你是个……

演员 李秉宪
是的，我想我比较认真。是的，我想我是个认真的演员，但是在现实生活中，我是相当有趣的家伙。而席安娜·米勒（编注：美国女演员，与李秉宪合演《特种部队》）也说……

《亚洲名人聊天室》安娜·科伦
对，她说过，席安娜·米勒也这么说。

演员 李秉宪
是的，她说我是相当有趣的家伙。

《亚洲名人聊天室》安娜·科伦
导演史蒂芬·桑莫斯也这么说。他说你有种调皮的幽默感。我想你总是在搞恶作剧。

演员 李秉宪
是的，那就是真实的我。

《亚洲名人聊天室》安娜·科伦
在《共同警备区》成功之后，李秉宪接着出演广受好评的电影《不悔》及 2008 年在戛纳影展首映的《神偷、猎人、断指客》。但是就像李秉宪自己说的，他的最佳作品尚未

Notes & Vocabulary

describe A as B
将 A 描述成 B

describe 搭配 as 的句型除了有本文中的 describe A as B 之外，也可在 describe as 后面加上形容词或 V-ing，即"将某人事物描述成……（的样子）"。

· She described her ex-boyfriend as a cheat.
她形容她的前男友是个骗子。

· He is often described as looking like a movie star.
常有人说他看起来像电影明星。

critically acclaimed
大获好评

每当有书籍、影片或专辑等获得大部分专业评论家（critic）的好评、赞赏（acclaim）时，便可用 critically acclaimed 来形容，也可用 to critical acclaim 或 critical success 来表达。

· Stephen King has written numerous novels to critical acclaim.
史蒂芬·金写过许多大获好评的小说。

8. **wicked** [ˈwɪkɪd]
adj. 淘气的；调皮的；邪恶的
The story features a wicked stepmother as the main antagonist.

影视娱乐

时尚生活

政治财经

体坛文艺

hun went on to star in the critically acclaimed *A Bittersweet Life* and *The Good, The Bad, The Weird*, which premiered[9] at Cannes in 2008. But as Byung-hun himself points out, his best work is yet to come.

I understand that you are your harshest critic, that you're never fully happy with your performance. Why is that?

LEE BYUNG-HUN, ACTOR
I'm trying to be perfect, especially in the shooting place, because I have a lot of responsibility to the audience, because I'm not doing this job as a joke. I had to persuade the audience with my acting, with my emotions, so that's why I really want to be perfect. It's [a] good thing as an actor, but as a human in my real life, it's so bad sometimes.

ANNA COREN, TALK ASIA
In what way?

LEE BYUNG-HUN, ACTOR
I could not enjoy fully everything, because I always think about something. In my real life, I try to have a lot of fun and I try to be natural.

ANNA COREN, TALK ASIA
How do you have fun? What do you do to unwind[10]?

LEE BYUNG-HUN, ACTOR
Watching movies, as [well as] drinking wine. That's my best time.

ANNA COREN, TALK ASIA
Do you miss being anonymous[11]? Are there ever

诞生。

我了解你是对自己最严厉的评论家，你从未对自己的表现感到相当满意。为什么呢?

演员 李秉宪

我对试着做到完美，尤其在拍摄现场，因为我要对观众负责任，因为我做这份工作不是因为做着好玩的。我必须用我的演技和情感来说服观众，所以这就是我想做到完美的原因。当演员很棒，但是作为一个人，我的真实生活有时并不好受。

《亚洲名人聊天室》安娜·科伦

在哪方面呢?

演员 李秉宪

我没办法完全享受每件事，因为我总是在思考。在我的真实生活中，我试着开心玩乐，试着自然一点。

《亚洲名人聊天室》安娜·科伦

你会如何娱乐?你如何放轻松?

演员 李秉宪

看电影、喝点酒，这是我最棒的时光。

《亚洲名人聊天室》安娜·科伦

你怀念默默无闻的时候吗?有没有过那种日子，让你希望自己可以在街上走而没人认得你?

9. premiere [prɪˈmɪr]
   v. 首次播映、演出
   The play premiered to rave reviews.

10. unwind [ʌnˈwaɪnd]
    v. 放轻松；松开
    After work, Michael unwinds on the couch with a glass of wine and a book.

11. anonymous [əˈnɑnəməs]
    adj. 匿名的；不知名的
    An anonymous caller tipped off the police to a crime in progress.

李秉宪荣获法国文化艺术勋章

毕业于韩国汉阳大学法语系的李秉宪，曾在 2004 年韩法建交 100 周年时，被任命为第一位法国宣传大使。而同年 10 月，法国驻韩大使在第十一届釜山国际电影节的相关活动中，授予李秉宪法国文化艺术勋章中的"骑士荣誉勋章"。

法国文化艺术勋章是法国文化部针对在艺术和文学领域创下突出成绩的外国人，所颁发的勋章，始于 1957 年，分为"大十字勋位"、"大军官勋位"、"司令勋位"、"军官勋位"和"骑士勋位"五个等级。

曾被授予此勋章的国际影星还有罗伯特·德尼罗、莎朗·斯通、乌玛·舒曼、巩俐、莱昂纳多·迪卡普里奥，以及布鲁斯·威利。

影视娱乐 时尚生活 政治财经 体坛文艺

days that you wish that you could just walk down the street and go unrecognized?

LEE BYUNG-HUN, ACTOR

What I really wanted to do was ~~driving~~ [to drive a] taxi. I borrowed a taxi from my friend. He was the boss of the taxi company, and I borrowed the taxi and I ~~drived~~ [drove] for like a few days. It was so fun and so interesting [an] experience.

ANNA COREN, TALK ASIA

So you were picking up people and taking them.

LEE BYUNG-HUN, ACTOR

Yeah. Nobody recognized me.

ANNA COREN, TALK ASIA

That's fantastic.

LEE BYUNG-HUN, ACTOR

But, nobody recognized me because I was hiding everything.

ANNA COREN, TALK ASIA

How did it feel for those couple of days being normal, being anonymous?

LEE BYUNG-HUN, ACTOR

It was so interesting and that was so weird, the experience to me, because I'm used to be . . . live as an actor, so that was strange to me.

正常 *MP3-Track10* / 慢速 *MP3-Track40* ❙ *Taking Hollywood by Storm*

演员 李秉宪

我真正想做的是开出租车。我曾跟朋友借了
辆出租车，他是出租车公司的老板。我借那
辆出租车开了几天。那真的是好玩又有趣的
经历。

《亚洲名人聊天室》安娜·科伦

你真的接送客人啊。

演员 李秉宪

对啊，没人认得我。

《亚洲名人聊天室》安娜·科伦

那真是太棒了。

演员 李秉宪

不过没人认得我是因为我把自己全遮起来
了。

《亚洲名人聊天室》安娜·科伦

那几天你可以当个正常人，没人认得，感觉
如何？

演员 李秉宪

对我来说，那真是有趣又不可思议，因为我
已经习惯⋯⋯以演员的身份生活。所以那对
我来说真的很奇特。

李秉宪 代表作

电视剧

1999《Love Story》

2001《美丽的日子》

2003《真爱赌注（All In）》

2009《IRIS》

电影

2000《JSA 共同警备区》

2004《三更 II》

2004《谁都有秘密》

2009《特种部队：眼镜蛇的崛起（G.I.
Joe: The Rise of Cobra）》

影视娱乐

时尚生活

政治财经

体坛文艺

Chasing a Dream

Talk Asia Exclusive
Interview with Korean Film Star
Jang Dong-Gun

图片提供：Reuters

ANJALI RAO, TALK ASIA

Hi, I'm Anjali Rao in Seoul. My guest today is the movie star heartthrob and the most recognizable[1] face in South Korea, Jang Dong-Gun. This is Talk Asia.

Things really started to take off for you in 2000 when you had a starring role in the movie *Friend*, which at the time was the highest-grossing[2] Korean film ever. What was it like being a part of something so huge?

正常 MP3-Track11
慢速 MP3-Track41

名人小档案 ▼ 张东健

韩国演员及歌手张东健（1972—），除了以英俊的外貌著称，其出色的演技更被广泛认同，他多次夺得各项网络投票评比的第一名，例如：白色情人节最佳伴侣、明星塑身之王、最不希望结婚的男星、最想见的艺人等等。张东健以《天桥风云》和《爱上女主播》等电视剧在亚洲大受欢迎。之后转战电影界参与演出的《朋友》为他赢得亚太影展最佳男配角。《太极旗飘扬》则让他荣获青龙奖最佳男主角的称号。也许是因为张东健高中时期就开始接触佛教著作，在韩国演艺圈内，他是出了名的"三好先生"——演技好、性格好、品行好。

Jang Dong-Gun

《亚洲名人聊天室》安姿丽

大家好，我是安姿丽，在首尔为您带来今天的节目。我今天的来宾是电影偶像明星，也是韩国最多人认识的面孔：张东健。欢迎收看《亚洲名人聊天室》。

你在 2000 年主演《朋友》之后，事业就开始起飞，当时《朋友》也是有史以来票房最高的韩国影片。参与如此庞大的一场盛事有什么感觉？

Notes & Vocabulary

take off
（事业）起飞

take off 原意是"（飞机）起飞"或"突然离开"，此处引申表示"（观念、计划、产品等）在短时间内迅速获得大家喜爱"的意思。

- That movie really **took off** among young viewers.
  那部电影大受年轻观众欢迎。

1. **recognizable** [ˈrɛkəɡˌnaɪzəbl]
   adj. 认得出的
   Brad Pitt is one of the most recognizable American actors today.

2. **gross** [ɡros]
   v. 收入；赚得
   The company grossed much more than last year.

关于韩国的"青龙电影节"

青龙电影节（**Blue Dragon Film Awards**）是韩国一年一度的大规模电影颁奖典礼，于 1963 年开始，由韩国的体育日报举办。青龙电影节只评审过去一年的大片或有高度艺术价值的受欢迎影片。在选拔过程中，大约有 40 部影片会被选出作为提名作品，并免费供公众欣赏。筛选完成后，颁奖典礼便随之开幕。其中"人气明星赏"一奖由网友投票选出。此外，每年颁奖典礼举行前一星期，上一届的获奖者会一起参加印手印的仪式，象征得奖的荣誉将永远持续。

影视娱乐 时尚生活 政治财经 体坛文艺

JANG DONG-GUN, KOREAN ACTOR

When I first chose the film, even after we'd filmed the entire movie, no one really expected—I certainly didn't expect, nor did any of the actors expect—that it would be so well received[3]. My intention for the film was to show a different side of myself. I actually believed that it was more of an artistic[4] film in that sense, but because it became so popular at the time, I somehow think that the popularity[5] may have, in a sense, undermined[6] the true artistic value that the movie might actually have.

ANJALI RAO, TALK ASIA

That movie though paved the way for your starring role in *Taegukgi* about the Korean War, which again smashed all known box-office record[s]. Tell us about your experiences of that film.

JANG DONG-GUN, KOREAN ACTOR

The theme of the movie is the Korean War. The Korean War was one of the most significant[7] historical events in modern Korean history. I think that its significance is something that could be well expressed and presented in a film. Personally, my

韩国演员 张东健

我一开始选择这部影片的时候，甚至直到片子杀青之际，都没有人想到——我完全没想到，其他演员也都一样——根本没想到这部影片会这么受欢迎。我当初出演这部影片是为了要展示自己不同的一面。我其实认为这部影片比较像是艺术片，但因为后来非常热门，所以就某种程度来说反而降低了这部片真正的艺术价值。

《亚洲名人聊天室》安姿丽

不过，那部电影让你后来有机会主演《太极旗飘扬》这部关于朝鲜战争的电影，而且又再次打破了所有的票房纪录。请告诉我们你拍摄这部影片的经历。

韩国演员 张东健

这部影片的主题是朝鲜战争。这是韩国现代史当中最重要的一个历史事件。我认为电影能够充分表达并且呈现这个事件的重要性。就我个人来说，我在片中饰演的角色很吸引

Notes & Vocabulary

in a sense
在某种意义来说
sense 原本是"知觉；观念；意识"的意思，这里则是指某件事物传达或显示的"意义；涵义"。

· **In a sense**, David has achieved all he had hoped for in life—a wonderful wife, beautiful kids and a successful career.
就某种意义说来，大卫已经实现他对人生所有的期望了——家有贤妻、可爱儿女和成功的事业。

近义词
· in a way
· in a manner of speaking
· so to speak

pave the way for . . .
为……铺路
pave 是指"铺设"街道等，pave the way 在字面上是"铺路"的意思，比喻"预做安排或准备"或"达到条件或取得进展"。

· Jackie Robinson paved the way for African American players in Major League Baseball.
杰克·罗宾森为大联盟的非裔美籍球员打开了道路。

英文谚语
The road to hell is paved with good intention.
通往地狱之路往往是由善意铺成的。
（比喻做事若一味出于好意而不问结果，结果可能反而害了人。）

3. receive [rɪˋsiv] v. 接受；欢迎
4. artistic [ɑrˋtɪstɪk] adj. 艺术性的
5. popularity [ˌpɑpjəˋlærətɪ] n. 受欢迎；人气；名气
6. undermine [ˌʌndəˋmaɪn] v. 削减；损害
7. significant [sɪgˋnɪfɪkənt] adj. 意义重大的

影视娱乐 时尚生活 政治财经 体坛文艺

role in the film's was quite appealing to me, and I was quite keen on doing it. And my grandfather's birthplace is in North Korea, and I had heard many stories about the Korean War as a child when I was growing up.

ANJALI RAO, TALK ASIA

So in 2006 you staged a one-man protest in front of the general assembly[8] here against the government's new policy on domestic films[9]. Didn't last very long though, only a couple of minutes before you got swamped[10] by thousands of fans. Are you concerned about the current[11] state of the film industry in South Korea, as so many others are?

JANG DONG-GUN, KOREAN ACTOR

Many think the industry is stagnating[12], but I differ in opinion. In total I've had 15 years of acting, and in the film industry I've had 10 years of experience. Looking back on those 10 years, I can see there'd always been ups and downs within the industry. And when you say things are slow and not going well in the field, the difference rather depends on how many good Korean films have been made.

我，因此非常希望参与演出。而且我的祖父出生于朝鲜，所以我小时候听过很多朝鲜战争的故事。

《亚洲名人聊天室》安姿丽
2006 年，你在这里的国会议事堂展开一个人的示威活动，反对政府对国产影片的新政策。不过没有持续太久，因为几分钟后你就被数以千计的影迷困住了。你和许多人一样对韩国电影产业的现状感到忧虑吗？

韩国演员 张东健
许多人认为韩国电影产业已经陷入停滞，但我不同意。我总共已经演了 15 年的戏，在电影方面也有 10 年的经验了。回顾这 10 年，我可以看到这个产业一直都有高低起伏。如果说这个领域各方面发展缓慢，情况不好，这其实取决于最近究竟拍出了多少部好的韩国影片。

Notes & Vocabulary

be keen on sth.
渴望某事物
keen 在这里是指"热衷的；热切的；渴望的"，后面可以加上 on + sth.，表示渴望的事物。也可以加上不定词 to V.，表示极想做的事。keen 另外还可以形容"锐利"或"敏锐"。

- Allen is keen on starting college this fall.
艾伦对于今年秋天即将上大学感到非常期待。
- The chef sharpened the knife to a keen edge.
厨师把那把刀的刀锋磨锋利。

补充
as keen as mustard
此语字面上是"像芥末一样激烈"的意思，比喻某人"非常热切渴望"的状态。

look back on
回顾
look back 意思是"回头看"，引申为"回顾；回想"过去，后面经常用介词 on 加上过去的一段时间，表示思考那时发生的事情。

- Barry looks back on his high school days with nostalgia.
贝瑞带着怀旧的心情回顾自己的高中时光。

8. **general assembly** [ˈdʒɛnerəl] [əˈsɛmblɪ] *n.* 国会；立法机构

9. **domestic film** [dəˈmɛstɪk] [fɪlm] *n.* 国产影片

10. **swamp** [swɑmp] *v.* 淹没
Irate customers swamped the service department with angry phone calls.

11. **current** [ˈkɜənt] *adj.* 目前的；现今的

12. **stagnate** [ˈstæɡˌnet] *v.* 停滞；萧条
The actor's career stagnated after his last movie flopped.

影视娱乐 | 时尚生活 | 政治财经 | 体坛文艺

As of now, the reduced quota[13] of films, the rising wages[14], and also because of the poor performance of the Korean films this year, people are saying things are going bad. I think it only means good films have not been produced lately, that's all. So I still have a positive[15] outlook[16], and I believe as more good films are made, positive sentiments[17] will be picked up quickly.

张东健的获奖记录

2007 第十五届春史大奖：韩流文化大奖

2004 青龙电影节：最佳男主角（《太极旗飘扬》）

2001 亚太影展：最佳男配角（《朋友》）

1999 青龙电影节：最佳男配角（《不留情面》）

1997 青龙电影节：最佳新人奖（《败者复活》）

1997 韩国文化广播公司：TV 最佳演员奖

1997 百想艺术奖：最受欢迎男主角奖

1994 百想艺术奖：最佳电视演员

正常 *MP3-Track11* / 慢速 *MP3-Track41* ❙ *Chasing a Dream*

就目前而言，由于影片配额减少，工资提高，再加上韩国影片今年表现不佳，所以很多人就说这个产业已经开始走下坡路。我认为这只是表示最近没有拍出好的影片而已。所以，我对未来的展望还是乐观的，而且我认为只要拍出多一点的好片子，正面的情绪就会很快被带动起来。

13. **quota** [ˈkwotə] *n.* 配额

14. **wage** [wed.] *n.* 薪资

15. **positive** [ˈpɑzətɪv]
    adj. 正面的；积极的
    The self-help book allowed Janice to make several positive changes in her life.

16. **outlook** [ˈautˌluk]
    n. 前景；展望

17. **sentiment** [ˈsɛntəmənt]
    n. 情绪

"抗议国产电影配额制"事件

2006 年 2 月，韩国政府与美国达成自由贸易协议（free trade agreement），修订施行 40 年的电影配额制度（quota system），将国产电影的院线上映天数由 146 天减为 73 天。电影人士组成"抗议电影配额电影人对策委员会"计划发动示威（protest），担任会长的演员安基顺为避免错失时机（timing），于 4 日起进行示威接力（relay），由朴仲勋、张东健、崔岷植接棒。

张东健于 6 日下午出现在美国使馆（embassy）前，举牌写着"请与国产电影配额做'朋友'，让'太极旗'飘扬全世界"，以他主演的片名串成口号（slogan），三分钟即吸引了两千多名影迷及记者，之后为了安全，大家步行至国会正门后即结束。

2 月 8 日正式示威在首尔光华门（Kwanghwamun）前举行，包括金喜善、车太贤、元彬、李秉宪、李准基等约一千人到场。但韩国政府仍然自 2006 年 7 月起施行（enforce）新制度，让韩国电影人对国产电影的未来感到担忧。

影视娱乐

时尚生活

政治财经

体坛文艺

Butt-Kicking Beauty

A Talk Asia Exclusive Interview with Action Star Michelle Yeoh

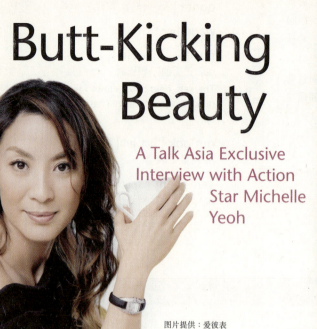

图片提供：爱彼表

ANJALI RAO, TALK ASIA

Hi, I'm Anjali Rao. My guest today is the movie star Michelle Yeoh. This is Talk Asia.

So, you're one of Asia's most internationally recognized actresses. How did you get where you are?

MICHELLE YEOH, ACTRESS

Well, ever since I was a little girl, I never thought that one day I would be an actress, to be honest. My big love was dance. I was a ballerina[1] since I was four years old and I always had the . . . I think I always geared towards[2] that side.

Then I went to England to study ballet. I did a degree in dance. So my parents, you know, bless them, they're very liberal[3] in that sense. They're very traditional Chinese parents, but at the same

正常MP3-Track12
慢速MP3-Track42

名人小档案▼ 杨紫琼

杨紫琼（1962—）出生于马来西亚怡保，选美出身的她后来在香港影坛发展，成为国际明星，获奖无数。1998 年受邀出演"007"系列电影《007 之明日帝国（Tomorrow Never Dies）》的女主角。2000 年，出演李安导演的《卧虎藏龙》，再次扬名国际。杨紫琼 2001 年受马来西亚霹雳州苏丹册封拿督，也是马来西亚第一位受此封衔的华裔女演员。

Michelle Yeoh

Notes & Vocabulary

标题扫描

butt-kicking
很厉害；很棒

kick butt/ass 的直译是"踢屁股"，俚语中表示"痛击；打败"或"很厉害；很有效"。butt-kicking 当形容词是说某人或事物"很厉害；很棒"，当名词则表示"狠狠教训；痛击"。标题 butt-kicking beauty 意指杨紫琼是个会武术的美女，也是个令人惊艳的美女。

When it comes to organizing a party or event, Melody kicks butt.
讲到筹划聚会或活动，梅洛迪是个中高手。

1. **ballerina** [ˌbæləˈrinə]
   n. 女芭蕾舞者

2. **gear towards** 朝……调整、发展
   The television program is geared towards teaching English to young children.

3. **liberal** [ˈlɪbərəl] adj. 开明的

影视娱乐　时尚生活　政治财经　体坛文艺

《亚洲名人聊天室》安姿丽

大家好，我是安姿丽。今天的来宾是影星杨紫琼。这是《亚洲名人聊天室》。

您是亚洲最知名的国际女星之一。你是如何取得今日的成就呢？

女星 杨紫琼

老实说，我小时候不曾想过有一天会成为女演员。以前我最爱的是跳舞。我从 4 岁就开始跳芭蕾舞，也一直朝着这方面努力。

我曾到英国学习芭蕾舞蹈，也拿到一个学位。我的父母，愿上帝保佑他们，他们在这方面很开明。他们是很传统的中国父母，不

time they always had this attitude whereby[4] they thought that, you know, your career is what you choose. So they've always been very supportive of what I wanted to do.

ANJALI RAO, TALK ASIA

You were crowned Miss Malaysia back in 1983, and the pageant[5] world is often made out to be this hideous[6], sort of shallow, kind of nightmare world of, you know, sequins[7] and feathers. What was it like for you?

MICHELLE YEOH, ACTRESS

Well, I was a little resistant, you know, to do it, and it really was my mom. And so she sort of like spoke some sense, I would say, into me and said, "You know, look, this is the only period of your life that you can do something like this, and just think of it as an experience on stage."

ANJALI RAO, TALK ASIA

Did you particularly want to break into Hollywood?

MICHELLE YEOH, ACTRESS

Actually, it really was Terrance Chang, John Woo, 'cause they really were the ones in my books that went out to Hollywood in, I would imagine, the early '90s, that were knocking on the door, you know, trying to make Hollywood wake up and see the talent that ~~are~~ [is] out here in Asia and to recognize that the Asian market is growing. And I think it was not easy for them.

There were only the elite[8] group that watched Asian films, like the Quentin Tarantino, and at that time, you know, he was still a video guy, right? He was still a store keeper. He was taking in[9] all these, like, fabulous[10] things that were coming out from the East. And even for then, you know, for John Woo

过他们一直采取这种态度，认为从事什么行业是你的选择。所以，我想做什么他们一直都很支持。

《亚洲名人聊天室》安姿丽

你在 1983 年荣获马来西亚小姐桂冠，而选美界常被认为是个丑陋、有点肤浅、像是噩梦一样，你知道，充斥着亮片跟羽毛的世界。当时那对你来说是什么感觉？

女星 杨紫琼

我当时有点不太愿意做这件事，之所以参加都是因为我母亲的关系。可以说是她灌输了我一些观念，她跟我说，"你想想，你只有在人生中的这个时期才能做这种事，就把它当做是上台表演的经验。"

《亚洲名人聊天室》安姿丽

你是特别想要打进好莱坞的吗？

女星 杨紫琼

实际上，这得归功于张家振和吴宇森。据我所知，他们在 20 世纪 90 年代初期远赴好莱坞发展。我能想象他们敲着好莱坞的大门，试图让好莱坞觉醒，看到亚洲这里人们的才华，并且察觉亚洲市场正在成长。这对他们来说并不容易。

那时只有"精英集团"会看亚洲电影，例如昆汀·塔伦提诺，而他当时还是个出租录像带的家伙，对吗？他当时还是录像带出租店的店员，吸收了来自东方全部这些了不得的东西。而即使在当时，吴宇森刚出头的时

Notes & Vocabulary

in one's books
依某人之见
这个俚语是"依某人之见；在某人看来"的意思，与 in one's opinions 同义，最早出现于 19 世纪中期，book 是指"名册"或个人"手札；笔记"。

· In my book, there is nothing better than cold lemonade on a hot day.
在我看来，热天里最棒的莫过于冰凉的柠檬汁。

4. whereby [hwɛrˋbaɪ]
   conj. 通过

5. pageant [ˋpædʒənt]
   n. 盛大场面；庆典；游行

6. hideous [ˋhɪdɪəs]
   adj. 丑陋的；令人厌恶的
   Helen wore a hideous dress to the spring formal.

7. sequin [ˋsikwən]
   n.（衣着装饰）亮片

8. elite [eˋlit] *n.* 精英；上层集团

9. take in 吸收
   Brenda took in her pastor's sermon on the importance of charity.

10. fabulous [ˋfæbjələs]
    adj. 极好的；惊人的
    Walter received several fabulous gifts for his eighteenth birthday.

影视娱乐

时尚生活

政治财经

体坛文艺

when he first went out, you know, there was only an elite group that appreciated ~~what he~~ his talent. And I remember the first meeting I took, the first, always the question is, "Oh my God, you speak English!" Um, yes, I do.

ANJALI RAO, TALK ASIA

So, I guess when you have a waxwork[11] of yourself, is that how you know that you've really arrived? And it says that you are "known for roles that combine both glamour[12] and toughness[13]."

MICHELLE YEOH, ACTRESS

Yes!

ANJALI RAO, TALK ASIA

Do you feel like a sort of, you know, a trailblazer[14] in a way, because you were really the first sort of, you know, butt-kicking Bond girl? All the others just sort of, you know, stood there looking hot.

MICHELLE YEOH, ACTRESS

It was very apparent to me that, you know, there were certain molds[15] about referring to the Asian babes that needed to be completely broken, whereby, you know, we are the Ming vases, just fragile and in the background. You know, be seen and not heard, and just . . . or the femme fatale, youknow, prostitute[16] from Chinatown.

ANJALI RAO, TALK ASIA

Right, Suzie Wong.

MICHELLE YEOH, ACTRESS

Yeah. You know, those images were updated, and it's necessary to show what, you know, the girls are like, the ladies are like out here. They're smart. They're independent. You know, they're tough without being—(clearing throat) the B-word. Right?

96

候，也只有"精英集团"欣赏他的才华。我还记得第一次参加会议，第一个被问到的问题都是，"天啊！你会讲英文！"嗯，是啊，我会。

《亚洲名人聊天室》安姿丽
我想，当你有了自己的蜡像，是不是就知道自己有多成功了呢？这上面说你以"饰演兼具魅力与刚毅的角色而闻名"。

女星 杨紫琼
好极了！

《亚洲名人聊天室》安姿丽
你会不会觉得自己在某方面来说有点像个拓荒者呢？因为你的确是第一个会拳脚功夫的邦德女郎。其他都只像是站在那儿，看起来性感火辣。

女星 杨紫琼
在我看来，有些亚洲女郎的特定典型显然需要彻底破除，我们被塑造成像是明朝花瓶，脆弱易碎、摆在背景当装饰。你知道，用来观赏而不是听她们想说什么，就只是……不然就是演红颜祸水的女子，譬如唐人街的妓女。

《亚洲名人聊天室》安姿丽
没错，像是苏丝黄。

女星 杨紫琼
就是啊。但是那些形象已经变了，我们必须呈现当下的女孩们、女士们是什么样子。她们聪明能干、独立自主，她们强悍但不是那种——（清喉咙）嚣张的泼妇（注1）。对吧？

Notes & Vocabulary

femme fatale
红颜祸水
femme fatale [ˈɛfəmfˈtæl] 是法语，意思是"带来灾祸的女人"，通常指性感美艳、具有致命吸引力的女人，令男人受诱惑而导致灾祸，例如特洛伊的海伦、商纣王的妲己、埃及艳后等等。

11. waxwork [ˈwæksˌwək] *n.* 蜡像

12. glamour [ˈglæmə] *n.* 魅力

13. toughness [ˈtʌfnəs]
    n. 坚强；刚毅

14. trailblazer [ˈtreɪˌbleɪzə]
    n. 开拓者；先驱

15. mold [mold] *n.* 模子；模型；类型

16. prostitute [ˈprɑstəˌtjut] *n.* 娼妓

注1
指 Bitch，是性别歧视、骂人的字眼，旧义为"贱货；烂货"，现在常指"狂妄、嚣张的女性"，因为不雅故意省略说成 B-word。

杨紫琼 代表作

1997《宋氏三姐妹》

1997《007 之明日帝国》

2000《卧虎藏龙》

2005《艺妓回忆录》

2008《木乃伊 3》

影视娱乐
时尚生活
政治财经
体坛文艺

ANJALI RAO, TALK ASIA
  Right.

MICHELLE YEOH, ACTRESS
  And I think it's very important to realize that when women are tough, they can be very sexy as well. So when we . . . when they figured out that Bond girl, then they wanted her to be Asian, it was important that, you know, we communicated with, you know, the producers, Barbara Broccoli. And she's a very independent . . . you know, she's smart and she understands what women represent.

ANJALI RAO, TALK ASIA
  Right.

MICHELLE YEOH, ACTRESS
  So she didn't just want like a Bond babe because if you look at this new generation—or the last two decades of the Bond girls, they've been tougher. They've been, you know, more sassy[17] . . .

ANJALI RAO, TALK ASIA
  Exactly. Yeah.

MICHELLE YEOH, ACTRESS
  Without just being the sexual innuendos[18], you know, without just being the girls in the bikini. They can be in a bikini looking fantastic.

ANJALI RAO, TALK ASIA
  Halle Berry.

MICHELLE YEOH, ACTRESS
  Yeah, exactly, but, you know, they're smart. They're what we are today.

正常*MP3·Track12* / 慢速*MP3·Track42* | *Butt-Kicking Beauty*

《亚洲名人聊天室》安姿丽
没错。

女星 杨紫琼
我认为让大家知道女人可以很强悍，同时又很性感，这件事很重要。所以，当我们……他们在构思这个邦德女郎的时候，他们希望她是个亚洲人，那么跟制作人沟通就很重要了，譬如芭芭拉•布罗科利。而她是个很独立自主的人……她很明智，她知道女人代表的意义。

《亚洲名人聊天室》安姿丽
是的。

女星 杨紫琼
所以她不想要个邦德宝贝，因为如果你看看新一代的或近20年来的邦德女郎，会发现她们越来越强悍了。她们变得越来越有个性……

《亚洲名人聊天室》安姿丽
一点也没错。

女星 杨紫琼
她们不只是引人遐想的对象，不只是穿着比基尼的女人。她们可以穿着比基尼，但看起来非常了不得。

《亚洲名人聊天室》安姿丽
譬如哈莉•贝瑞。

女星 杨紫琼
对，就是这样，而且她们精明干练，就是我们当今女性的形象。

Notes & Vocabulary

17. **sassy** [ˈsæsɪ]
adj. 有个性的；桀骜的

18. **innuendo** [ˌɪnjəˈwɛndo]
n. （讥讽的）影射

杨紫琼重要经历

1979 取得英国皇家舞蹈学院戏剧舞蹈专业学士

1983 当选马来西亚小姐、澳大利亚墨尔本蒙巴小姐

1984 分别与成龙、周润发拍摄广告，加入德宝电影拍摄首部电影《猫头鹰与小飞象》

1985 以《皇家师姐》成为武打女星（girls with guns）类型电影头号人物

1988 与德宝电影创办人潘迪生结婚淡出影坛

1992 离婚后以《警察故事 3：超级警察》复出，成为亚洲片酬最高女星

1997 受邀演出《007 之明日帝国》，入选《人物（People）》全球排行五十名美女

1999 担任柏林影展评审委员

2000 与李安合作《卧虎藏龙》再次扬名国际

2001 第一位受马来西亚政府册封"拿督"（Datuk）的女艺人

2002 担任戛纳影展评审委员，成立"神话电影"公司，拍摄《天脉传奇》、《飞鹰》等影片

2004 结识现任男友法拉利车队经理尚•托特

2008 担任国际汽车联合会"公路安全"大使

影视娱乐 时尚生活 政治财经 体坛文艺

Zhou Xun

Talk Asia Interview with the Quirky[1] Queen of Chinese Cinema

图片提供：AP

ZHOU XUN, ACTRESS AND SINGER

I am Zhou Xun. I'm getting my makeup done right now, and I'm going to attend the movie premiere for *Confucius*. Tonight the movie will be screened at the premiere. There will be a lot of friends coming to watch the movie, and it's also my first time watching the movie. I'm very much looking forward to it.

ANJALI RAO, TALK ASIA

You have two big movies coming out, one right after the other. You've got *Confucius* and then *True Legend*. How are you feeling about everything? That sounds like a bit of a nerve-wracking prospect[2].

CNN专访中国最具影响力的女演员周迅

名人小档案▼ 周迅

周迅（1974— ）出生于中国浙江杭州，15 岁时被导演谢铁骊发现，以电影《古墓荒斋》出道。1998 年对周迅来说是关键的一年，她主演的电影《苏州河》让她获得了第十五届巴黎国际电影节最佳女主角奖。2006 年，周迅凭借电影《如果爱》先后获得香港电影金像奖及台湾电影金马奖等多项最佳女主角奖。2009 年，她的作品《李米的猜想》则获得中国电影金鸡奖最佳女主角奖。至此周迅成为华语电影界中第一位包揽中国最高电影奖项影后桂冠的演员。

Zhou Xun

Notes & Vocabulary

come out
发表；出版

come out、release、bring out 均可指"发表；出版"，但 come out 通常以产品作为主语。

- The author's latest book **comes out** next week.
  那位作者的新书将于下周出版。

1. **quirky** [ˋkwɜkɪ]
   adj. 多变的；古怪的
   The designer is known for her quirky fashion creations.

2. **prospect** [ˋprɑspɛkt]
   n. 前景；机会
   With no prospect of victory in sight, the army decided to surrender.

影视娱乐

时尚生活

政治财经

体坛文艺

女演员兼歌星 周迅

我是周迅，我现在正在化妆，待会儿要出席《孔子》的首映式。今晚这部电影就要进行首映。很多朋友都会来看，这也是我第一次看这部影片。我很期待。

《亚洲名人聊天室》安姿丽

你有两部大片连续上映，先是《孔子》，接着是《苏乞儿》。你对这一切有什么感觉？听起来压力很大。

图片提供：山水国际娱乐

101

ZHOU XUN, ACTRESS AND SINGER

I'm quite excited because I play two very different characters in these movies. I've never played a mother or a significant historic figure[3] before, so everything was brand new[4] to me. Also, both films were produced by groups of very talent[ed] people, so I hope the audience will enjoy them as well.

ANJALI RAO, TALK ASIA

For somebody that is still so young—you're only 35—you've been in this industry for a long time, nearly 20 years now. So, you know, you're the perfect person to tell us about what it's like within the industry here in China.

ZHOU XUN, ACTRESS AND SINGER

Being an actress is a very interesting job because I don't even consider it as my job, but as my life now. Being an actress in China, I'm actually a very lucky actress. I think just be yourself and it should be fine, especially now that Chinese movies are becoming more diverse[5] with more viewers overseas—stepping onto the global stage. So, just be a responsible actress.

I'm currently in a recording session for a song for my latest movie, *True Legend*, or in Mandarin, *Su Qi Er*.

ANJALI RAO, TALK ASIA

You are also a singer as well. You've got two CDs to your name so far. What is it about singing particularly that you love? Why would you not just want to stick to acting?

女演员兼歌星 周迅

我很兴奋，因为我在这两部影片里扮演了两个非常不同的角色。我从没演过母亲或是重要的历史人物，所以一切对我来说都是全新的体验。此外，这两部影片的制作团队都非常杰出，希望观众也会看得开心。

《亚洲名人聊天室》安姿丽

你才 35 岁，对某些人来说还很年轻，却已经在这个行业里打拼了将近 20 年。所以，由你来告诉我们中国电影圈的情况再适合不过了。

女演员兼歌星 周迅

演员是个很有趣的工作，因为我并不认为这是一份工作，而是我的人生。作为中国的演员，我其实非常幸运，我认为我只要忠于自我就行了，尤其现在中国电影随着海外观众增加、并逐步踏上国际舞台而变得越来越多元化。所以，只要当个负责任的演员就可以了。

我现在正在为我的新片《苏乞儿》录制一首歌。

《亚洲名人聊天室》安姿丽

你也是歌星，目前已出了两张唱片。歌唱有什么地方是让你特别喜欢的？为什么不想只是演戏呢？

Notes & Vocabulary

stick to
坚持（做某事）

动词 stick 原有"刺入；黏住"的意思，常与不同介词连用构成动词短语，常见搭配如下：stick to "持续；坚持做（本文用法）"、stick out "伸出；吐出"、stuck up "竖起"。

Even though Brian wanted to act in movies, he stuck to stage productions to gain more experience.
尽管布莱恩想在电影里参演，他还是坚持在舞台剧的表演中吸取更多经验。

3. **figure** [ˈfɪgjə] *n.* 人物

4. **brand new** 全新的
Andrew bought a brand new car with his sales bonus.

5. **diverse** [daɪˈvɜs]
adj. 各式各样的；形形色色的
Ben's diverse experience makes him a perfect candidate for the job.

ZHOU XUN, ACTRESS AND SINGER

I like singing because it's another way to express myself. I've enjoyed singing since I was little. Also, because I am an actress, I have the opportunity to sing, so it's quite good. Music is like a kind of medicine that has the power to cure. When you are sad or happy, it can make you forget sadness or be even happier.

ANJALI RAO, TALK ASIA

Away from the singing, away from the acting, how do you deal with the celebrity[6] side of things with, I guess, you know, people following you around and you can't walk down the street?

ZHOU XUN, ACTRESS AND SINGER

This is what I'm trying hard to adjust[7] to because I don't like being followed or noticed when I'm not working, but I can't do anything about it. So I try not to let it bother me too much when I get upset[8], but this adjustment process takes quite a long time, and this type of paparazzi culture in China is getting more severe[9] as well.

ANJALI RAO, TALK ASIA

Let's go way back. You did come from a very average[10] background I guess it's fair to say. Was fame something that you had a burning[11] desire for?

ZHOU XUN, ACTRESS AND SINGER

No. Because I was born in a very small town outside of Hangzhou, and even though there was a cinema in our town, movies still seemed very far away to me. I didn't know the production process at all, so I never expected[12] to become an actress. But ever

女演员兼歌星 周迅

我喜欢唱歌，因为唱歌是表现自己的另一种方式。我从小就喜欢唱歌。此外，作为演员让我有了唱歌的机会，这样很好。音乐就像一种具有疗效的药物。在悲伤或是快乐的时候，音乐可以让人忘却悲伤，或是变得更快乐。

《亚洲名人聊天室》安姿丽

先不管唱歌与演戏的事，你怎么应付身为名人的生活，例如许多人到处跟着你，你不能随意走在街上？

女演员兼歌星 周迅

我一直努力要适应这一点，因为我不喜欢有人在我不工作的时间跟着我或是注意我，可是我没办法改变这种现象。所以，我尽量不让这种情况过度影响我的心情。不过，这种调节过程需要相当长的时间，而且八卦文化的现象在中国也越来越严重。

《亚洲名人聊天室》安姿丽

我们来回顾一下。你的出身算是相当平凡，成名是不是你所极度渴望的目标？

女演员兼歌星 周迅

不是。因为我出生在杭州城外一个很小的小镇里，虽然镇上也有电影院，但电影在我心目中却仍是非常遥不可及的东西。我完全不知道电影的制作过程，所以也从来没想过要

Notes & Vocabulary

deal with
处理；应付

deal with 是指"处理；应付"，后面多接麻烦、棘手的状况。不过 deal with 还有另外一个意思就是"关于；涉及"，例如书籍、电影等的内容。

- Brenda always **deals with** the store's more difficult customers.
布伦达总是应付店里那些较难应对的客人。

6. celebrity [sə`lɛbrətɪ] n. 名人

7. adjust [ə`dʒʌst] v. 调适；调整
After her first month of college, Jan adjusted to being away from her family.

8. upset [ʌp`sɛt] adj. 不愉快的；生气的
Amy was upset that her brother wouldn't be at the party.

9. severe [sə`vɪr] adj. 严重的
The businessman faced severe punishment for his actions.

10. average [`ævərɪdʒ] adj. 普通的；一般的
Phil was an average student in high school.

11. burning [`bɜnɪŋ] adj 迫切的；强烈的
Jenny has a burning need to be up-to-date on the latest fashions.

12. expect [ɪk`spɛkt] v. 预期；预计
Alex expects to receive the results of his test any day now.

影视娱乐

时尚生活

政治财经

体坛文艺

since I was young, I loved singing and dancing, and then I was admitted[13] into a dance academy[14]. After I was admitted, a director spotted[15] me to become an actress. So, it was almost that I was destined[16] to act.

ANJALI RAO, TALK ASIA

Which has been the role that's pushed[17] you the most as an actress?

ZHOU XUN, ACTRESS AND SINGER

~~Li Mei~~ [Gu Xiaomeng] in *Feng Shang* (*The Message*). I played a taxi driver in *The Equation*[18] of *Love and Death*, and I played a spy in *The Message*.

ANJALI RAO, TALK ASIA

The Message is a World War II espionage[19] film. Is it true that you had an emotional breakdown[20] when you were filming it?

ZHOU XUN, ACTRESS AND SINGER

Yes. The role in *The Message* was the first time that I needed to hold things in[21] and withdraw[22] a bit when acting. It is relatively[23] easier to let go of emotions and have that release when acting, but it's hard to withdraw and hold things in. Also, the character was constantly living on the edge and facing death, so I felt the pressure from the role as well.

正常*MP3-Track13* / 慢速*MP3-Track43* ❙ *Zhou Xun*

成为演员。不过，我从小就热爱唱歌和跳舞，后来也进了舞蹈学院。我进入舞蹈学院之后，一位导演发现了我，让我成为演员。所以，感觉上就像是我命中注定要演戏。

《亚洲名人聊天室》安姿丽
你演过的哪个角色对你最有挑战性？

女演员兼歌星 周迅
《风声》里的顾晓梦。我在《李米的猜想》里饰演出租车司机，在《风声》里则是扮演间谍。

《亚洲名人聊天室》安姿丽
《风声》是一部关于第二次世界大战的谍战电影。你在拍摄期间真的发生了情绪崩溃的情况吗？

女演员兼歌星 周迅
确实如此。《风声》里的角色是我第一次必须以情绪内敛、稍微与角色分离的方式演出。表演的时候，直接释放情感比较简单，要内敛、压抑则比较难。此外，这个角色也一直处于险境，随时面对死亡的威胁，所以我也会感受到这个角色的压力。

Notes & Vocabulary

let go of sth.
放弃（想法、控制、情感等）
此短语可改写成 let + N. + go。而不及物的 let go 还可指心理上的"释怀；放松"。

Nadine **let go of** her need for constant reassurance from her peers.
纳丁对于必须永远寻求同辈人认同的想法释怀了。

13. **admit** [əd`mɪt]
    v. 接受（入学）；准许加入（组织）
    After graduating at the top of his class, Greg was admitted to a prestigious law school.

14. **academy** [ə`kædəmɪ]
    n. 专科院校；私立学校；学会

15. **spot** [spɑt] *v.* 发现；找出
    Peggy spotted a rare mushroom while walking in the forest.

16. **destine** [`dɛstɪn] *v.* 注定
    Even in elementary school, teachers knew Jim was destined for greatness.

17. **push** [pʊʃ] *v.* 迫使；敦促
    The coach pushed the players to try harder.

18. **equation** [ɪ`kweʒən] *n.* 方程式

19. **espionage** [`ɛspɪə‚nɑʒ]
    n. 间谍活动

20. **breakdown** [`brek‚daʊn] *n.* 崩溃

21. **hold in** 抑制（感情、情绪）

22. **withdraw** [wɪθ`drɔ]
    v. 退缩；疏离
    Annette withdrew from her friends and family after the death of her cat.

23. **relatively** [`rɛlətɪvlɪ]
    adv. 相对地；相当地

影视娱乐

时尚生活

政治财经

体坛文艺

Transplanted[1] Talent

Talk Asia Sits Down with Actor-Director Daniel Wu

图片提供：AP

ANJALI RAO, TALK ASIA
Daniel, welcome to Talk Asia.

DANIEL WU, ACTOR AND DIRECTOR
Thank you very much.

ANJALI RAO, TALK ASIA
Now, you're coming up on 50 movies in your 12-year career. You're also a businessman. You own a pool hall[2], which is why we're here.

DANIEL WU, ACTOR AND DIRECTOR
We're in it.

❶❹ 无心插柳的星路奇缘——CNN专访吴彦祖

名人小档案 ▾ 吴彦祖

吴彦祖（1974— ）出生于美国旧金山，在加州成长，毕业于美国俄勒冈大学建筑学系，是著名的演员、导演兼制作人。他于 1997 年前往中国香港，开始他的电影及模特工作。之后在 2004 年，他凭借《新警察故事》中的表演赢得金马奖最佳男配角奖。2007 年又凭《四大天王》一片，在第 26 届香港电影金像奖中夺得新晋导演奖。

Daniel Wu

Notes & Vocabulary

1. transplant [ˌtræns`plænt]
   v. 使迁移；使移居
   Ted transplanted his family from New York to California.

2. pool hall [pul] [hɔl]
   n.【美】台球场
   The rough pool hall was filled with students.

吴彦祖 代表作

1998《新古惑仔之少年激斗》

1999《特警新人类》

2002《新扎师妹》

2004《旺角黑夜》、《新警察故事》

2006《四大天王》

2007《天堂口》

2009《窃听风云》

2010《如梦》

2011《窃听风云 II》

《亚洲名人聊天室》安姿丽
丹尼尔，欢迎来到《亚洲名人聊天室》。

演员兼导演 吴彦祖
非常谢谢你。

《亚洲名人聊天室》安姿丽
你 12 年来的演艺生涯已经累积了 50 部电影作品，而且你还同时在做生意，拥有一家台球场，所以我们才会在这里。

演员兼导演 吴彦祖
我们就在我的台球场里。

ANJALI RAO, TALK ASIA

Now, if somebody had said to you back in the day, you know, you're not gonna be an architect like you trained to be, you're gonna be a famous movie star, what would you have thought?

DANIEL WU, ACTOR AND DIRECTOR

I wouldn't have believed it. I mean it really, the whole thing just fell in my lap and then I went with[3] it. And, you know, studying architecture, you never think that you would get into film or movies or this whole business that I'm in, and it was just a surprise.

I feel I've had lucky, lucky, lucky turn[s] of events in my life, that a lot of people, you know, strive[4] and struggle to be there and can't get there, and then someone like me, it just falls in my lap. So [I] just try and make the best of it and appreciate what I have, you know?

ANJALI RAO, TALK ASIA

You were born in the U.S. to Chinese parents, but even though you weren't raised in Asia, did you still feel that connection to this part of the world?

DANIEL WU, ACTOR AND DIRECTOR

Yeah, definitely. I mean, I felt growing up in San Francisco there's all the huge Chinese community there and a lot of my friends growing up in high school that were also Chinese. I didn't speak the language that well when I was there, but I learned a lot from my parents who always instilled[5] in me: No matter that you're an American, you're always also a Chinese. So they always pushed that in my mind.

《亚洲名人聊天室》安姿丽

当初如果有人告诉你，你不会依从自己的专业成为建筑师，而会成为知名电影明星，你会怎么想？

演员兼导演 吴彦祖

我一定不会相信。我说真的，因为这一切突然就降临在我身上，我只是跟着命运走而已。况且，学建筑的人绝不会想象自己会走进电影或娱乐行业，所以这的确是意外。

我觉得我人生中碰到许多非常幸运的转折。很多人拼命奋斗都还不一定进得了演艺圈，但我的机会却是从天而降。所以，我尽量做到最好，也对自己拥有的一切心怀感恩。

《亚洲名人聊天室》安姿丽

你父母是中国人，但你在美国出生。虽然你不是在亚洲长大，还是觉得自己和亚洲有紧密的关系吗？

演员兼导演 吴彦祖

没错，的确如此。我在旧金山长大，那里有庞大的华人社区，我高中的许多朋友也都是华人。我在美国的时候，中文说得不太好，但我从父母身上学到了很多。他们总是这么教我：你虽然是美国人，却也永远是中国人。他们总是对我灌输这样的观念。

Notes & Vocabulary

fall in one's lap

不劳而获；从天而降

fall in/into one's lap 字面上是"掉在腿上"的意思，表示坐着、不费力就有收获，比喻"（珍贵事物）不劳而获；从天而降"。

- Great opportunities seem to **fall in Betty's lap**.

  大好机会似乎都会降临在贝蒂身上。

3. **go with** 顺从……的趋势

   When booking a room, Rob goes with the cheapest option.

4. **strive** [straɪv]

   v. 努力；奋斗；力争

   Maggie strives to improve herself.

5. **instill** [ɪn`stɪl] *v.* 灌输（观念等）

   The coach instilled a sense of pride in his team.

吴彦祖的重要经历

1997 年 回到香港见证香港回归。开始担任模特儿，拍摄广告。

1998 年 被杨凡发掘出演第一部电影《美少年之恋》，以《新古惑仔之少年激斗》入围香港金像奖新人奖。

1999 年 出演《紫雨风暴》、《特警新人类》、《新扎师妹》。

2004 年 以《新警察故事》获得金马奖最佳男配角。

2006 年 推出《四大天王》流行音乐纪录片，并于 2007 年获得第 26 届香港电影金像奖新晋导演奖。

2010 年 与长跑 8 年的女友 Lisa S. 于南非低调完婚。

It wasn't until I came to Hong Kong that Hong Kong people started calling me "guai zai,"—which means "white boy," right ~~which~~ [that] I started to feel that I wasn't necessarily the same. And I realized it is different, you know? Now I don't really feel that I'm either actually anymore. I just kind of think of myself as a person of this world, you know, really. And I think that's the most important thing, is if you can relate to other people, other cultures and just be open, you get much further in society, yeah.

ANJALI RAO, TALK ASIA

You won Best New Director at the Hong Kong Film Awards in 2007 for *The Heavenly Kings*, which was a popumentary about a boy band called Alive that is ironic[6] in itself because it never was alive: it never existed. What was your motivation[7] for that project and what was it like having to pretend to be in a boy band for two years?

DANIEL WU, ACTOR AND DIRECTOR

It was embarrassing, really embarrassing, because it's . . . I mean, you know, we're ~~satiring~~ [satirizing][8] basically the pop music industry, and at that time there were a lot of boy bands who were very popular. And on the side, me and my friends, we kind of laugh at that, that sort of scene, because I grew up in America. I grew up listening to, you know, punk rock and rock and hip-hop, and real interesting dark, heavy music. And then [to] see this

直到我来到香港，开始被人叫做"鬼仔"——也就是"白人小子"的意思——我才意识到自己似乎和别人不一样。于是，我开始产生不同的感受，不再认为自己是中国人或美国人，只觉得自己是个世界公民。我认为这才是最重要的事情。如果你能够放开心胸，认同其他人和其他文化，你在社会上就能更有发展。

《亚洲名人聊天室》安姿丽

你在 2007 年的香港电影金像奖赢得新晋导演奖，得奖作品是《四大天王》这部流行音乐纪录片，内容讲述一个叫 Alive 的男子组合的故事。这个组合的名称本身就带有反讽意味，因为这个组合从来不曾"活过"——从来不曾存在过。你拍摄这部影片的动机是什么？假装身为男子组合的成员达两年之久又有什么感觉？

演员兼导演 吴彦祖

很尴尬，真的很尴尬，因为其实我们基本上是在嘲讽流行音乐，当时有许多当红的男子组合。另一方面，由于我在美国长大，所以我和我的朋友都把那股风潮当成笑话看。在成长过程中，我听的都是朋克摇滚、摇滚、嘻哈及黑暗、沉重却很有趣的音乐。因此，

Notes & Vocabulary

popumentary 流行乐纪录片

popumentary 是个新词，其构词源自于 rockumentary，这个词最早出现于 1969 年，是指"（关于摇滚乐或摇滚乐手的）摇滚纪录片"，这个词的构成是：

> rock music + documentary
> = rockumentary 摇滚纪录片

再来看 popumentary 的构词

> pop music + documentary
> = popumentary 流行音乐纪录片

另一个常见的词还有 mockumentary "伪纪录片"，后来 -umentary 常被用来自行造词，如：dog-umentary "狗纪录片"、bike-umentary "自行车纪录片"、stalk-umentary "跟踪纪录片"等。有趣的是，后来有人把既有词变成 doc-umentary，表示"医生日志"。

on the side 另一方面；秘密地

on the side 字面意思是"在旁边；另外的"，可用来指"秘密地；非法地"，另外也可指正常工作之外的"兼职或副业"。口语中则常用来指点菜时的"附餐"，也就是配菜（side dish），如 I want some salad on the side.（我要点色拉当配菜）。

David often praises his boss at the meetings, while on the side he ridicules his management style.
大卫常在会议上称赞老板，但却会在私下偷偷取笑他的管理风格。

6. ironic [aɪˌrɑnɪk]
   adj. 讽刺的；挖苦的

7. motivation [ˌmotəˈveʃən] n. 动机

8. satirize [ˈsætəˌraɪz] v. 讽刺；讥讽

light, poppy[9], boyish[10] music with girls running after people and screaming and crying was very foreign[11] to me.

And so we wanted to sort of poke fun at that as well as poke fun at the industry in general. We thought about making a movie that we'd actually be playing these characters, but I felt like the point wouldn't get across as well as us actually doing it and actually using ourselves to make fun of what we were talking about.

So it was difficult because we couldn't tell anybody, so even some of our friends didn't know. And they were like, "You're in a boy band now? What's goin' on? I think you need to work on your dancing skills a little bit." You know, stuff like that. And it was, I mean, it was embarrassing really, but we knew what we were doing it for, so it made it worth it in the end.

ANJALI RAO, TALK ASIA
You and Lisa have been together for, you know, a long time now, but you've been able to largely keep your relationship out of the public eye. How do you do that?

DANIEL WU, ACTOR AND DIRECTOR
I don't really like to talk much about my ~~public~~ [private] life in general, because I really do believe that if you know too much about that stuff, it kind of takes away the magic of what you see an actor do on screen. And so, yeah, I mean it's a matter of just keeping things private, and, you know, special moments for special things. I don't think everything

看到这种肤浅幼稚的流行音乐，还有女孩追在偶像身后尖叫呐喊的情形，对我来说是非常奇怪的事。

因此，我们想要嘲讽这种现象，也想嘲讽整个娱乐产业。我们本来想拍一部电影，由我们来扮演这些角色，但我觉得我们如果不实际去做，不亲自去嘲弄我们所谈论的那些事物，就不可能让观众体会我们的观点。

所以，整个过程很不容易，因为我们不能告诉别人，甚至某些朋友也不知道。很多人说："你加入了男子组合？发生什么事了？我觉得你的舞技要多练练。"或是其他类似的反应。实在是很尴尬，但我们知道自己这么做是为了什么，最后的结果也让我们的付出很值得。

《亚洲名人聊天室》安姿丽
你和 Lisa 已经交往很长一段时间了，但你们俩的关系大都能远离观众的视线。这是怎么做到的？

演员兼导演 吴彦祖
我一般不喜欢多谈自己的私生活，因为我认为大家一旦知道演员太多的私生活，观看演员在银幕上的表演时就会难以入戏。所以，我认为重点就是保持私密，只在特别的时刻才做特别的事情。我不认为一切事情都应该

Notes & Vocabulary

poke fun at
拿……开玩笑；嘲弄
poke 是指"推；捅；戳；探"，poke fun at sb./sth. 则是指"拿……开玩笑；嘲弄……"，通常是暗地里取笑或无厘头地嘲弄。

- The story **pokes fun at** several sacred institutions, like religion and the government.
这个故事嘲讽了许多神圣的机构组织，像是宗教组织及政府。

9. **poppy** [ˈpɑpɪ] *adj.* 流行音乐的
The singer's latest single has a very poppy sound.

10. **boyish** [ˈbɔɪʃ]
adj. 孩子气的；幼稚的
Even at age 40, Steve has very boyish looks.

11. **foreign** [ˈfɔrən]
adj. 陌生的；外来的
Failure is a foreign concept to Justine.

吴彦祖与Alive

Alive 由吴彦祖、尹子维、陈子聪、连凯四人组成，曾公开演唱，并投资 6 万港币录制唱片《阿当的抉择》，且在 Alive 自设的官方网站可以免费下载；但 Alive 却在其后声称唱片未推出前已被非法上传到网络上。2006 年 Alive 曾传出不和，并把互骂片段放在其网站上。当时 Alive 正拍摄由吴彦祖执导、以纪录片形式拍摄的电影《四大天王》，当《四大天王》上映，传媒发现所谓不和，实际是由吴彦祖自导自演，以达到宣传的目的的手段。

影视娱乐

时尚生活

政治财经

体坛文艺

is meant for everybody. You know, I've got to keep some things treasured to myself.

ANJALI RAO, TALK ASIA

Now, Asian movies are churned out in rapid succession[12]. You've got three coming out this year alone I understand. What else is on the horizon for you?

DANIEL WU, ACTOR AND DIRECTOR

I'm now kind of expanding[13] business-wise[14]. I mean, we're here in my . . . in one of the sort of bars that I've invested in. And I just want to expand my business based on the ideology[15] of doing what I think is right or doing what I think is fun and interesting rather than for a monetary[16] return.

So, I started my own management company, Revolution Talent Management, and we're starting a new music division[17] soon, and we're . . . you know the music industry's changing, and we want to try different ideas on how to make successful musicians out there, and also non-mainstream musicians. I have a lot of friends who have a lot of talent but don't necessarily fit into the typical Hong Kong pop star mode, and I want to give them a chance to show their talents.

And whether they make money or not is not important to me. It's really about getting the passion out there and getting people to have a choice and a variety and not just be spoon-fed[18] entertainment, but given a choice to select what they want to see, you know.

正常 *MP3 - Track14* / 慢速 *MP3 - Track44* ▌ *Transplanted Talent*

让所有人知道，有些事情必须珍藏起来，只属于我自己所有。

《亚洲名人聊天室》安姿丽

亚洲电影推出的速度是又多又快。据我所知，你光今年就将推出 3 部作品。接下来你还有些什么其他计划？

演员兼导演 吴彦祖

我现在正在扩张自己的生意版图。我们现在所在的地方，就是我投资的一种类似酒吧的一个地方。我扩张生意版图的方向，主要还是以我本身的理念为基础，也就是做我认为正确的事情，做我觉得有趣的事情，而不只是为了赚钱。

所以，我创立了一家经纪公司，叫做"革命人才经纪公司"，而且我们也即将成立一个新的音乐部门。音乐界正在转变，因此我们想尝试以不同的方式培养成功的音乐人及非主流的音乐人。我有很多朋友都相当有才华，却不一定符合香港流行歌星的模式。我希望能为他们提供展示才华的机会。

对我来说，他们赚不赚钱并不重要，重点是发挥热情，让大家拥有不同的选择，不再只是被动接受演艺圈灌输给他们的娱乐方式，而是有机会选择自己想看的东西。

Notes & Vocabulary

on the horizon
即将来临的；即将发生的
horizon 是"地平线；海平面"的意思，当看到物体升至地平线或海平面上，进入视线范围内，可用 on the horizon 来表示，引申形容某种新的事物或现象"即将发生"。

· Todd has several business projects on the horizon.
托德有好几个商业项目即将完成。

比较

over the horizon
未来
over the horizon 则指还在地平线或海平面另一端，表示视线范围以外、看不见的未来。

· It's difficult to know what challenges might wait for us over the horizon.
未来会有什么挑战等着我们难以预料。

12. **succession** [sək`sɛʃən]
   n. 一连串；连续

13. **expand** [ɪk`spænd] v. 扩张；扩展
   The company expanded its reach into new territories.

14. **-wise** [waɪz]
   adv. 在……方面；以……方式

15. **ideology** [ˌaɪdi.ɑlədʒɪ]
   n. 意识形态；观念形态

16. **monetary** [`mɑnəˌtɛrɪ]
   adj. 货币的；金钱的
   Phil enjoys playing music for no monetary gain.

17. **division** [dɪ`vɪʒən] n. 部门；部分

18. **spoon-feed** [`spunˌfid]
   v. 填鸭式灌输
   Hannah believes many people are spoon-fed information by the media.

影视娱乐

时尚生活

政治财经

体坛文艺

Ballad of John and Yoko

Rock Legend's Widow Remembers Lennon on His 70th Birthday

图片提供：AP

ANDERSON COOPER, AC 360°

Tonight, a 360 exclusive we're really excited to bring you—Yoko Ono. She doesn't give many interviews, but she recently agreed to sit down with me to talk about her life with John Lennon. As you probably know, Lennon would have turned 70 years old this month.

Ono has been remastering[1] his music, and she celebrated the anniversary[2] of his birthday in Iceland, where she performed with the Plastic Ono Band, which is still making music after all these years. It is hard to believe that Yoko Ono is 77 now. She looks amazing.

正常MP3-Track15
慢速MP3-Track45

名人小档案▼ 小野洋子

小野洋子（1933—）生于日本东京，其父为银行家及古典钢琴家，其祖先小野镇幸是日本战国时代大名（daimyo）立花宗茂的重臣。第二次世界大战后洋子14岁时因父亲派驻美国移民，定居纽约斯卡代尔镇，就读莎拉劳伦斯学院。20世纪60年代初期，她在文学、哲学和电影创作等方面引起广泛关注，成为"激浪派"（Fluxus）重要代表人物。她的艺术创作包括绘画、作曲、表演艺术、影片、装置艺术等。洋子于1956年与作曲家一柳慧结婚，1962年离婚；次年与安东尼·考克斯结婚，育有一女Kyoto，1969年离婚；同年与约翰·列侬结婚，育有一子Sean。

Yoko Ono

Notes & Vocabulary

标题扫描

Ballad of John and Yoko
约翰与洋子之歌

标题出自甲壳虫乐队的单曲"The Ballad of John and Yoko"（1969），主要由约翰·列侬创作，是一首穿插叙事诗"narrative poem"的摇滚歌曲，内容描述两人的婚姻及携手发起的运动，例如蜜月期间在旅馆进行的反越战床上和平静坐（Bed-Ins for Peace）。

1. **remaster** [riˈmæstə]
   v. 将母带重新编录处理
   The band remastered its early recordings.

2. **anniversary** [ˌænəˈvɜːsərɪ]
   n. 纪念日；周年纪念

《360° 全面视野》安德森·库珀

今晚，我们很高兴能为你带来小野洋子的独家专访。她不太经常接受访问，但她最近答应与我一同坐下聊聊她和约翰·列侬的生活。也许你知道，列侬在这个月就要70岁了。

小野重新录制了列侬的音乐。她在冰岛庆祝了他的诞辰，和"塑料小野乐队"一同登台演出，这个乐队这些年来仍持续创作音乐。很难相信小野洋子现在已经77岁了。她看起来仍相当有魅力。

艺术上的激进派

Fluxus "激进派"这个名词源于拉丁文，有"水的流动"的意思。激进派为活跃于20世纪60年代的国际性艺术组织，其成员来自各国，主要受到达达主义运动的影响，与其在精神上有着一脉相承的关系，主要想把个人在生理上、精神上、政治上的压抑感释放出来，对抗秩序、对抗规则、对抗文化。英国著名评论家里德爵士曾表示"激进派是无政府主义的行动"，可见其社会性的目的比美学目的更强。"激进派"的演出形式不只限于现场演出，邮递艺术（以邮寄分发作品）等各种艺术形式都同时出现，并无明确目的，彼此也不连贯，但它破除习俗，成为行为、影像等艺术的先驱。

影视娱乐

时尚生活

政治财经

体坛文艺

In December, it's gonna be 30 years since Lennon was murdered, shot dead outside the Dakota apartment building here in New York where he and Ono lived.

As news of his death broke, a crowd gathered outside the Dakota. Mourners stayed throughout the night. Ono vividly[3] remembers hearing them singing the night she was widowed[4]. She still lives at the Dakota today, and just across the street in Central Park is Strawberry Fields, the memorial[5] dedicated to Lennon five years after his murder on what would have been his 45th birthday.

Thirty years. That terrible day is still vivid for Ono. We talked about what she remembers and how she managed to move on.

There's a lot I want to ask you about, both your work now, what's coming up, and also just, given that this is the anniversary for John's birthday, how did you first meet? How did you first meet John?

YOKO ONO, ARTIST AND WIDOW OF JOHN LENNON
Oh, OK. Well, I was doing a show, my own art show in Indica Gallery in Mason['s] Yard in London. And John just came in, just walked in with the owner of the gallery. And I was a bit upset[6] about it, because, you know, I told the owner that nobody should get in before the opening. And it was just before the opening. I said, "What is he doing?"

ANDERSON COOPER, AC 360°
You didn't know he was a Beatle?

今年 12 月，距离列侬被谋杀的日子将满 30 年，他在他和小野居住的纽约达科塔大楼外遭到枪杀。

当他过世的消息传开之后，群众便聚集在达科塔大楼外面。哀悼者待了一整夜。小野很清楚地记得丧偶的那晚听到他们在唱歌。她现在还住在达科塔大楼，对面就是中央公园，里面有个草莓园，那是列侬遇刺的 5 年后人们向他致献的纪念园地，当时是他的 45 岁诞辰。

30 年了。那恐怖的一天对小野而言仍是历历在目。我们谈到她所记得的一切和她怎么走出悲伤继续生活。

我想问你许多事情，包括你现在着手的工作、接下来的计划，还有因为这是约翰诞辰周年纪念，能否谈谈你们当初是怎么认识的？你第一次见到约翰是什么情景？

艺术家兼约翰·列侬遗孀 小野洋子
好的，我当时正在筹办一场展览，我在伦敦梅森苑的因迪卡画廊举办自己的艺术展。然后约翰进来了，和画廊的老板一同走进来。我对此有点不高兴，因为我告诉老板在开幕前任何人都不可以进来。而那时就是在开幕之前。我说，"他在这做什么？"

《360° 全面视野》安德森·库珀
你不知道他是甲壳虫的成员？

Notes & Vocabulary

manage to V.
勉力完成；设法应付
manage 原本是指"管理；控制；照管"，另外还有"（勉强）应付；努力做成"的意思，加上不定词 to V. 表示"设法做成某事"。而根据上下文，有时可贬抑地表达"即使做了一番努力，还是……"。

- If you can manage to pick up some eggs and milk at the grocery store, I'd appreciate it.
如果你可以去杂货店买些鸡蛋和牛奶，我会很感激的。

3. vividly [ˈvɪvɪdlɪ]
   adv. 清晰地；生动地

4. widow [ˈwɪdo]
   v. 使成为寡妇或鳏夫；丧偶
   The wars in Iraq and Afghanistan widowed thousands of women in the U.S. and U.K.

5. memorial [məˈmorɪəl]
   n. 纪念物（碑、像等）

6. upset [ˌʌpˈsɛt]
   adj. 不高兴的；生气的
   Benny's low grades upset his parents.

约翰·列侬遭枪杀事件

来自美国的马克·大卫·查普曼（1955–）于 1980 年 12 月 8 日枪杀了约翰·列侬。人们一般相信他患有精神病，是披头士的狂热歌迷。然而根据 Discovery 频道的节目访查，他杀害列侬的原因可能是由于列侬曾表示"披头士比耶稣更有名"，侵犯了他的信仰而引起杀机。他向列侬连开 5 枪，4 颗全数打在列侬背上。列侬倒地不起，而这名男子却神情自若地站在原地读起了《麦田捕手》。

影视娱乐

时尚生活

政治财经

体坛文艺

YOKO ONO, ARTIST AND WIDOW OF JOHN LENNON

Of course not. Of course not. I don't know how to put it, but I thought he was [a] very elegant[7], very beautiful guy. I saw his face and I thought, well, he's rather, you know, elegant. But I, you know, and I thought, well, I could think of having an affair[8] with somebody like that, but I didn't want to because I'm too busy, that's what I said, because I was really busy at the time. So, you know, forget it.

ANDERSON COOPER, AC 360°

So what . . . when was there that connection? When was there the moment of, "Oh, OK, I recognize you?"

YOKO ONO, ARTIST AND WIDOW OF JOHN LENNON

Well, I started to feel that he did sort of have a special feeling for me, probably, in 1967 when he visited my apartment. And the way he visited was kind of nice. You know, he just suddenly appeared.

ANDERSON COOPER, AC 360°

Why do you think there was such prejudice[9]? Why did so many . . . you know, I guess some of it stems from people saying that you broke up the Beatles, but I mean, the Beatles were on their way to breaking up before you were . . .

YOKO ONO, ARTIST AND WIDOW OF JOHN LENNON

They didn't think about that. I think that I was used as a scapegoat[10], and it's a very easy scapegoat. And Japanese woman and, you know, whatever.

艺术家兼约翰·列侬遗孀 小野洋子

当然不知道，真的不知道。我不知道怎么讲，但我觉得他很优雅，是个很俊美的男子。我看见他的长相，觉得他相当斯文。然后我想，我可以想象和那样的人谈场恋爱，但是我当时并不想，因为我太忙了，我这样告诉自己，因为我当时真的很忙。所以，就算了吧。

《360° 全面视野》安德森·库珀

所以……什么时候才有交集的？到了什么时候你才觉得，"嗯，好吧，我接受你"？

艺术家兼约翰·列侬遗孀 小野洋子

嗯，我开始觉得他对我有种特殊的情感，大概是在 1967 年他到我的公寓拜访。他来访的方式还挺不错的，你知道，他就突然出现了。

《360° 全面视野》安德森·库珀

你觉得为什么会有这样的成见？为什么有这么多……你知道，我猜有些是因为人们谣传是你害甲壳虫解散的，但我想甲壳虫在你出现之前就有解散的迹象了……

艺术家兼约翰·列侬遗孀 小野洋子

他们并没有那么想。我想我只是个代罪羔羊，现成的代罪羔羊。我是个日本女人等等，你知道，随便怎么说。

Notes & Vocabulary

stem from

起源于；因……造成

stem 原本是植物的"茎干；柄；梗"，当不及物动词是指"起源于"，常与 from 连用，表示某事物的结果源自某原因。

- Polly's dislike of seafood stems from a case of food poisoning she had several years ago.
波利对海鲜的厌恶起因于几年前的一次食物中毒。

同义词

- result from
- arise from

---

7. elegant [ˈɛlɪgənt]
adj. 优雅的；优美的
Daphne attended an elegant garden party after the polo match.

8. affair [əˈfɛr]
n. 短暂恋情；风流韵事
Jill accused her husband of having an affair with her best friend.

9. prejudice [ˈprɛdʒədəs]
n. 偏见；成见
It's hard to get rid of ingrained prejudices.

10. scapegoat [ˈskepˌgot]
n. 代罪羔羊；替罪者
Caught up in international politics, he was sacrificed as a scapegoat.

影视娱乐

时尚生活

政治财经

体坛文艺

ANDERSON COOPER, AC 360°

You think there . . . some of it was sexism[11], racism[12]?

YOKO ONO, ARTIST AND WIDOW OF JOHN LENNON

Sexism, racism, but also just remember that the United States and Britain were fighting with Japan in World War II. It was just after that in a way. So I can understand how they thought.

ANDERSON COOPER, AC 360°

Did it hurt?

YOKO ONO, ARTIST AND WIDOW OF JOHN LENNON

Well, it did in a way. But you know, it was sort of like a distant[13] thing in a way, because John and I were so close. And we were just totally involved in each other and in our work. You know, I just kept on being . . . getting ideas, and he was, too. So that was much more exciting.

ANDERSON COOPER, AC 360°

What do you think he would have been like at 70?

YOKO ONO, ARTIST AND WIDOW OF JOHN LENNON

John was an incredibly spiritual[14] and intelligent guy, but aside ~~of~~ [from] that, he was a very attractive guy, and you know, he would not have changed. I'm sure of that, because, you know, he had this kind of like cheekbone[15] and the bone structure that would not [have] failed in years.

And, of course, he would not be retiring. I mean, he would never have . . . well, he did think about retiring. He said, "In the end we should be in

《360° 全面视野》安德森·库珀

你会觉得……有部分原因是性别歧视，或种族歧视吗？

艺术家兼约翰·列侬遗孀 小野洋子

性别歧视，种族歧视，但也别忘了美国和英国在第二次世界大战中和日本对立。好似那种对立的延续。所以我可以理解他们的想法。

《360° 全面视野》安德森·库珀

那会伤人吗？

艺术家兼约翰·列侬遗孀 小野洋子

嗯，在某种程度上确实是。但就某方面来说，那些传言其实也有点毫不相干，因为约翰和我非常亲密。我们深爱着彼此并全心投入我们的工作。你知道，我就是不停地……汲取新的灵感，而他也是。那样的关系更令人兴奋。

《360° 全面视野》安德森·库珀

你觉得他 70 岁时会是怎样的人？

艺术家兼约翰·列侬遗孀 小野洋子

约翰是个非常崇尚心灵层面的聪明男子，但除此之外，他非常迷人，他不会有太大的改变。我相当确信，因为他有那样的颧骨，那样的骨架好几年也不会老。

而且，当然，他也不会退休。我是指，他不会……嗯，他确实想过退休一事。他曾说，"最后我们会待在康沃尔，坐在摇椅上等待

Notes & Vocabulary

aside from

除……之外

aside 是副词"在一旁；到一旁"的意思，aside from 则是介词短语，指"不包括……；除了……之外"。

· Aside from Woody Allen movies, Pete doesn't like comedies.
皮特不喜欢喜剧片，除了伍迪·艾伦的电影。

同义词
· apart from
· besides
· except for

其他与 aside 连用的短语

set aside sth.   把……放置一旁

· The two leaders set aside their differences and worked on the peace treaty.
这两位领导人撇开分歧，一同努力订立和平条款。

11. **sexism** [ˈsɛkˌsɪzəm]
n. 性别歧视

12. **racism** [ˈreɪˌsɪzəm]
n. 种族歧视

13. **distant** [ˈdɪstənt]
adj. 遥远的；疏远的
Success seemed a distant memory to the faded movie star.

14. **spiritual** [ˈspɪrɪtʃəwəl]
adj. 心灵（层面）的；精神的
Becky had a spiritual awakening after college.

15. **cheekbone** [ˈtʃikˌbon]
n. 颧骨；颊骨

影视娱乐
时尚生活
政治财经
体坛文艺

Cornwall, you know, in rocking chairs and waiting for Sean's postcard or something." Well, that didn't happen.

And I'm sure that, if he got to be 70, then he would have forgotten all of that. No, we have to do something now. And I'm sure this is when he would have been totally activist[16].

ANDERSON COOPER, AC 360°
Why did you decide to stay at the Dakota?

YOKO ONO, ARTIST AND WIDOW OF JOHN LENNON
Well, because it is our home. You know, you don't just leave home. And also for Sean, that was the only home that he knows with . . . having time with his father. You know? Everything in the house really reminded us of[17] him. Every room is where he touched. How're you gonna leave that?

ANDERSON COOPER, AC 360°
I would find it hard. I mean, after my brother died, we moved from the building, because I . . . I don't know, my mom and I both found it just really hard. But for you it gives you strength.

YOKO ONO, ARTIST AND WIDOW OF JOHN LENNON
For me it gives me . . . it's the reminder of love that we had, too. You know? It gives me power.

ANDERSON COOPER, AC 360°
Do you still come here to Strawberry Fields often?

肖恩的明信片或其他东西。"嗯，但这并没有发生。

我很确信，如果他活到 70 岁，他可能会忘记所有的这些事。不，我们现在一定会做什么，我很确信现在他会完全活跃于各种运动中。

《360°全面视野》安德森·库珀
你为什么决定继续住在达科塔大楼？

艺术家兼约翰·列侬遗孀 小野洋子
嗯，因为那是我们的家。你知道，你不能就这样离家而去。对肖恩来说也是如此，那是他所知道的唯一的家……他和父亲在那里共度了时光。你知道吗？屋内的每件物品都让我们想起他。每个房间都有他生活的痕迹，你怎么舍得丢下这些呢？

《360°全面视野》安德森·库珀
我觉得那并不容易。我是说，在我哥哥过世之后，我们搬离了那个家，因为我……我不知道，我母亲和我都觉得在那里生活真的会触景伤情。但是对你而言，那个家给了你力量。

艺术家兼约翰·列侬遗孀 小野洋子
对我而言，它给了我……它让我不断想起我们曾有过的爱。你知道吗？它给了我力量。

《360°全面视野》安德森·库珀
你还经常到草莓园这儿来吗？

Notes & Vocabulary

16. **activist** [ˈæktɪvɪst]
    adj. 参与社会运动的；激进活跃的
    With all her activist pursuits, Silvia barely has time for her family.

17. **remind sb. of . . .**
    使某人想起……
    What does this picture remind you of?

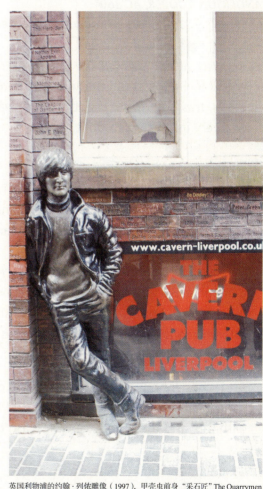

英国利物浦的约翰·列侬雕像（1997），甲壳虫前身"采石匠"The Quarrymen 乐队于 1957 年在这里首度登台，并于 1961 年在此被发掘。

图片提供：George Groutas

影视娱乐

时尚生活

政治财经

体坛文艺

YOKO ONO, ARTIST AND WIDOW OF JOHN LENNON
Well, you know, when I take a walk—I walk a
lot because it's very good for your health and
everything. So when I take a walk in the morning,
I . . . of course I pass here, just checking, you know.
Everything's all right, you know, that kind of thing,
yeah.

ANDERSON COOPER, AC 360°
What's your feeling when you come here?

YOKO ONO, ARTIST AND WIDOW OF JOHN LENNON
Well, I feel good that I made this tribute to John. I
mean, this is a tribute to John, and I realize that it
was very important to do it.

ANDERSON COOPER, AC 360°
I mean, we all remember the day, the night he died,
and people coming spontaneously[18] and thousands
of people outside singing. Did you hear those songs?

YOKO ONO, ARTIST AND WIDOW OF JOHN LENNON
Of course. Because I was . . . my bedroom was right
in front of it. I'm right next to it. And so all night I'm
listening to them singing or sometimes they'd play
the radio, John singing.

And when John was singing, it just made me feel
strange because I mean he's supposed to be in bed
with me, and then, you know. It wasn't very easy.

ANDERSON COOPER, AC 360°
Was it helpful? Did it make it harder?

艺术家兼约翰·列侬遗孀 小野洋子

嗯，我散步时会——我经常散步，因为那对健康什么的都很好。我早上散步时，我……我当然会经过这里，就只是稍微看一看。一切都很完好，就大概看看，对。

《360° 全面视野》安德森·库珀

当你到这里来时，你有什么感觉?

艺术家兼约翰·列侬遗孀 小野洋子

嗯，我觉得我为约翰设计了这样的纪念园地很好。我是说，这是献给约翰的追思地，我知道这非常重要。

《360° 全面视野》安德森·库珀

我们都记得那天，他过世的那个晚上，许多人自发地前来，数千人在外面唱歌。你听到那些歌唱了吗?

艺术家兼约翰·列侬遗孀 小野洋子

当然听到了。因为我……我的房间就在群众正前方，我人就在那旁边。所以整个晚上我都听到他们唱歌，有时他们会播放收音机，放约翰唱的歌。

约翰的歌声传过来的时候，我觉得很奇怪，因为他应该在我身旁共寝，但那时……你知道，那实在不好过。

《360° 全面视野》安德森·库珀

大家聚集唱歌有任何帮助吗? 还是让一切变得更难受?

Notes & Vocabulary

tribute

致敬（尤指对死者）；献礼

tribute 原指"贡品；贡金"，后来引申表示"致敬"，**pay tribute to** 表示"对……表示敬意；致敬"。其同义词组为 **pay homage to**。

- Community leaders paid tribute to local soldiers serving overseas.
  社会领袖向在海外服役的本国军人表示感谢。

- The statue pays homage to the soldiers who fought in World War II.
  这座雕像是为了向在二次世界大战中奋勇作战的士兵们致敬。

18. **spontaneously** [spɑnˋteniəslɪ]
    adv. 自发地
    Teddy's headache stopped spontaneously.

古巴哈瓦那的约翰·列侬纪念公园，最著名的是靠近 17 街与 6 街的座椅上有一座列侬雕像。

影视娱乐

时尚生活

政治财经

体坛文艺

YOKO ONO, ARTIST AND WIDOW OF JOHN LENNON
It made it very hard. Yeah.

ANDERSON COOPER, AC 360°
And now, I mean, on this 70th birthday, what do you want people to celebrate? What do you want people to do tonight?

YOKO ONO, ARTIST AND WIDOW OF JOHN LENNON
His spirit, and the fact that there's so much that he gave to us and to sort of thank him. And I know that people love him for what he has given them, you see, because he did give a lot.

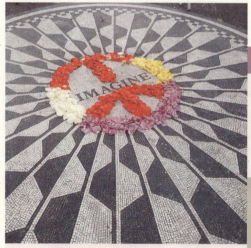

← 纽约中央公园的草莓园（1985），地面马赛克圆环中央有一个和平图案。草莓园原是约翰·列侬童年住所附近的一家孤儿院，也是甲壳虫乐队歌曲《永远的草莓园》（Strawberry Fields Forever）（1967）的灵感来源。

→ 冰岛雷克亚维克的 Imagine Peace Tower（2007），由小野洋子筹划兴建，塔上刻有 24 种语言的 Imagine Peace 字样，每年 10 月 9 日约翰·列侬生日时她会在此点灯，至 12 月 8 日遇刺日熄灯。

正常 *MP3-Track15* / 慢速 *MP3-Track45* | *Ballad of John and Yoko*

艺术家兼约翰·列侬遗孀 小野洋子
那让一切变得更难受。是的。

《360° 全面视野》安德森·库珀
现在，在他 70 岁的诞辰之际，你希望人们
庆祝什么？你希望人们今晚做什么？

艺术家兼约翰·列侬遗孀 小野洋子
缅怀他的精神，事实上他给了我们很多，然
后就是类似说感谢他。我知道人们爱他是因
为他给了他们许多启发，因为他真的贡献了
许多。

图片提供：David Shankbone

Plastic Ono Band 塑料小野乐队

起源

起源：小野洋子与约翰·列侬尝试制作与甲壳虫截然不同的前卫（avant-garde）电子乐，
推出《Unfinished Music No.1: Two Virgins》（1968）与《Unfinished Music No.2: Life
With the Lions》（1969）专辑。某次小野表演想用 4 个塑料台摆上录音机当乐队成员，约
翰提出"塑料小野乐队"的名称。

首支单曲：
"Give Peace a Chance"（1969），
于蒙大拿旅馆房间录制。

创始成员（1969－1975）：
Eric Clapton、Klaus Voormann、
Alan White、甲壳虫乐队的 George Harrison
和 Ringo Starr 等人。

复出成员（2009－　）：
Sean Lennon、Cornelius、Yuka Honda。

甲壳虫乐队的成员约翰·列侬、保罗·麦卡特尼、乔治·哈
里森和林戈·期塔尔（前排由左至右）1964 年抵达美国
肯尼迪机场受到热烈欢迎。

Notes

时 尚 生 活
Fashion & Life

A Partnership in Fashion

Love and Business Intertwine for Style Icons Dolce and Gabbana

图片提供：Reuters、JAYfre01TM、
　　　　　PRNewsFoto/Dolce & Gabbana

NARRATOR

The Italian idyll[1] of Portofino.

UNIDENTIFIED MALE

Welcome to Fantasy Island.

NARRATOR

Designers Domenico Dolce and Stefano Gabbana are relaxing at their cliff-top retreat[2]. Leopard skin sofas, the dogs—the home they share tells the story of a creative partnership where love and business are intertwined[3].

STEFANO GABBANA, DESIGNER

We buy [bought] the house nine years ago and we come just for the weekend usually because it is so

134

正常MP3-Track16
慢速MP3-Track46

名人小档案 ▼ D&G

D&G 品牌（Dolce & Gabbana）由意大利设计师杜梅尼科·多尔奇（1958—）与斯蒂芬诺·嘉班纳（1962—）创办，两人的姓氏也是品牌名称的来源。D&G 的设计在好莱坞十分受欢迎。他们曾为麦当娜、凯莉·米洛等人设计服装。目前这个品牌的总公司位于米兰。

Dolce &
Gabbana

Notes & Vocabulary

1. **idyll** [ˈaɪdl]
   n. 恬静愉快的乡村生活；田园诗

2. **retreat** [rɪˈtrit]
   n. 隐居处；僻静处
   After working so hard, Tina spent a weekend at a relaxing retreat.

3. **intertwine** [ˌɪntəˈtwaɪn]
   v. 纠缠一起；紧密联结
   The lives of Jeff and his twin brother were intertwined from birth.

旁白
意大利有如田园诗般美丽的菲诺港。

不知名男士
欢迎来到梦幻岛。

旁白
设计师杜梅尼科·多尔奇和斯蒂芬诺·嘉班纳正在他们的悬崖顶上的别墅里休息。豹皮沙发和狗，他们共有的房子诉说着创新的合作故事，故事中交织着爱情和事业。

设计师 斯蒂芬诺·嘉班纳
我们 9 年前买了这栋房子，而我们通常只会来这过周末，因为这里和米兰相当近。只有

影视娱乐

时尚生活

政治财经

体坛文艺

135

close to Milan. It's just one hour, two hour[s] by car. We take the car, and we arrive with my dog. It's very relaxing. When I arrive here by boat I say, "Wow, finally!"

NARRATOR

Domenico and Stefano were romantically involved until 2005. Since the breakup, they have never stopped working together, a liaison[4] which is the backbone[5] of the multimillion-dollar Dolce & Gabbana brand. The relationship began in a Milanese design studio 30 years ago.

HILARY ALEXANDER, DAILY TELEGRAPH FASHION EDITOR

When Stefano and Domenico first came on the scene, it was quite unusual to have, you know, designers as a pair, you know, a couple, for example. I think right from the beginning, it was obvious that Dolce and Gabbana were going to be a major force.

NARRATOR

Out of the passion and hard work was born the first line of women's wear.

DOMENICO DOLCE, DESIGNER

At the first show, Dolce & Gabbana Woman, we produce[d] a lot. We organize[d] a show in one small studio, and we organize[d] the show for the real woman. We didn't have money for paid model[s], and we ask[ed] all my friend[s]. We didn't have money, too, for any shoes, bag[s], belts, and all the people use[d] the personal accessory[6]. And this [was the] way it is [was] at Dolce & Gabbana.

一两个小时的车程。我们开车带着狗一起抵达这里。实在是相当惬意。如果我乘船来这里，我会说，"哇，终于到了！"

旁白

杜梅尼科和斯蒂芬诺维持恋人的关系直到2005年结束。分手之后，两人一直没有停止合作。这层合作关系是市值数百万美元 D&G 的品牌基础。他们的关系始于30年前在米兰的一家设计工作室。

《每日电讯报》入时尚编辑 希拉里·亚历山大

斯蒂芬诺和杜梅尼科首次跨入时尚界时，当时二人组的设计师很少见，而且还是一对恋人。我想从一开始就很明显杜梅尼科和嘉班纳将成为时尚界的主力。

旁白

从热情和辛勤工作中诞生了第一个女装系列。

设计师 杜梅尼科·多尔奇

在第一场服装展览中，那是 D&G 女装系列，我们制作了许多作品。我们在一家小工作室规划了一场展览，而我们所规划的展览是给女性观众的。我们没钱请模特儿，所以我们向所有的朋友求助。我们也没钱买鞋子、背包、皮带，所以大家都是用他们私人的配饰。D&G 公司就是这样开始的。

Notes & Vocabulary

come on the scene
出现；到场

scene 指"事发现场；场面"，come on the scene 可表示出现在某地或处在某种处境。scene 还有"领域；圈；界；坛"之意，文中是指两人"出现在时尚界"。

The band came on the scene at the height of the soul music revival of the late 1970s.
这个乐队在20世纪70年代晚期灵魂乐复苏的时候登上的乐坛。

4. **liaison** [liˈeˌzɑn]
   n. 交流合作；联系

5. **backbone** [ˌbækˈbon]
   n. 骨干；基础

6. **accessory** [ɪkˈsɛsərɪ]
   n. 配饰；配件
   A beach bag is this summer's must-have fashion accessory.

影视娱乐

时尚生活

政治财经

体坛文艺

NARRATOR

In the years of success which have followed, the faces of Domenico and Stefano have become synonymous[7] with their brand. Domenico is reluctant[8] to be photographed, but plays along[9] for the photo shoot.

DOMENICO DOLCE, DESIGNER

I prefer my clothes. I work for my clothes. I don't care about Domenico Dolce. I am Domenico Dolce. I work for Dolce & Gabbana. I would like one day that people remember my label, not my face.

NARRATOR

Since today is a celebration of the past two decades of Dolce & Gabbana Menswear[10] models will include Tony Ward and Enrique Palacios, stars of the very first campaigns[11].

ERIQUE PALACIOS, MODEL

And actually my first job was with Domenico and Stefano. Every time I have shared time with them, we have been in [on] vacation or we go somewhere, it is like being with my family. Even that [though] they're not together, they [are] still a couple. That's what I want you to understand. That's how it is.

NARRATOR

The collection represents six months of collaboration[12] between the designers, but they do not always agree.

STEFANO GABBANA, DESIGNER

When you fight . . . I express myself, he express[es]

旁白

在接下来成功的日子里，杜梅尼科和斯蒂芬诺的面孔成为了他们品牌的代名词。杜梅尼科不太愿意拍照，但是面对杂志摄影还是勉强配合。

设计师 杜梅尼科·多尔奇

我喜爱我创作的服装。我为了我的服装而工作。我一点也不在意杜梅尼科·多尔奇是谁。杜梅尼科·多尔奇只是我个人。我为 D&G 公司工作。我希望有一天人们记得的是我的品牌，而不是我的面孔。

旁白

因为今天是 D&G 男装成立 20 周年的庆祝活动，模特将包括托尼·沃德和恩里克·帕拉西奥斯，他们是最开始的品牌代言人。

模特 恩里克·帕拉西奥斯

我的第一份工作确实是和杜梅尼科与斯蒂芬诺合作。每次我和他们一同共度时光，我们一起度假或是去别的地方，那就像是和我的家人相处一样。虽然他们不在一起了，但是他们仍旧是很好的伙伴。那是我希望你们了解的。他们之间就是这样。

旁白

这次的系列时装代表了这两位设计师 6 个月来的合作成果，但是他们却不总是意见一致。

设计师 斯蒂芬诺·嘉班纳

人们吵架时……我表达自己的想法，他表达他自己的意思，我为我的想法辩驳，而他也

⑯ 永远的时尚伙伴——CNN 专访 D&G 创始人

Notes & Vocabulary

7. synonymous (with) [sɪˋnɑnəməs]
adj. 同义的；等同于……的

8. reluctant [rɪˋlʌktənt]
adj. 不情愿的；勉强的

9. play along 顺从配合

10. menswear [ˋmɛnzˌwɛr] *n.* 男装

11. campaign [ˌkemˋpen]
n. 宣传、造势；参加活动

12. collaboration [kəˌlæbəˋreʃən]
n. 合作；合作成果

D&G

1980 年　两人同在米兰一家艺术工作室（atelier）担任助理而结识。

1982 年　合伙成立 Dolce & Gabbana 设计公司。

1985 年　创立 Dolce & Gabbana 品牌。

1986 年　两人正式结为伴侣，推出第一个 Dolce & Gabbana 女装系列，受到业内赞赏（acclaim）。

1989 年　于日本东京开设第一家连锁精品店（boutique）。

1990 年　推出第一个 Dolce & Gabbana 男装系列；于米兰开设第一家女装精品店；担任米兰 Genny 集团旗下 Complice 品牌设计师。

1994 年　推出第二品牌 D & G 男、女装及家居系列，走年轻开放的都市（urban）休闲风格。

2001 年　推出童装系列。

2006 年　两人结束伴侣关系，但在生活与工作上继续相互扶持。

2008 年　两人恢复他们的感情关系。

影视娱乐　时尚生活　政治财经　体坛文艺

139

himself, and I defend my opinion, and him too. I don't know. Maybe he tried to convince me to do it red and I try to convince him to make it white, and maybe in the end we do it black.

NARRATOR
VIP guests are whisked off to an aftershow party at the Piazza della Scala in Milan, where the mayor of the city has given over[13] the town hall in honor of Dolce & Gabbana.

LETIZIA MORATTI, MILAN MAYOR
When you talk about Milan, you talk about fashion. When you talk about fashion, you talk about the big names, and Dolce and Gabbana are among those.

NARRATOR
The party seems a fitting[14] tribute to two of the key players in Milan's foremost[15] industry. Dolce and Gabbana are a powerhouse[16] of design in a country where beauty and style will always be beacons[17] of national pride.

STEFANO GABBANA, DESIGNER
Fashion is, first of all, an expression of life. You know, I put all [of] myself in my fashion. It's a mirror. It is an expression about Domenico and Stefano.

DOMENICO DOLCE, DESIGNER
I want to ~~talk with~~ [ask] Jesus, "Why [did] you make this combination?" I don't know. I think we are destiny. I think this one desire is that me and Stefano are together.

正常*MP3-Track16* / 慢速*MP3-Track46* ❙ *A Partnership in Fashion*

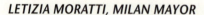

这么做。我不知道。他也许试着要说服我做成红色的，而我试着要说服他做成白色的，结果到最后我们是做成黑色的。

旁白

贵宾迅速被接送到位于米兰斯卡拉广场举办的展览后宴会。米兰市长提供市政厅向 D&G 致敬。

米兰市长 莱迪兹·莫拉蒂

当你提到米兰，你会谈论时尚。当你谈论时尚，你会谈起许多大人物，其中会包括多尔奇和嘉班纳。

旁白

这场宴会像是为米兰最重要产业的两大主角打造的献礼。在这个永远以美丽与风格为国家荣耀象征的国度，多尔奇和嘉班纳这个团队是个精力旺盛的设计强队。

设计师 斯蒂芬诺·嘉班纳

首先，时尚是生活的表述。我将自己的全部放入我的时尚之中。时尚是一面镜子。这是关于杜梅尼科和斯蒂芬诺的表述。

设计师 杜梅尼科·多尔奇

我想问问耶稣，"为什么你会做这样的组合？"我不知道。我想我们是命中注定的。我想我和斯蒂芬诺就是要在一起。

Notes & Vocabulary

whisk off
迅速送走
whisk 当动词时常指"快速搅动"，另外还有"快速送走、带走"的意思，whisk off 则指"快而轻地掸去；拂去"，后面可用 to 加上地点，表示迅速送至某处。

- The limousine **whisked** Alfonso **off** to the airport.
  一辆礼宾车迅速把阿方索接送至机场。

in honor of
向……致敬、祝贺；纪念……
honor 是"崇敬；敬意"的意思，in honor of 则是对某件事或某个人表达敬意。

- The retirement party was held **in honor of** Ted's long career with the company.
  举办这场退休聚会是为了向泰德长期以来为公司的贡献致敬。

13. **give over**
    交出某物（特定用途）；交托
    The school gave over its gymnasium for the dance.

14. **fitting** [ˈfɪtɪŋ]
    adj. 恰当的；合适的
    The speech was a fitting tribute to the honored guest.

15. **foremost** [ˈfɔr.most]
    adj. 最重要的；最著名的
    Will is the foremost expert on prehistoric cultures.

16. **powerhouse** [ˈpauɚ.haus]
    n. 强大的集团；积极能干的人

17. **beacon** [ˈbikən]
    n. 灯塔；指标；象征

影视娱乐

时尚生活

政治财经

体坛文艺

Putting Your Best Face Forward

Behind the Scenes with
Makeup Artist
Bobbi Brown

图片提供：美商怡佳

MAGGIE LAKE, CNN ANCHOR

Well, in the business world, image is very important and the face that you present can make or break your professional reputation[1]. Makeup artist Bobbi Brown has been creating polished[2] looks for women for almost 20 years. Hard to believe. We went behind the scenes with her to see how she puts her skills into action.

BOBBI BROWN, FOUNDER, BOBBI BROWN

I'm here at our 20-something annual boot camp[3], which is where my best artists from all over the globe are here. And I teach and I train and I talk.

Good morning, everybody.

正常MP3-Track17
慢速MP3-Track47

名人小档案 ▼ 波比·布朗

波比·布朗（1957—）出生于美国芝加哥，当她还是一个小女孩时，就已经被化妆品迷住了。年轻时，她曾尝试经营小型化妆店铺，后来她就读于爱默生学院，攻读舞台化妆专业，开始正式的专业训练。毕业后，她随即前往纽约成为专业化妆师。她的才华赢得各方赞赏，她开始与知名摄影师合作，为《时尚》、《悦己》等杂志的模特儿化妆。创立公司之后，波比将她的彩妆王国延伸至全球超过300个柜台。在不断扩张的事业版图中，波比继续秉持自己的理念，推出时尚、历久弥新的高级彩妆，并教导每位女人成为自己的彩妆师。

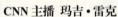

CNN 主播 玛吉·雷克

在商界，形象是非常重要的，而你所呈现的形象可能是你专业信誉的成败关键。化妆师波比·布朗为女性打造光鲜亮丽的脸庞将近20年。实在是令人难以置信。我们私下探访她，看看她是如何发挥专业技术的。

BOBBI BROWN 创办人 波比·布朗

我现在在第二十几届的培训班，我旗下来自世界各地的顶尖化妆师都齐聚在此。我在这教课、培训和演讲。

各位早。

Notes & Vocabulary

标题扫描

behind the scenes
在幕后；秘密地

scene 指"舞台布景；（电视）镜头"，behind the scenes 的字面意思即表示"在幕后"，也可延伸指"秘密地；私下"。

Ben's dad works behind the scenes in the entertainment industry.
本的父亲在娱乐圈做幕后工作。

make or break . . .
是……成败关键

这个押韵的词组，最早使用于狄更斯（Charles Dickens）的小说中，用来表示某事可能让人不是成功就是失败，即"是……的成败关键"。

The important deal would make or break the company.
这宗重要交易将是该公司成败的关键。

1. reputation [ˌrɛpjəˈteʃən]
   n. 名誉；名声
   The scandal stained the actor's clean-cut reputation.

2. polished [ˈpɑlɪʃt]
   adj. 润饰过的；润色的
   The children all looked fresh and polished on the first day of school.

3. boot camp [but] [kæmp]
   n. 新兵训练营

I didn't get to see everyone last night. And if anybody has any pictures of me dancing and if it is on YouTube or Facebook, you're fired!

We've grown so much that in order for to get the message out all over the world and to be able to have not only women understand how to do their own makeup, but makeup artists understand the brand and the products; the way to do that is really with my ambassadors. That's basically the only market research I really enjoy, is hearing about what my artists are saying and what the customers are saying.

What did you guys think of the new products yesterday?

Yeah? What are you the most excited about seeing? Concealer[4]?

We're gonna start with a hydrating[5] eye, and that's natural.

Well, the BOBBI BROWN look, to me, is really simple. It's got to be makeup that's right for a woman's style, but the colors have to be natural to a woman's skin and they have to look like skin.

But can you see, already? I mean, for you guys on this side, it just . . . now it's flawless[6].

The company is 20 years old, and I started this company with a lipstick—a lipstick that looked like lips. You have to have a product first of all, or an idea that doesn't exist in the market. There are too many me-too things happening out in the world,

我昨晚没办法跟各位一一照面。如果你们谁拍到任何我跳舞的画面，而且如果放上 YouTube 或 Facebook 的话，你就被解雇了！

我们已经有了长足的发展，为了将信息传遍全世界，为了要让女性顾客了解如何使用化妆品，还要让化妆师了解这个品牌和产品，要达到这些目标需要依赖我的大使们了。基本上，我最喜欢的市场调查便是倾听我的化妆师和顾客的意见。

你们觉得昨天的新产品如何？

嗯？你们最想看到哪样产品？遮瑕膏？

我们从画一个水嫩的眼睛开始，那很自然。

对我而言，BOBBI BROWN 的妆容其实是非常简单的。那必须是符合女性风格的化妆品，但色彩在女性的肌肤上要很自然，看起来就像肌肤一样。

你们看出来了吗？我的意思是，从坐在这边的人看来，现在几乎是完美无瑕的。

这家公司已经 20 年了，而我是以一款唇膏创办了这家公司——擦起来很像自然唇色的唇膏。首先，你必须有市场上没有的一项产品或一个点子。世上有太多效仿的产品，而

Notes & Vocabulary

4. **concealer** [kənˈsilə]
   n. 遮瑕膏

5. **hydrate** [ˈhaɪˌdret]
   v. 使吸入水分
   Derrick hydrated by drinking water during a break in the game.

6. **flawless** [ˈflɔləs]
   adj. 完美的；无瑕的
   The dancer put on a flawless performance.

影视娱乐

时尚生活

政治财经

体坛文艺

and you need something that is needed, and then it's much easier to, you know, figure out what to do from there. I thought, wow, what a great idea: a makeup company that's actually been created from a makeup artist.

The best trait[7] I have, being an entrepreneur[8], is that I am very naive[9]. I never thought that I wouldn't succeed. I know it sounds a bit intense[10], because it's makeup, but if you can take a woman and show her a product that makes her look less tired, makes her look fresher, prettier, there's no better feeling in the world.

Pass it around and feel it, and it's really warm, by the way.

I am incredibly passionate about creating new products and colors. You know, how lucky am I that I get to have an idea and it could be an idea coming from nowhere. I get to come in and tell a group of people, that I really enjoy their company, about this idea. We work together and we keep meeting on the same idea.

KAT DELUNA, R&B RECORDING ARTIST
So, Bob?

BOBBI BROWN, FOUNDER, BOBBI BROWN
Yeah? Whoo! Hey, guys, everyone know my friend, Kat?

How are ya? How are ya?

你需要找到大家真正需要的东西，从那儿想出接下来的点子便容易得多。我当时想，哇，这是很棒的点子：一家由化妆师所创立的化妆品公司。

作为企业家，我拥有的最佳特质是我很天真。我从来没想过我会失败。我知道这听起来有点极端，因为这是化妆品市场，但如果你能向一位女性展示有个产品能让她看起来更有精神、更年轻、更美丽，世上没有比这更棒的感觉了。

向后传，摸摸看，顺便提一下，它的色调相当柔和。

我非常热衷于开发新产品和新色彩。我是多么的幸运，我灵机一动，便能有个绝无仅有的点子。然后我进公司将我的想法告诉一群人，我真的很高兴有他们一起。我们一同努力，一同开会讨论这个点子。

R&B 唱片歌手 凯特·德鲁娜
波比？

BOBBI BROWN 创办人 波比·布朗
嗯？哇！各位，大家都认识我的朋友凯特吗？

你好吗？你好吗？

Notes & Vocabulary

figure out
想出；算出

figure sth./sb. out 表示"理解某事或某人"，也就是类似中文的"弄明白；搞清楚"的意思。

· Jake figured out the solution to the problem.
杰克想出了那个问题的解决办法。

7. trait [tret] n. 特征；特质
8. entrepreneur [ˌɑntrəprəˈnɜ]
   n. 创业者；企业家
9. naive [naˈiv] adj. 天真的；率直的
10. intense [ɪnˈtɛns]
    adj. 激烈的；极端的

护肤品功效的形容词

moisturizing 保湿

long-wear / long-lasting 持久

tinted 润色

sun-proof 防晒

whitening / brightening 美白

concealing 遮瑕

correcting 修饰

影视娱乐 时尚生活 政治财经 体坛文艺

KAT DELUNA, R&B RECORDING ARTIST

Very good. Excited to see you.

BOBBI BROWN, FOUNDER, BOBBI BROWN

Our surprise guest, you know, Kat DeLuna who is an up-and-coming[11] star. I think she's gonna be a superstar, I really do. I met her last year at an event. We became friends. She happened to yesterday, say she's gonna be in the neighborhood, could she stop in? I said, absolutely. I knew my artists would, you know, get a kick[12] and a thrill out of meeting her.

There is no average working day for me, at all. Everyday is different, and, you know, my biggest problem in life is that I have too many great things going on all the time.

彩妆产品 相关词汇

concealer 遮瑕霜

loose powder / face power 蜜粉

❶ foundation 粉底液

❷ cream compact foundation 粉凝霜

❸ powder compact 粉饼

❹ blush 腮红

❺ eye shadow 眼影

❻ eye palette 眼彩盘

❼ gel eyeliner 眼线膏

❽ mascara 睫毛膏

❾ brow pencil 眉笔

正常MP3-Track17 / 慢速MP3-Track47 | Putting Your Best Face Forward

R&B 唱片歌手 凯特·德鲁娜
很好。很期待看到你。

BOBBI BROWN 创办人 波比·布朗
我们的神秘嘉宾凯特·德鲁娜是位新秀。我认为她会成为巨星，我真的这么觉得。我去年在一个场合中认识她，我们成为朋友。刚好昨天她说她会到这附近，可不可以顺道来看看？我说，当然好啊。我想我的化妆师见到她会相当兴奋、激动。

对我而言，没有平淡无奇的工作日，完全没有。每天都不一样，我生命中最大的难题是，我总是有太多很棒的事情在进行。

Notes & Vocabulary

stop in
顺便拜访

stop in 指 "顺道拜访；短暂停留"，其他同义短语还有 stop by、drop in/by。不过要注意的是，stop in 及 drop in 都特别指到室内的拜访。

- Megan **stopped in** at her old office to visit her former co-workers.
  梅根顺便到以前的公司拜访老同事。

11. **up-and-coming**
   [ˈʌpˌændˈkʌmɪŋ]
   adj. 有前途的；前程似锦的

12. **kick** [kɪk] *n.* 极度刺激；极度兴奋

⑩ lip gloss 唇蜜
⑪ lip palette 唇彩盘
⑫ brush 刷具
⑬ makeup sponge 化妆海绵
⑭ eyelash curler 睫毛夹
⑮ tweezer 修眉夹
⑯ lipstick 唇膏
⑰ puff 粉扑
⑱ blotting papers 吸油面纸
⑲ makeup remover 卸妆油

影视娱乐

时尚生活

政治财经

体坛文艺

时尚生活 ⑱ 台湾设计师吴季刚——打造自己的时尚舞台

Dressing for Success

Fashion Upstart[1] Jason Wu's Star Continues to Rise

图片提供：Reuters 、GENERAL IMAGING

CHARLES HODSON, CNN ANCHOR

One year ago he burst onto the fashion scene[2], catapulted[3] to stardom[4] by one ~~infamous~~ [famous] dress. Today, the designer Jason Wu is fresh from showing his latest collection at New York Fashion Week. Alina Cho spoke to him about a stellar[5] year and how he's expanding his brand.

ALINA CHO, CNN CORRESPONDENT

The carpet was pink but the ticket red hot[6]. The show: Jason Wu.

JASON WU, FASHION DESIGNER

Five years ago, it was a rack of clothes and Jason Wu, the person, you know? And now, it's about Jason Wu the brand.

正常MP3-Track18
慢速MP3-Track48

名人小档案 ▼ 吴季刚

吴季刚（1982—）是一名旅美的台湾服装设计师，出生于中国台湾省云林县，9岁移居加拿大，于东京就读初中，并在当时学习雕塑，高中则在纽约帕森设计学院主修设计。16岁时以自由职业的身份开始为玩具公司设计玩偶的衣服。18岁投资自己曾工作的玩具公司。19岁就读设计学院时自行开设计公司。毕业后，为了投入到时尚设计圈，他参与了纽约时尚周，还投资10万美元办时装秀，以提高自己的知名度。吴季刚的作品既现代又高雅，简约而华丽，深受众多好莱坞女星的喜爱。

Jason Wu

CNN 主播 查尔斯·霍德森

一年前他闯进时尚圈一炮而红，他以一件出色的女装一战成名，现在吴季刚才刚刚在纽约时尚周推出最新系列，爱丽娜·秋和他谈到了成名的一年，还有他要如何拓展他的品牌。

CNN 特派员 爱丽娜·秋

地毯虽然是粉红色，但是入场券可是红得发烫呢。节目主角：吴季刚。

时尚设计师 吴季刚

5年前，这是一架子的衣服和一个闻闻无名的吴季刚，现在吴季刚可是个服饰品牌呢。

burst onto sth.
突然出现在……
短语 burst onto 有"突然出名"或"突然走红；蹿红"的意思，常与 the scene 连用。

The artist burst onto the scene in the early 1980s.
这位艺术家在 20 世纪 80 年代初期走红。

1. upstart [ˈʌpstɑːt]
   n. 骄傲的新手；狂妄的新起之秀

2. scene [sin]
   n. 圈；界；领域

3. catapult [ˈkætəpʌlt]
   v.（被）猛掷；猛扔
   The movie catapulted the young actress to stardom.

4. stardom [ˈstɑːdəm]
   n. 明星地位

5. stellar [ˈstɛlə]
   adj. 优秀的；杰出的

6. red hot 极红的；极热门的

影视娱乐

时尚生活

政治财经

体坛文艺

ALINA CHO, CNN CORRESPONDENT

The brand got the boost[7] fashion designers dream of when First Lady Michelle Obama wore Wu's one-shoulder gown on inauguration[8] night. That made this Taiwanese-born 27-year-old an overnight star. In the 13 months since then . . .

JASON WU, FASHION DESIGNER

Well, I mean, it's been really crazy. I've been offered reality shows. I've been offered, you know, all sorts of[9] product endorsements[10].

ALINA CHO, CNN CORRESPONDENT

But Wu, always mindful about not growing his company too fast, said no.

JASON WU, FASHION DESIGNER

This is a feather-covered, encased-in-silk-tulle[11] dress.

ALINA CHO, CNN CORRESPONDENT

What he has done is move into a 9,000-square foot studio, more than four times the size of his old one.

They're gonna have to name the building after you?

JASON WU, FASHION DESIGNER

Well, I was told that if I take over[12] another floor, it would be named after me. So, you know, I'm working on that in the next couple of years.

ALINA CHO, CNN CORRESPONDENT

Expanding the brand beyond clothes—sunglasses, shoes come next. He's even designing cameras for General Electric.

CNN 特派员 爱丽娜·秋

这个服饰品牌得到时尚设计师们梦想得到的帮助。第一夫人米歇尔在就职晚宴上穿着吴季刚设计的单肩礼服，让出生于台湾省、当时 27 岁的吴季刚一夜之间成为明星，13 个月过去后……

时尚设计师 吴季刚

这一路都非常疯狂，有人邀请我出演真人秀，有各式各样的产品找我代言。

CNN 特派员 爱丽娜·秋

但是一直都小心谨慎不愿让公司成长太快的吴季刚都拒绝了。

时尚设计师 吴季刚

这是一件包裹着羽毛、外罩丝质薄纱的礼服。

CNN 特派员 爱丽娜·秋

他换到一家 9 000 平方英尺的工作室，这是他以前的工作室的 4 倍大。

他们会以你的名字来为这栋大楼命名？

时尚设计师 吴季刚

他们跟我说，如果我再租下另一层楼，这栋大楼就会以我来命名，我接下来几年会努力这么做的。

CNN 特派员 爱丽娜·秋

将该品牌拓展到服饰以外的领域——太阳镜、鞋子随后推出。他还曾经帮通用电气公司设计过相机。

Notes & Vocabulary

an overnight star
一夜成名的人或物
overnight 有"隔夜的"的意思，所以 an overnight star 指"一夜成名的人或事物"，有"一炮而红"的意思。

name after
以……命名
name 当动词时是"命名；取名"的意思。"给（某人）取名……"可用 name (someone) + 名字。be named after (someone) 则为"被以（某人）的名字来命名"，也可用 be named for 来表示。
George's parents named him after the first U.S. president.
乔治的父母以美国总统的名字来为他取名。

7. **boost** [bust]
   n. 帮助；激励

8. **inauguration** [ɪnˌɔgjuˋreʃən]
   n. 就职典礼
   The singer was paid an undisclosed sum to perform at the president's inauguration.

9. **all sorts of** 各式各样的
   Sally collects all sorts of Disney-themed toys.

10. **endorsement** [ɪnˋdɔrsmənt]
    n. （公开的）赞同；支持；宣传；背书
    The restaurant received a ringing endorsement from a top critic.

11. **tulle** [tul] *n.* 薄纱

12. **take over** 接管；占领
    The band took over an old farmhouse and converted it into a studio.

影视娱乐 时尚生活 政治财经 体坛文艺

Do you ever worry about spreading yourself too thin?

JASON WU, FASHION DESIGNER

I think there's always worry—you know, am I doing too much or am I doing too little or am I doing just enough. And, you know, the challenge is—you know, I've always gone with my gut[13] feeling on certain things and, you know, I go for it.

CINDI LEIVE, EDITOR-IN-CHIEF, GLAMOUR MAGAZINE

What he got at the inaugural ball was an incredible moment, a real chance, but it was his to make something of it or to squander[14]. And I think he's really built on it in an intelligent way.

ALINA CHO, CNN CORRESPONDENT

But he has taken his knocks.

The New York Times said of your collection, the evening dresses were one of those weird runway surprises that make you look down at the floor. Fair?

JASON WU, FASHION DESIGNER

Well, I think opinions are opinions. And I think when you put your art . . . your work out there, and you're going to have people who like it [and] who will dislike it. This is fashion.

ALINA CHO, CNN CORRESPONDENT

The whirlwind[15], as he calls it, has taught him to stay grounded[16].

你曾经担心过拓展不足吗？

时尚设计师 吴季刚
我想永远都有担心的事，我做过头了，还是太少了，还是刚刚好，挑战其实是……我一直都跟着我的直觉走，直觉对了我就去做。

《魅力》杂志主编 辛迪·雷夫
就职晚宴给了他让人难以置信的时刻，一个真正的机会，但是决定把握住还是浪费掉这个机会的人是他自己，而我认为他用了很聪明的方式来利用这个机会。

CNN 特派员 爱丽娜·秋
但他也有运气不好的时候。

《纽约时报》说在你的系列中，晚礼服是展台上让人惊讶的怪异作品，让你抬不起头来，这样说公平吗？

时尚设计师 吴季刚
我想见仁见智吧，当你把你的艺术作品呈现出来时，就要面对有人喜欢有人不喜欢的情形，这就是时尚。

CNN 特派员 爱丽娜·秋
他口中所谓的旋风教会他要忠于自己、脚踏实地。

Notes & Vocabulary

take a knock
遭受到（重大）挫折
knock 是指"撞击"，take a knock 原本是指"受到重击"，也可比喻心理上"遭受重大的挫折、打击"。
- Clarice took a lot of hard knocks in her early career.
克拉丽斯早年在职场上遭遇到许多重大的挫折。

13. **gut** [gʌt] *adj.* 直觉的；本能的
Michael had a gut feeling something was wrong when his wife was late for dinner.

14. **squander** [ˈskwɑndə]
v. 浪费；挥霍
The musician squandered his talent with drugs and alcohol.

15. **whirlwind** [ˈwɜlwɪnd] *n.* 旋风

16. **grounded** [ˈgraʊndɪd]
adj. 踏实的；务实的
Bennie managed to stay grounded in spite of his success.

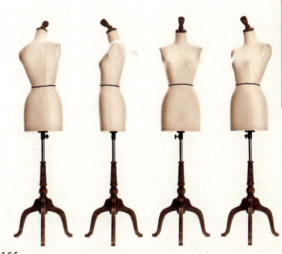

影视娱乐

时尚生活

政治财经

体坛文艺

JASON WU, FASHION DESIGNER

You know, I was in the airport and this group of Chinese kids came up to me and they . . . they were like, you know, I'm really proud because you are an Asian designer who is doing something that isn't traditionally acceptable and, you know, stood your ground and did it.

ALINA CHO, CNN CORRESPONDENT

Inspiring the next generation, even as he continues to live in the moment.

But you're still nervous, aren't you?

JASON WU, FASHION DESIGNER

Oh, I'm always nervous. It's like that piano recital[17]—and I used to play the piano—and it's like right before and just hope you don't make a mistake.

ALINA CHO, CNN CORRESPONDENT

Me, too.

正常 *MP3-Track18*／慢速 *MP3-Track48* ▌ *Dressing for Success*

时尚设计师 吴季刚

有一次我在机场，一群中国孩子朝我走来，他们表现得就像是在说，我非常骄傲，因为你是亚裔设计师，你在做一些非传统的事情并且坚持做下去。

CNN 特派员 爱丽娜·秋

即使在舞台上，他还是在启发下一代。

但你还是很紧张吧，不是吗？

时尚设计师 吴季刚

我一直都很紧张，就像是钢琴独奏会，我以前也弹钢琴，就像是挑战就在眼前，而你希望不要出错。

CNN 特派员 爱丽娜·秋

我也希望。

Notes & Vocabulary

stand one's ground
坚持立场
字面上的意思是"站在某人的土地上"，引申为"坚持自己的立场；坚持己见"，stand 也可用 hold 代替。

The small company held its ground rather than selling out to a larger company.
这家小公司坚持不卖给大公司。

17. recital [rɪˋsaɪt]
n. 独奏会
The child revealed himself to be a budding talent at the piano recital.

影视娱乐 时尚生活 政治财经 体坛文艺

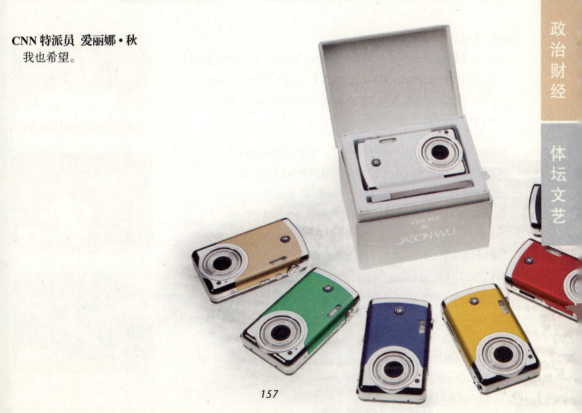

Wok on the Wild Side

Talk Asia Goes into the Kitchen with Celebrity Chef Bobby Chinn

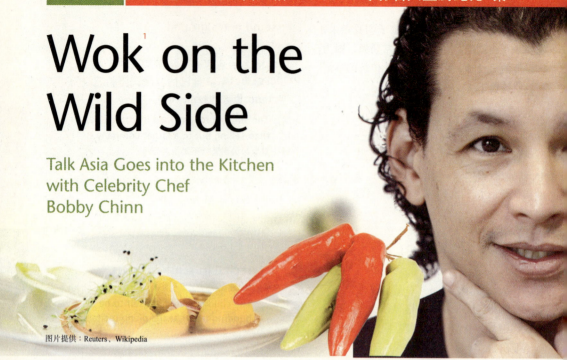

图片提供：Reuters、Wikipedia

ANJALI RAO, TALK ASIA

My guest today was once a Wall Street trader[2] and a stand-up comic. Today, he's one of Asia's most celebrated chefs. We're in the kitchen with Bobby Chinn. This is Talk Asia.

He's high-energy[3] and clearly has a passion for cooking, but Bobby Chinn's path to culinary[4] success is a winding[5] tale. He was born in New Zealand to a Chinese father and an Egyptian mother, educated in England and for a time called San Francisco home. He tried his hand as a trader on the floor[6] of the New York Stock Exchange and even took a crack at being a stand-up comic, but his restless soul eventually led him into the kitchen,

正常MP3-Track19
慢速MP3-Track49

名人小档案 ▼ 鲍比·秦

以烹调越南菜闻名的厨师鲍比秦（1966— ），是著名的主厨，其身影常出现在旅游频道中，他也曾带领观众尝遍亚洲各地的知名小吃。他出生于新西兰，在英国求学。在进入餐饮业之前他曾从事金融业，当过华尔街的交易员，也做过脱口秀主持人。他对烹饪的兴趣与天分促使他在越南开创了真正的事业。他位于河内的一家的餐厅，几乎是每个欧美观光客必定造访之地，连美国前第一夫人希拉里都曾是宾客。

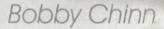

Bobby Chinn

《亚洲名人聊天室》安姿丽

我今天的来宾曾经当过华尔街交易员和脱口秀表演者，而现在他则是亚洲最受推崇的大厨之一，我们现在正和鲍比·秦一起在厨房里，欢迎收看《亚洲名人聊天室》。

他活力十足，且对烹饪明显有着一股热情。不过鲍比·秦的名厨成功之路却是个曲折的故事。他出生于新西兰，父亲是中国人，母亲是埃及人。他在英国受教育，有段时间以旧金山为家。他曾尝试在纽约证券交易所担任交易员，甚至也尝试过当一名脱口秀演员。但是他不羁的灵魂终究还是将他带进了厨房，他在这个天地中将想象力发挥到极

Notes & Vocabulary

take a crack at sth.
尝试做某事

crack 在口语中可指"尝试"，所以 take a crack at sth. 便指"尝试做某事"。文中的 try one's hand at sth. 则表示"初次尝试做某事"。

· Jim took a crack at fixing his wife's computer.
吉姆试着修理妻子的电脑。

1. wok [wɑk] *n.* 铁锅

2. trader [ˈtredə] *n.* 交易员；商人

3. high-energy [ˈhaɪ ˌɛnɜdʒɪ]
adj. 有生气的；有力的
The movie features several high-energy dance routines.

4. culinary [ˈkʌlə‚nɛrɪ] *adj.* 烹饪的
Jeff likes to show off his culinary skills by cooking for his friends.

5. winding [ˈwaɪndɪŋ]
adj. 曲折的；迂回的

6. floor [flɔr]
n. （交易所中的）交易场地

影视娱乐　时尚生活　政治财经　体坛文艺

where he put his imagination to the test. In 1995, Bobby Chinn set his sights on Vietnam. Today, he runs his namesake[7] restaurant in the heart of Hanoi. He's also the host of a successful cooking and travel show and author of a recently released cookbook.

I just want to know what first attracted you to the culinary arts.

BOBBY CHINN, CHEF
I guess I always liked food. That's helpful. And I didn't realize food could be a horrible experience until I went to English boarding school. So I was brought up by two really great grandmothers that can cook and I was always intrigued[8] by how they made food really good—one being Egyptian, the other one being Chinese.

When I left Wall Street, I wanted to do something a little creative, and I saw chefs in a completely different light than I've seen them in the past, you know, wearing white jackets, looking like doctors. My mother wanted me to be a doctor, so this was as close as I was going to get. And they had, like, the command of everybody, like they were gods in this little space—"Give me this, give me that." And I like kind of like that world and the ability to create.

ANJALI RAO, TALK ASIA
You know, there are so many celebrity chefs that are out there these days. How do you set yourself apart? How do you make sure that you're different?

致。1995 年，他决心在越南发展。现在，他在河内市中心开了一家以他的名字命名的餐厅，同时他也是一个热门烹饪旅游节目的主持人，身兼作者的他最近刚出版了一本烹饪书。

我想知道最初是什么吸引你投入烹饪艺术。

大厨 鲍比·秦

我想我一直都很喜欢食物，这很有帮助。直到我去读英国的寄宿学校，才知道食物可以有多难吃。抚养我长大的奶奶和外婆都很了不起，她们的厨艺都很棒，我一直很好奇她们怎么把食物做得这么好吃，一位是埃及人，一位是中国人。

离开华尔街之后，我想做有一点创意的事。而我对厨师的看法和以前大不相同，他们穿着白上衣，就像医生一样。以前我妈妈希望我当医生，所以这是我能做的最接近的一种工作。而且他们可以对大家发号施令，像是这个小空间里的神一样，指使人"给我这个，给我那个。"我喜欢像那样的世界以及可以发挥创造的能力。

《亚洲名人聊天室》安姿丽

现在外面有很多名厨，你如何让自己与众不同？你又如何知道你真的和别人不一样？

影视娱乐

时尚生活

政治财经

体坛文艺

BOBBY CHINN, CHEF

You know, each one has their idiosyncrasies[9]. You know, Jamie Oliver's very good at being the guy next door and being sweet and being very knowledgeable and cooking very simple food, and everybody loves Jamie. Gordon Ramsay—I don't think you have a better chef on television. [Anthony] Bourdain—you know, that New York . . . kind of like, you know, Keith Richards.

I'm just kind of like the ethnic mutt[10], a person that's kind of like shooting from left field[11], where people kind of like, you know, they look at me like, "Oh!" And I can be engaging[12], I guess, so . . . and I think that my ethnicity[13] and my upbringing and my education will always send me from a different angle than other people and I think that's what separates me.

ANJALI RAO, TALK ASIA

You are though sometimes portrayed as this sort of in-your-face[14], really full-on[15] publicity magnet[16]. How fair do you think that characterization of you is in terms of who you really are?

BOBBY CHINN, CHEF

I don't know. I think that people are looking for a new face. There haven't been really many Asian chefs to speak of, and I've been able to generate that. But I don't know. I mean, like, it's just a machine that, you know, feeds on people like me and then spits me out when my time's done, and you just go with the flow.

ANJALI RAO, TALK ASIA

So, three top Bobby Chinn tips for anybody that's at home and wants to make Vietnamese food.

Notes & Vocabulary

9. **idiosyncrasy** [ˌɪdɪəˈsɪŋkrəsɪ]
   n.（个人的）气质、习性

10. **mutt** [mʌt] *n.* 有混血血统者

11. **left field** [lɛft] [fɪld]
    n. 非主流；非典型
    The charges against the politician seemed to come out of left field.

12. **engaging** [ɪnˈgedʒɪŋ]
    adj. 迷人的
    The talk show host is known for his engaging interview style.

13. **ethnicity** [ɛθˈnɪsətɪ]
    n. 种族特点（背景、渊源）
    The disease does not discriminate between ethnicity or gender.

14. **in-your-face** [ˈɪnˈjurˈfes]
    adj. 咄咄逼人的；态度挑衅的
    Jaime prefers thoughtful dramas to in-your-face action movies.

15. **full-on** [ˈfulˌɑn] *adj.* 全面的
    Company is planning a full-on revamping of its brand image.

16. **magnet** [ˈmægnət]
    n. 有吸引力的人或物；磁铁

影视娱乐

时尚生活

政治财经

体坛文艺

大厨 鲍比·秦

每个人都有自己的风格，吉米·奥利弗善于营造邻家男孩的形象，他亲切且知识丰富，善于烹调非常简单的食物，大家都喜欢他。戈登·拉姆齐，我想你找不出比他更适合上电视的大厨。安东尼·波登，有点纽约风格……像滚石乐团吉他手基斯·理查兹。

我则有点像是个混血儿，像是非主流出身的人。人们会看到我，然后叫着，"哦！"而且我也可以是很迷人的，我猜的……我的种族背景、成长经历和所受的教育都让我和其他人有不同的地方，我想这就是我的独特之处。

《亚洲名人聊天室》安姿丽

你有时候会被说成是个盛气凌人、乐于曝光的大众万人迷，你觉得这样的描述对真正的你来说公平吗？

大厨 鲍比·秦

我不知道，我想人们总是在找新面孔，一直以来都没有什么亚洲大厨可讲，而我可以制造话题。不过，我也不知道，其实就像有台机器要让我这种人去发动，等把我消耗殆尽，就把我吐掉，反正就从善如流吧。

《亚洲名人聊天室》安姿丽

那么，给那些想在家自己做越南菜的人提供三个鲍比·秦的烹饪秘诀吧。

163

BOBBY CHINN, CHEF

You've gotta have a great fish sauce—first press, just like olive oil. No food coloring, aged—that's key. Fresh ingredients—very important. Fresh herbs.

And then the right cooking vessel for whatever you're cooking. I mean you're not going to make a soufflé[17] in a bread and butter plate. You know, you gotta have the right equipment, so if you're gonna make something in a clay pot, let it be a clay pot. If it's a wok, cook it in a wok.

ANJALI RAO, TALKASIA

Bobby, it has been a great treat meeting you. Thank you very much, indeed.

BOBBY CHINN, CHEF

Thank you.

大厨的私房菜

Sautéed Beef with Rice Noodles and Salad 生蔬牛肉河粉

材料（ingredients）

菲力牛肉薄片 100 克

河粉 100 克

混合蔬菜 50 克

豆芽菜 50 克

牛肉高汤（stock）2 小匙　　植物油 1 小匙

紫苏 20 克　　　　　　　　蒜末 1 小匙

香菜（coriander）5 克

糖醋酱（sweet-and-sour sauce）2 小匙

腌料（marinade）

植物油 1 小匙

柠檬香茅草（lemon grass）细末 1 小匙

装饰（garnish）

白芝麻（sesame）1 小匙

烤花生 1 小匙

油酥（crispy-fried shallots）1 小匙

大厨 鲍比·秦

要有很棒的鱼露，鲜榨的，就像橄榄油一样。别用染色的、放得太久的食物，这是重点。新鲜食材很重要。新鲜的香料。

要用正确的容器来烹调食物，你不会想拿装面包和奶油的盘子来装蛋奶酥吧。你一定要有适当的器皿，如果你需要用一个砂锅做菜，那就用砂锅；如果得用炒锅，那就用炒锅来做。

《亚洲名人聊天室》安姿丽

鲍比，很高兴认识你，真的很谢谢你。

大厨 鲍比·秦

谢谢！

做法

1 将菲力牛肉薄片涂上植物油，裹上（coat）柠檬香茅细末，腌制（marinate）15 分钟。

2 取大碗放入香菜末、混合蔬菜和河粉。

3 炒锅倒入植物油，待油热倒入腌好的菲力牛肉薄片，略有焦色时翻面，翻炒（stir）至受热均匀（evenly cooked），将蒜末倒入锅中快炒（sauté）。

4 保持高温，倒入牛肉高汤，刮铲（scrape）锅中炒肉留下的深色焦底，使之与高汤混合，做成棕色酱汁。

5 倒入豆芽菜，盖上锅盖焖煮一分钟，加入糖醋酱。

6 将牛肉、豆芽菜舀进碗里，淋上锅中酱汁。

7 撒上油酥、白芝麻和烤花生即完成。

Architect for the Ages

Norman Foster Looks to the Past, Present and Future of Building Design

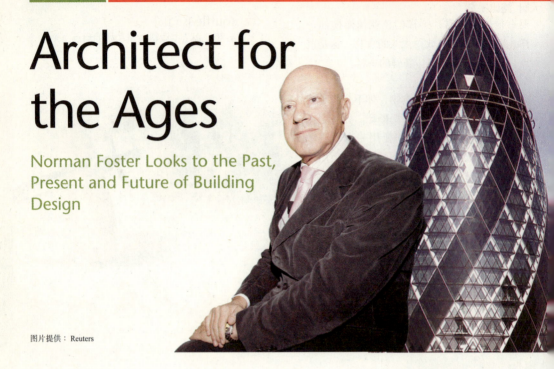

图片提供：Reuters

CNN ANCHOR

Now, he's arguably[1] responsible for more of the world's instantly recognizable buildings than any other architect.

CNN ANCHOR

Certainly here in London and around Europe, but what drives[2] the designs of Norman Foster and what does he make of today's age of architecture is part of this month's *Spirit of Architecture* program. Becky Anderson sits down with the master designer.

正常MP3-Track20
慢速MP3-Track50

名人小档案 ▼ 诺曼·福斯特

诺曼·福斯特（1935—）生于英国曼彻斯特，1961 年自曼彻斯特大学毕业，到耶鲁大学攻读硕士学位。1967 年创立自己的事务所 Foster Associates。1983 年获得皇家金质奖章，1990 年受封爵士；1997 年被英国女王列入杰出人士名册，获功绩勋章；1999 年，获封终身贵族"泰晤士河岸的福斯特男爵"（Baron Foster of Thames Bank）。福斯特是高技派（high-tech）建筑师的代表人物，以设计金融证券类商业建筑和机场建筑而闻名。他曾两次获得斯特林奖，也是 1999 年普利兹克建筑奖的得主。

Norman Foster

CNN 主播

这位建筑师的作品包括许多世界上一眼就能认出的著名建筑，可以说比起其他建筑师都多。

CNN 主播

至少在伦敦和欧洲确实如此，而本月的《建筑精神》节目，就要介绍诺曼·福斯特建筑设计背后的动力，还有他对当今这个时代建筑的看法。贝基·安德森访问了这位设计大师。

Notes & Vocabulary

标题扫描

look to
注意；关注

look to 在此是指"注意；关注"，注意 to 为介词，后面须加上名词。另外还可表示"指望、依赖某人／事物"，后面用 for sth. 或 to V. 表示希望对方提供的东西或做的事。

· Jack took time off from work to **look to** family matters.
  杰克从工作中抽出点时间照料一下家事。

· Judith **looks to** her personal assistant to manage her daily schedule.
  朱迪思靠个人助理来安排她每天的行程。

1. **arguably** [ˈɑrgjuəblɪ]
   adv. 可以认为地
   David was arguably the greatest magician of all time.

2. **drive** [draɪv]
   v. 驱动；驱使
   A sense of personal pride in his work drives Alan to excel in his job.

影视娱乐
时尚生活
政治财经
体坛文艺

BECKY ANDERSON, CNN CORRESPONDENT

He may be based in London, but his appeal[3] and attitude[4] is truly international. I caught up with Lord Norman Foster in Barcelona and began by asking him what the purpose of architecture is.

NORMAN FOSTER, ARCHITECT

Since man came out of the cave, [he] needed to be protected from the elements[5], and then it becomes apparent that the quality of that environment affects the quality of your life, so the other dimension[6]. In that sense, it's about society; it's about civilization[7]; it's about a social agenda[8]. It also is about symbolism[9]. It's about the things that you can't measure[10]. How do you measure the quality of the light, a view, sunshine?

BECKY ANDERSON, CNN CORRESPONDENT

When you look at a building, what makes you feel happy and what makes you feel angry?

NORMAN FOSTER, ARCHITECT

What makes me feel good is when the environment, if I use it in the broadest sense, has been taken seriously by everybody involved, and they've insisted on quality. And quality is not about money; it's about attitude; it's about the quality of the thinking.

You go to Rockefeller Center—you know, that's a public space; there's a place there. You go to Central Park; it's an extraordinary thing. You can't think of New York without Central Park. It's part of the infrastructure.[11]

CNN 特派员 贝基·安德森

他的事务所虽然位于伦敦，但他的吸引力和态度却超越了国界。我在巴塞罗那与诺曼·福斯特男爵（注）见面，第一个问题就是：建筑的目的是什么？

建筑师 诺曼·福斯特

人类不再居住在洞穴之后，就需要有其他东西遮蔽风雨。接着，我们发现自己居住的环境会影响生活的质量，其他层面也是一样。就这方面来说，建筑关乎社会，关乎文明，关乎社会进程。建筑也关乎象征，关乎你无法衡量的东西。你要怎么衡量光线、景色、日光的品质？

CNN 特派员 贝基·安德森

你看到一座建筑的时候，哪些东西会让你感到高兴，哪些东西又会让你感到气愤？

建筑师 诺曼·福斯特

最让我感到愉快的，就是参与一座建筑的所有人都认真看待这座建筑的环境，而且坚持品质。我所谓的环境，是指最广泛的定义而言；至于品质，也不是花钱多少的问题，而是态度，是指思考的质量。

你到洛克菲勒中心去，那是个公共空间，是个大家都可以去的地点。你到中央公园，那是个让人叹为观止的地方。想到纽约，就一定会想到中央公园。中央公园是纽约市容的一部分。

Notes & Vocabulary

3. appeal [ə`pil] *n.* 吸引力；感染力

4. attitude [`ætə͵tjud] *n.* 态度；看法

5. elements [`ɛləmənts]

   n. （恶劣的）气候情况（复数形式）

6. dimension [də`mɛʃən]
   n. 面向；方面

7. civilization [͵sɪvələ`zeʃən]
   n. 文明；文化设施

8. agenda [ə`dʒɛndɑ] *n.* 进程；事项

9. symbolism [`sɪmbə͵lɪzəm]
   n. 象征性；象征作用

10. measure [`mɛʒə] *v.* 测量；计量

11. infrastructure [`ɪnfrə͵strʌktʃə]
    n. 基础设施建设

注

根据英国封爵的等级，爵士（Knight）在姓名之前加 Sir 尊称，男爵（Baron）及子爵（Viscount）则加 Lord 尊称。

诺曼·福斯特建筑代表作

香港上海汇丰银行总行大厦（HSBC Main Building）

伦敦千禧桥（Millennium Bridge）

大伦敦市政府（Greater London Authority）

圣玛丽斧 30 号（30 St Mary Axe，瑞士再保险公司伦敦总部大楼 Swiss Re London Headquarters）

纽约赫斯特大楼（Hearst Tower）

伦敦温布利球场（Wembley Stadium）

北京首都机场（Beijing Capital International Airport）T3 航站大楼

苏格兰展览与会议中心（Scottish Exhibition & Conference Center）

影视娱乐　时尚生活　政治财经　体坛文艺

Of course, there are iconic buildings—overused[12] word—but buildings which over time still command[13] our respect and attention, and, you know, they roll off the tongue. There's the Seagram Building, you know? There's the Chrysler Building, the Empire State and so on.

BECKY ANDERSON, CNN CORRESPONDENT
Does every building that you're involved with have to be memorable and/or unique?

NORMAN FOSTER, ARCHITECT
I don't think it has to be memorable. If you come to our studio, you'll see schools, and we can talk about the way those schools have changed the lives of the children in terms of[14] their academic standard. You can measure that. You can measure it from the school they were in before. It's not just the architecture. It's also about the teaching.

BECKY ANDERSON, CNN CORRESPONDENT
How would you describe or characterize[15] the age of architecture that we're in at the moment?

NORMAN FOSTER, ARCHITECT
It's an age of rapid change. It's an age of rapid urbanization[16]. It's an age of extraordinary opportunity. And over time, I'm sure that, you know, future generations will sit back and say, "Well, they did that well. They did that, you know, not-so-well." It's a time of dynamic[17] change, and many approaches[18], but also extraordinary opportunities through competition systems which didn't exist in the past.

正常 *MP3·Track20* / 慢速 *MP3·Track50* ❙ *Architect for the Ages*

Notes & Vocabulary

当然，还有许多"代表性建筑"——这是陈腔滥调了——这些历时许久的建筑，仍然深受我们的仰慕和关注，大家经常挂在嘴边，例如西格拉姆大楼、克莱斯勒大厦、帝国大厦等等。

CNN 特派员 贝基·安德森

你参与过的建筑物是不是都一定要让人难忘或是充满独特性?

建筑师 诺曼·福斯特

我不认为我设计的建筑必须让人难忘。你到我们事务所可以看到我们设计的学校，而我们也会和你谈论这些学校对学生的学业成就有什么影响。这是可以衡量的东西。你可以和他们原本就读的学校比较。重点不只在于建筑，也在于对教学的影响。

CNN 特派员 贝基·安德森

你会如何描述当前这个建筑时代，或认为它有什么特色?

建筑师 诺曼·福斯特

这是个快速变化的时代，也是快速都市化的时代，同时也是充满机会的时代。以后，我相信我们的后代子孙会坐着闲聊，"当初那东西做得不错，但这个呢，就不怎么样了。"这是个变化频繁的时代，需要各式各样的不同做法，但前所未有的竞争体系也提供了许多非常好的机会。

---

over time 经过一段时间

over time 是指"经过一段时间"，有"经年累月"的意思，用于描述一个过程或事物的发展。

· **Over time**, Sandra got over her failed marriage.
过了一段时间后，桑德拉摆脱了她的失败婚姻的阴霾。

注意

overtime

adv. 加班；超时工作
n. 加班的时间；极讨厌的人（或事物）

over 和 time 合成一个词是"加班"，可当副词或名词，不要和短语 over time 混淆。

· Jenny often has to work **overtime**.
珍妮经常得加班。

roll off the tongue 常被提及

字面意思是"从舌头滚出来"，用来表示某事物"很容易说；容易被谈起"，也就是"常被提及"、"经常挂在嘴边"。

· Nathan wanted a name for his new company that would **roll off the tongue**.
内森想给他的新公司取个朗朗上口的名字。

12. **overuse** [ˈovəˈjuz]
v. 过度使用；滥用

13. **command** [kəˈmænd]
v. 博得；赢得

14. **in terms of** 在……方面

15. **characterize** [ˈkɛrɪktəˌraɪz]
v. 描述……的特性

16. **urbanization** [ˌɚbənəˈzeʃən]
n. 都市化

17. **dynamic** [daɪˈnæmɪk]
adj. 有活力的；有生气的

18. **approach** [əˈprotʃ]
n.（处理事情的）方法；态度

影视娱乐

时尚生活

政治财经

体坛文艺

Notes

政治财经
Politics & Finance

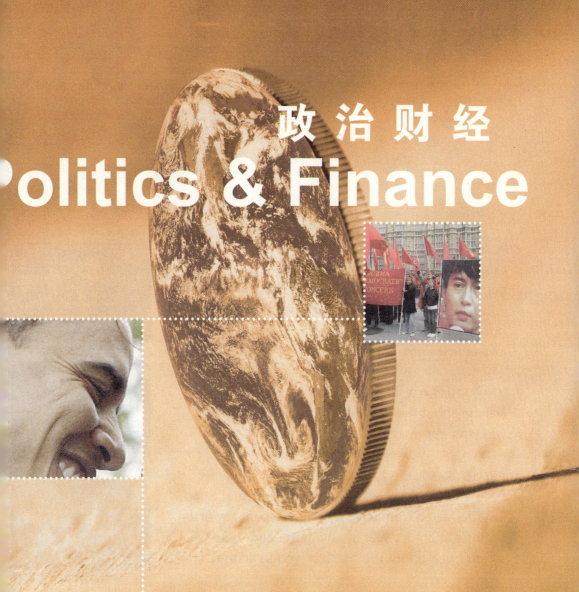

政治财经 ㉑ 第一夫人眼中的奥巴马

When Michelle Met Barack

First Lady Describes Her Initial Impressions[1] of the U.S. President

图片提供 : Reuters

CNN ANCHOR

In less than the three weeks, Michelle Obama becomes the nation's next first lady. In an interview with CNN's Suzanne Malveaux, she talks about how she first met Barack Obama, and why it wasn't love at first sight.

UZANNE MALVEAUX, CNN CORRESPONDENT

Tell me about the first time you met Barack. What was your impression?

MICHELLE OBAMA, U.S. FIRST LADY

I was a first-year associate[2] at Sidley & Austin. I had just graduated from law school, had spent my first summer as an . . . year as an intern[3], and there was all this buzz[4] about this hotshot[5] young first-year

正常MP3-Track21
慢速MP3-Track51

名人小档案 ▼ 米歇尔·奥巴马

美国非洲裔总统夫人米歇尔·奥巴马（1964—）本身是一名律师，出生于芝加哥南部，毕业于哈佛大学法学院。米歇尔早在 20 世纪 80 年代末期便已结识同于西德利与奥斯汀律师事务所工作的奥巴马，两人于 1992 年结婚，育有两个女儿。米歇尔非常注重自己的形象、举止及衣着品味，也经常被媒体评为衣着最佳的公众人物之一，更将之与美国已故第一夫人杰奎琳·肯尼迪比较。随着奥巴马成为全国性政治人物，米歇尔便开始成为流行文化的一部分。2006 年，米歇尔被生活杂志《元素》列为全球 25 位激励人心的女性，2008 年更被《名人》杂志称赞拥有"典雅及自信"的外表。

Michelle Obama

CNN 主播

再过不到三个星期，米歇尔·奥巴马就即将成为美国的下一位第一夫人。她在接受 CNN 的苏珊·马尔弗访问时，谈到自己和巴拉克·奥巴马初识的情景，也谈到他们当初为什么不是一见钟情。

CNN 特派员 苏珊·马尔弗

谈谈你和巴拉克初次认识的情形。你当时对他有什么印象？

美国第一夫人 米歇尔·奥巴马

当时我在西德利与奥斯汀律师事务所还是第一年的新人。我刚从法学院毕业，才当了一个夏天……一年的实习生，那时大家都在热切谈论着一个很厉害的年轻人，是个哈佛法

Sidley & Austin
西德利与奥斯汀律师事务所

1866 年创立于芝加哥，是全球历史最悠久的律师事务所之一。2001 年与 1914 年创立于纽约的 Brown & Wood 律师事务所合并为 Sidley Austin Brown & Wood LLP，2006 年改名为 Sidley Austin LLP "盛德国际律师事务所"，收入排名全美第六、全球第九，旗下有 1 800 位律师，遍布全球 16 个城市，对于商务交易（transaction）与诉讼（litigation）案件具有丰富的经验。

1. impression [ɪmˋprɛʃən]
   n. 印象
   It makes a very bad impression if you are late for an interview.

2. associate [əˋsoʃɪˏet]
   n. 伙伴；同事；合伙人
   Julia is the most media-savvy associate at the law firm.

3. intern [ɪnˋtɜn] *n.* 实习生

4. buzz [bʌz] *n.* 骚动
   The film generated considerable buzz before its release.

5. hotshot [ˋhɑtˏʃɑt]
   n. 要人；能人

影视娱乐

时尚生活

政治财经

体坛文艺

law student from Harvard. And everyone, I mean from the head of the firm on down, had talked about how brilliant[6] this guy was. And it was rare[7] that a firm as big as ours hired first-year students. So, he was gonna come in as a summer associate.

And they decided that I should be his adviser, probably because we both went to the same law school. We were both minority[8] students. So, I remember getting his bio[9].

 And I probably did what a lot of people do when they hear about Barack Obama. First, I thought, what kind of name is Barack Obama? And I found out that he grew up in Hawaii, and I found that strange as a girl who grew up on the South Side of Chicago. I had never met anybody who lived in Hawaii. That was always where you vacationed[10] and it wasn't where you were from.

SUZANNE MALVEAUX, CNN CORRESPONDENT
Right. Right.

MICHELLE OBAMA, U.S. FIRST LADY
And I found out that he was biracial[11]. So, my assumption[12] was, this guy has got to be kind of weird, right, probably a little nerdy[13]. I'd already sort of created an image of this very intellectual[14] nerd. And I was prepared to be polite and all that, and then he walked into my office on that first day, and he was cuter than I thought he would be.

So, that was a first positive impression, but I had to take him out to lunch on that first day, and we got to . . . we had to talk. And he told me more about his background, and he fleshed it out a bit more. I

学院一年级生。事务所里从上到下，每个人都在说这个家伙有多厉害。像我们那样的大事务所实在很少会雇用一年级学生，而他却要进来担任暑期助理。

然后，他们决定该由我负责指导他，也许是因为我们都上过同一所法学院吧。我们两人都是少数民族裔学生。我记得当时拿到了他的简历。

我大概和一般人听到巴拉克·奥巴马这个人的反应一样。我的第一个念头是，这是哪种名字啊？然后我发现他在夏威夷长大，对我这个在芝加哥南部长大的女孩来说这相当不寻常。我从没遇过住在夏威夷的人。夏威夷是大家去度假的地方，从没听过那里是哪个人的故乡。

CNN 特派员 苏珊·马尔弗
没错，没错。

美国第一夫人 米歇尔·奥巴马
接着，我发现他是混血儿。所以，我推测这个人一定会有点怪，说不定还有点书呆子气。那时候我就先在脑海里把他想象成一个聪明过人的宅男了。我准备好规规矩矩地接待他，然后他来的第一天走进我办公室，模样倒是比我想象的帅多了。

所以，第一印象还不错，可是第一天我还得带他去吃午餐，所以我们必须聊天。他又对我说了更多他自己的家庭背景，让我对他更加了解。我得知他的父亲来自肯尼亚，母亲

---

flesh out
使充实；使完善
flesh 原是名词，意思是"肉；肉体"，词组 flesh out 中的 flesh 是动词。按照字面意思，flesh out 就像是在骨骼上赋予血肉，引申为"使充实；使完善"。
● The writer needed more time to flesh out his story.
这名作家需要一些时间让他的故事更完善。

补充

put flesh on
为……充实内容
● Several reporters helped put flesh on the plane crash story.
几位记者帮忙完善了那则飞机坠毁的报道。

---

6. brilliant [ˈbrɪljənt]
adj. 杰出的；优秀的

7. rare [rɛr] *adj.* 稀有的；罕见的

8. minority [məˈnɔrɪtɪ]
n. 少数群；少数民族

9. bio [ˈbaɪoʃ] *n.* 自传

10. vacation [veˈkeʃən] *v.* 度假

11. biracial [ˌbaɪˈreʃəl]
adj. 混血的（尤指黑、白人种）

12. assumption [əˈsʌmpʃən]
n. 假定；设想

13. nerdy [ˈnɜdɪ]
adj. 书呆子的

14. intellectual [ˌɪntəˈlɛktʃəwəl]
adj. 聪明的

影视娱乐 时尚生活 政治财经 体坛文艺

found out that his father was from Kenya, his mother was a white woman from Kansas and that he had spent part of his life in Indonesia.

And I just found him intriguing[15] in every . . . in every way that you can imagine. He was funny. He was self-deprecating[16]. He didn't take himself too seriously. He could laugh at himself. I mean, we were . . . we clicked[17] right away. He was very down-to-earth[18], despite having come from this very exotic[19] background, compared to mine.

SUZANNE MALVEAUX, CNN CORRESPONDENT
Did he fit in into the . . . with your friends on the South Side? Did he fit in, or did he stand out in some way?

MICHELLE OBAMA, U.S. FIRST LADY
Yeah, no, he . . . he very much . . .

SUZANNE MALVEAUX, CNN CORRESPONDENT
What was that like, to meet your friends?

MICHELLE OBAMA, U.S. FIRST LADY
Yeah, he very much fit in.

是堪萨斯的白人妇女，而且他还在印度尼西亚住过。

然后我发现他在各方面都很令人好奇……你想知道的各方面。他很会说笑，会自嘲，不会把自己看得太了不起。他会开自己的玩笑。我是说，我们……一见如故。和我比较起来，他的成长背景虽然充满了异国经历，但是他却很踏实。

CNN 特派员　苏珊·马尔弗

他和你在芝加哥南部的朋友处得来吗？他能不能和他们打成一片，还是会比较突出？

美国第一夫人　米歇尔·奥巴马

嗯，他……他很……

CNN 特派员　苏珊·马尔弗

他和你的朋友见面的时候是什么样子？

美国第一夫人　米歇尔·奥巴马

嗯，他和他们相处融洽。

fit in
融入；处得来

fit 是指"容纳于"，fit in 引申为"被他人接受；相处融洽"的意思。fit in 还可以用来表示"安排、安插时间做某事"。

• Ryan fits in well with any crowd because of his easy-going personality.
莱恩的个性随和，所以跟任何人都相处得来。

• I'll try to fit you in my schedule for this week.
我会想办法将你安排进我这周的行程里。

stand out
突出；显眼

stand out 在这里指"突出；显眼"，指的是奥巴马是否因为他特殊的成长背景而显得与他人不同。

• With his unusual fashion sense, Ned always stands out in a crowd.
奈德特殊的时尚品位，使得他总是在人群中非常显眼。

15. intriguing [ɪnˈtrigɪŋ]
adj. 引人兴趣的

16. self-deprecating [ˌsɛlfˈdɛprɪˌketɪŋ] *adj.* 自我解嘲的

17. click [klɪk] *v.* 一拍即合；互相欣赏

18. down-to-earth [ˌdauntəˈɜθ] *adj.* 朴实的；谦虚的

19. exotic [ɛgˈzɑtɪk] *adj.* 异国情调的；奇特的

影视娱乐　时尚生活　政治财经　体坛文艺

You know, Barack is one of those people who is comfortable in his own skin. So, he's comfortable in every space that he's in. So, he was comfortable with my family that is very diverse in, you know, in opinions and perspectives[20].

But he was also very comfortable at Sidley & Austin, in a very upper-crust firm, but he was also comfortable in that church basement that he took me to, where he talked about the concept[21] of how you make the world as it is and the world as it should be one in [and] the same.

And that's what I liked about Barack—that he could very much be himself, but connect with people all over the place. And, then, as I got to meet his friends, and saw the diversity[22] of his . . . not just his family, but his friendships, the folks[23] in college and the kids, the folks that he grew up with in Hawaii, all very different people, but all basically the same.

正常 *MP3-Track21* / 慢速 *MP3-Track51* ▎ *When Michelle Met Barack*

你知道，巴拉克是那种对自己不觉得别扭的人。所以，他不论到哪里都很自在。像我家人的意见和观点都很不一样，可是他也与他们都相处自在。

不过他在西德利与奥斯汀事务所这个相当上层社会的公司里，还是一样很自在，还有他带我去过的教堂地下室。他在那里聊到了世界的现状是怎么形成的，还有如何塑造一个团结和谐的世界。

那就是我喜欢巴拉克的地方——他可以充分展现自我，但又能够和各地的人交流。然后，我认识了他的朋友，发现那种多元性……不只他的家人，还有他的朋友、大学同窗、在夏威夷一起长大的小孩、同伴，都是非常不一样的人，但基本上却也都具有相同的特质。

in one's own skin
做自己
in one's own skin 照字面意思是"穿着自己的皮囊"，抽象的意思就是"做自己"，文中指奥巴马一向很自在，不论他在何种环境下都是同一个样子，对他不会有太大的影响。

• Zach exudes confidence and seems quite comfortable in his own skin.
扎克散发出自信，他似乎对于做自己很自在。

upper-crust
一流的；顶尖的
crust 是指面包、蛋糕类最外层的表皮，upper-crust 是形容社会的最上层、社会顶尖的部分，有"上流阶级"的含意，也就是"一流的；顶尖的"的意思。

• Alice attended an upper-crust boarding school.
艾丽丝上的是一所顶尖的寄宿学校。

20. perspective [pɚˋspɛktɪv]
n. 看法；观点

21. concept [ˋkɑnsɛpt]
n. 概念；观念
Helen does not understand the concept of fairness.

22. diversity [daɪˋvɝsətɪ]
n. 差异；多样性
This gallery displays a diversity of work from many different artists.

23. folk [fok] n. 同学；人们；各位
Danny helps the old folks in the neighborhood.

影视娱乐

时尚生活

政治财经

体坛文艺

Step by Step 听懂 CNN 全球巨星专访

政治财经 ㉒ 为什么世界是"平"的？——CNN 专访作者托马斯·弗里德曼

The World Is Flat . . . so What Next?

Talk Asia Interview with Thomas Friedman

图片提供：Reuters

ANJALI RAO, CNN CORRESPONDENT
Thomas, great to have you on the program today.

THOMAS FRIEDMAN, JOURNALIST & AUTHOR
Good to be here.

ANJALI RAO, CNN CORRESPONDENT
Now, you're one of America's leading opinion makers.[1] Is there a sense of responsibility, do you think, that goes along with that? Or do you just say, "You know what? I'm gonna write what I like and you can take it or leave it?"

正常MP3-Track22
慢速MP3-Track52

名人小档案 ▼ 托马斯·弗里德曼

托马斯·弗里德曼（1953—）是一位犹太裔美国新闻记者、专栏及书籍作家，并是普利策新闻奖的三届获奖者。弗里德曼出生于美国明尼苏达州，自高中时即开始编辑校刊。1975 年他从布兰迪斯大学毕业，主修地中海地区事务，接着在牛津大学圣安东尼学院取得中东研究硕士学位。其中阿拉伯裔的教授 Albert Hourani 影响了弗里德曼终生的观点。弗里德曼以提倡巴以和平、阿拉伯世界现代化与全球化而受到瞩目，他偶尔会提及这些议题背后潜藏的危机。他的书从中立、新自由主义（neoliberal）的观点提出国际政治的不同面向。弗里德曼目前担任《纽约时报》的专栏作家，其专栏主要关注国际关系。

Thomas Friedman

Notes & Vocabulary

take it or leave it
接不接受随便你
这个短语常用来表示"接不接受随便你"，口语中会说"要就接受，不要就算了"，表示没有商量的余地，较文雅的说法是"悉听尊便"。
I'll give you $20 for the shirt. Take it or leave it.
我出 20 美元买那件衬衫。接不接受随便你。

1. **opinion maker**
   [ə`pɪnjən] [`mekə]
   n. 意见领袖；舆论制造者

影视娱乐　时尚生活　政治财经　体坛文艺

CNN 特派员 安姿丽
托马斯，今天很高兴能邀请你到节目里来。

记者兼作家 托马斯·弗里德曼
我很高兴能上这个节目。

CNN 特派员 安姿丽
你是美国非常重要的意见领袖之一。你觉得这个身份会伴随着很大的责任吗？还是你只会这么说，"反正我爱写什么就写什么，你们要接受就接受，不接受也随便你"？

THOMAS FRIEDMAN, JOURNALIST & AUTHOR

Well, the answer's really both. There's a huge sense of responsibility, you know, people will often come up and say, God, what's that like, to have that audience? Because I know that wide audience is out there, I wake up in the morning, after I've written a column, and I'm totally in agony. Did I get it right, you know? Did I say that exactly the way I wanted to say it? I agonize[2] over every column, precisely[3] 'cause I know it is gonna be read by a lot of people, and it's gonna be in Google, you know, forever. So, there is that sense of responsibility.

But at the same time, you do have to take the attitude of, "This is what I think, this is why I think it; I'm not in a popularity contest; if you like it, great, if you don't like it, please don't throw a shoe, okay?" But, you gotta believe what you say and say what you think, you know, so . . .

ANJALI RAO, CNN CORRESPONDENT

You've long traveled the planet investigating globalization[4]. How do you think that the current economic state of things is going to affect it?

THOMAS FRIEDMAN, JOURNALIST & AUTHOR

Well, you know, I wrote a book called *The World Is Flat*, and I wanna now apologize—I got it wrong. The current economic crisis tells me I got it wrong. The world is so much flatter than I thought. Who knew? Who knew that Iceland was a hedge fund[5] with glaciers[6]? Who knew that 15 British police

记者兼作家 托马斯·弗里德曼

其实两者都有。我的确会感受到一种庞大的责任感。常常有人问我说，老天，拥有那么多读者是什么感觉？正因为我知道自己有一大群读者，我写完一篇专栏之后早上醒来时心里都会很挣扎痛苦，想着自己写对了吗？我是否……我有没有确实表达出我想说的话？我撰写每篇专栏都深陷痛苦，就是因为我知道有很多人会看，而且这些文章会永远摆在谷歌上。所以，确实会有种责任感。

不过，我也必须保持强硬的态度，"这是我的想法，这是我这么想的理由。我不是在参加人气竞赛，所以如果你喜欢我的观点，当然很好，但你如果不喜欢，那么，请不要丢鞋子（注1），好吗？"总之，你必须确信自己说的话，也必须说出内心真正的想法，所以……

CNN 特派员 安姿丽

你为了探究全球化的现象，花了很长一段时间走遍世界各地。你认为当前的经济形势对全球化会有什么影响？

记者兼作家 托马斯·弗里德曼

你也知道，我写了一本书叫做《世界是平的》，现在我要道歉：我搞错了。当前的经济危机让我发现自己搞错了。世界比我想象的还要平坦得多。谁会知道？谁会知道冰岛是个覆盖着冰山的避险基金？谁知道英国 15 个警察局会把基金存在 ice-save.com（注2）这个冰岛的在线存款账户里？这种事情是编

in agony
处于精神痛苦的状态

agony 为名词，指"极度痛苦；苦恼"。短语 in agony 等同于 in pain、in grief、in misery。

· I need to see a dentist because I am in agony with this sore tooth.
  我得去看牙医，因为我的牙痛得要命。

2. **agonize** [ˈæɡəˌnaɪz]
   v. 感到苦恼；极度痛苦
   Jamie agonized over the decision of where to go to college.

3. **precisely** [prɪˈsaɪslɪ]
   adv. 确切地；正好
   When baking we need to measure ingredients more precisely than for cooking.

4. **globalization** [ˌɡloʊbələˈzeʃən]
   n. 全球化
   Many feel poor nations will get

5. **hedge fund** [hɛdʒ] [fʌnd]
   n. 避险基金；对冲基金

6. **glacier** [ˈɡleʃə] n. 冰河

注1
指美国前总统小布什 2008 年 12 月 14 日在巴格达遭一名伊拉克记者丢鞋羞辱的事件。

注2
icesave.com 是冰岛银行 Landsbanki 开设的网络银行，欧洲各地有数个分行及网站。其英国存款账户多达 30 万，包括数个地方政府与警察单位。2008 年 10 月 7 日 Landsbanki 银行宣告破产，存款账户遭到冻结，英国客户有超过 40 亿英镑存款无法提取。

影视娱乐 时尚生活 政治财经 体坛文艺

departments would be depositing[7] their funds in [an] Icelandic online saving account called ice-save.com? You couldn't make that up! Even I—who knew the world was flat—I didn't know it was that flat.

And that's really what we've learned in this crisis. For me, that's the real revelation[8]. I knew we were intertwined, I knew the world was flat, but what I've really learned is just how flat it's become. A minor variation[9] in interest rates between Iceland and Britain, led all this money, you know, to go from Great Britain to Iceland, of all places. So I think that's the real lesson here.

ANJALI RAO, CNN CORRESPONDENT
Your most recent book, *Hot, Flat and Crowded*, what is it precisely about that title that made you choose it?

THOMAS FRIEDMAN, JOURNALIST & AUTHOR
It's getting hotter, global warming; it's getting flatter, which is my metaphor[10] for the rise of middle-classes all over the world that are consuming and producing like Americans now, with all the energy and natural resource implications[11] that has. And we're in a world that's getting crowded, population-wise. When I look at these problems, what I see [are] incredible opportunities masquerading[12] as insoluble[13] problems.

Those opportunities are embedded[14] for me in an escalated[15] industrial revolution which I call ET—energy technology—the pursuit[16] of abundant[17], cheap, clean, reliable electrons[18] and molecules[19].

造不出来的！即便我早就知道世界是平的，却也没想到竟然有这么平。

这就是我们在这场危机里学到的东西。对我来说，这才是真正的启发。我早就知道所有人都密不可分，也知道世界是平的，但我真正学到的是，世界竟然已变得这么平。冰岛对英国的利率才出现些微变动，就导致这么多钱从英国跑到冰岛，而不是到其他地方去。我认为这就是最重要的教训。

CNN 特派员 安姿丽
你最新的著作叫做《世界又热又平又挤》。你为什么会挑选这个书名？

记者兼作家 托马斯·弗里德曼
世界越来越热，全球变暖。越来越平，我用这个意象比喻中产阶级在世界各地兴起的现象，这些人的消费和生产方式都和现在的美国人一样，对能源与自然资源造成的影响也相同。此外，就人口而言，我们的世界也越来越拥挤。这些问题在我眼中都是令人难以置信的机会，只不过表面上看来像是无法解决的问题而已。

在我看来，这些机会都潜藏在一种不断扩大的工业革命当中，我称之为 ET 能源科技——追求丰富、廉价、干净、可靠的电子与

-wise
就……方面；关于……方面
文中的 population-wise 并不是正式的英文单词，而是名词 population "人口" 加上词尾 -wise 变成副词，表示"就人口方面"。注意名词加上 -wise 可当副词或形容词。

Price-wise, this cell phone is a good bargain.
就价钱来说，这款手机很划算。

7. deposit [dɪˋpɑzət] v. 存款；存入

8. revelation [ˌrɛvəˋleʃən] n. 启发；显露

9. variation [ˌvɛriˋeʃən] n. 差异；变动

10. metaphor [ˋmɛtəˌfɔr] n. 意象；隐喻

11. implication [ˌɪmpləˋkeʃən] n. 含意；暗示；蕴含

12. masquerade [ˌmæskəˋred] v. 伪装；化装

13. insoluble [ɪnˋsɑljəbl] adj. 难以解决的；无法解决的

14. embed [ɪmˋbɛd] v. 埋入；嵌入

15. escalate [ˋɛskəˌlet] v. 升高；扩大

16. pursuit [pɚˋsut] n. 追求；寻求

17. abundant [əˋbʌndənt] adj. 充足的；大量的；丰富的

18. electron [ɪˋlɛkˌtran] n. 电子

19. molecule [ˋmalɪˌkjul] n. 分子

影视娱乐

时尚生活

政治财经

体坛文艺

And the country that owns ET, I believe, is gonna have the most energy security, national security, economic security, competitive industries, clean environment and global respect.

ANJALI RAO, CNN CORRESPONDENT
What should we expect from you, insofar as[20] tackling a new subject for your next book?

THOMAS FRIEDMAN, JOURNALIST & AUTHOR
Well, I'm a big believer of "If you don't go, you don't know," you know, so, I . . . that's really my motto[21]. I mean, I have the best job in the world. I get to be a tourist with an attitude. I get to go wherever I want, whenever I want, and I get to write whatever I want. It's a great job. I have the best job in the world. I mean, somebody has to have it. I've got it, and you don't, okay? And so, it's a great job.

But, with it, as we said, it comes a lot of responsibility and I really write my columns by following my notes. I . . . Why am I here in Hong Kong? It's not because an editor told me to go to Hong Kong. It's because I was basically sitting in America and in America, right now—I'm normally traveling all the time—I haven't been traveling, 'cause America is the greatest show on Earth right now.

Between Barack Obama coming in and the financial crisis which we started, basically, I don't wanna go anywhere, all right? But I said, no, if I'm gonna go anywhere, I'm gonna go to China right now, because we're not gonna get out of this without cooperating and working closely with China. And it's the G2, now. I mean, at the end of the day, it's

分子。我相信拥有 ET 的国家就会拥有最高程度的能源保障、国家安全、经济稳定、富有竞争力的产业、洁净的环境，以及全球的尊重。

CNN 特派员 安姿丽

我们对你该有什么期待呢？你下一本书会探讨什么新主题？

记者兼作家 托马斯·弗里德曼

我深信这句话，"不到现场，就不可能知道。"这句话可以说是我的座右铭。我是说，我拥有世界上最棒的工作。我可以是个带着自身观点的游客。我想去哪里就去哪里，时间任我自己安排，而且可以写我自己想写的东西。这个工作很棒。我拥有全世界最好的工作。这个工作总是会落到某个人手上，刚好就被我拿到了，不是你，对不对？所以，这个工作确实很棒。

不过，就像我们说的，这个工作伴随着很大的责任，我的专栏文章其实都是按照笔记写的。我现在为什么在香港？不是因为某个编辑要我到香港来，而是因为我本来在美国——我平常几乎都在四处奔波——但我在美国已经有好一阵子没有旅行了，因为美国现在就是全球最精彩的节目。

从奥巴马上任到这场金融危机的这段时间，我可是哪里都不想去。但我心想，不对，如果我要到其他地方去，那我就要去中国。因为我们如果不和中国密切合作，就不可能摆脱这片泥沼。现在是 G2 两大工业国了（注3），我是说，归根究底，关键就在奥巴马和胡锦涛两人身上。说来很有趣，胡锦涛担

189

---

at the end of the day
到头来；终究
此语字面的意思是"一天结束时"，常在口语中用来表示"到头来；终究；说到最后"的意思。

· **At the end of the day**, what matters is that you still have your job.
到头来，重要的是你仍然还有工作。

20. **insofar as**
在……的范围内；到……的程度
I will keep working insofar as I'm able to.

21. **motto** [ˈmɑto] *n.* 座右铭
"Never settle for less than you deserve" is my personal motto.

注3
世界各大工业国不时会举行高峰会，例如 G8、G20 等等，随着经济发展其成员国也会有调整。弗里德曼在这里以 G2 指出美国和中国对全球经济发展的重要性，未来将会由这两国的领袖决议来主导。

影视娱乐
时尚生活
政治财经
体坛文艺

gonna be Barack Obama and Hu Jintao. And it's very interesting, you know, when you think about it—Hu Jintao's second term overlaps[22], as president of China, almost perfectly with Barack Obama's first term. And I have a feeling these two guys are gonna get to know each other really well. I hope it'll be for the benefit[23] of both countries.

I'm an optimist[24] at heart, you know. I was in Israel a couple of years ago, and um, the editor of the *Haaretz Newspaper* where my column runs in Israel, [we] had a dinner party, and I asked him what . . ., "Why do you guys run my column?" And he said, "Tom, it's 'cause you're the only optimist we have." But I do live by the motto that pessimists[25] are usually right. Optimists are usually wrong, but all the great change in history was done by optimists. So, I'm gonna go down swinging with optimism.

ANJALI RAO, CNN CORRESPONDENT
Thomas, it's been a real delight having you on this show, and enlightening[26] to boot.

托马斯·弗里德曼著作

《从贝鲁特到耶路撒冷》(From Beirut to Jerusalem, 1989)——记述他 20 世纪 80 年代被派驻贝鲁特的中东经历。

《凌志汽车橄榄树：理解全球化》(The Lexus and the Olive Tree: Understanding Globalization, 1999)——以凌志汽车与橄榄树的意象，比喻全球化过程中高科技与传统相互较量且共生的关系。

《经度与态度》(Longitudes and Attitudes: Exploring the World After September 11, 2002)—— 911 事件后谈论中东情势与恐怖主义。

正常*MP3-Track22* / 慢速*MP3-Track52* | The World Is Flat . . . so What Next?

190

任中国国家主席的第二任任期几乎和奥巴马的第一任完全重叠。我觉得他们两人一定会和对方很熟。希望这样的情况对两国都会有利。

我其实是个乐观主义者。我几年前到以色列去。在那里，我的专栏都登在《国土报》。那家报社的编辑举办了一场晚宴，我问他，"你们为什么登我的专栏？"他说，"托马斯，因为你是我们唯一的乐观主义者。"但我的座右铭是：悲观主义者的观点通常是正确的。乐观主义者通常会看走眼，但历史上所有的重大变革都是乐观主义者打造的结果。所以，我要抱着乐观的态度。

CNN 特派员 安姿丽

托马斯，能够邀请你到节目来真是开心，也非常具有启发性。

go down swinging
绝不放弃；努力到最后
go down swinging 是指明知可能会失败，但还是不轻言放弃，也就是"努力到最后一刻"和"绝不放弃"的意思。

- The team won't give up. If they lose, they'll go down swinging.
  那个球队不会放弃。即使他们会输，还是会努力到最后一刻。

to boot 此外；而且
boot 在这里当名词，不是指"靴子"，而是"（附加）利益；等值之物"，to boot 表示"此外；另外"，等于 in addition to 或 besides 的意思。

- Mandy is very intelligent, with good looks to boot.
  曼迪很聪明，而且也很漂亮。

22. **overlap** [ˌovəˈlæp] v. 与……重叠
23. **benefit** [ˈbɛnəˌfɪt] n. 好处；利益
24. **optimist** [ˈɑptəmɪst] n. 乐观主义者
25. **pessimist** [ˈpɛsəmɪst] n. 悲观主义者
26. **enlighten** [ɪnˈlaɪtn̩] v. 启发；启迪

《世界是平的》(The World is Flat: A Brief History of the 21st Century, 2005) ——以"世界正被贸易活动与科技抚平"为核心论点，讨论 21 世纪初期的全球化过程。

《世界又热又平又挤》(Hot, Flat, and Crowded: Why We Need a Green Revolution and How It Can Renew America, 2008) ——从全球变暖（热）、中产阶级暴增导致市场需求扁平化（平），与人口爆炸（挤）这三种现象，进一步探讨全球化议题，并强调绿色革命才是改造人类生活与地球环境的最佳方式。

Notes

体 坛 文 艺
Athletics & Art

Going the Distance

Ultra-marathoner Scott Jurek Pushes Mind and Body to the Edge of Endurance[1]

图片提供: AP

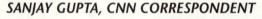

SANJAY GUPTA, CNN CORRESPONDENT

Scott Jurek has been called the "King of Pain" and the greatest ultra-marathoner ever. Ultra-marathons[2] can be 125 miles longer than a typical 26-mile marathon.

Scott finished his first in 1994, and since then, he's dominated the sport. Today he holds records for these races that cover more than 150 miles and last over 24 hours straight. A notoriously[3] tough ultra-marathon is the 135-mile Badwater in Death Valley, California. In 2005, to get through the 130-degree heat, Scott was dunked[4] in this king-sized cooler full of ice water.

正常MP3-Track23
慢速MP3-Track53

名人小档案 ▼ 斯科特·尤雷克

有"超级马拉松之神"美称的斯科特·尤雷克（1973—）出生于美国明尼苏达州普罗克托市，是一名超级马拉松选手、物理治疗师及教练。他是多项长跑纪录的保持者，包括 2005 年坏水河超级马拉松（Badwater Ultra-marathon），其纪录是 24 小时 36 分，以及 2004 年美西 100 英里耐力赛（Western States Endurance Run），其纪录是 15 小时 36 分。

Scott Jurek

CNN 特派员 桑杰·古普塔

斯科特·尤雷克被人们称为"痛苦之王"，也是史上最了不起的超级马拉松选手。比起一般 26 英里长的马拉松，超级马拉松的长度可能要多出 125 英里。

斯科特在 1994 年跑完他的第一场超级马拉松赛跑，此后就称霸了这项运动。如今他在超过 150 英里及连续 24 小时以上的比赛中都是纪录保持者。其中一场特别艰苦的超级马拉松比赛，就是在加利福尼亚死亡谷举行的 135 英里坏水河超级马拉松。2005 年参赛时，斯科特为了挨过 130℃的高温，全身浸泡在这个装满冰水的大型冰桶里。

Notes & Vocabulary

标题扫描

go the distance
坚持到底
原本是指赛跑"跑完全程"，后来也表示任何比赛"打完、赛足全场"，引申为做事"坚持到底，直到成功"。

- Vincent went the distance and finished the race.
  文森特坚持到底跑完全程。

. . . straight
连续地；不间断地
straight 在文中是副词，放在连续的事物之后修饰前词，若当形容词用则放在数字之后、量词之前，如文中"连续 24 小时"，则写法如下：

24（数字）+ hours（单位）+ straight（副词）
= 24（数字）+ straight（形容词）+ hours（单位）

- The contestants danced for 10 hours straight.

= The contestants danced for 10 straight hours.
参赛者连续跳舞跳了 10 个小时。

1. endurance [ɪn`durəns]
   n. 忍耐；耐力

2. ultra-marathon [`ʌltrə`mærəˌθɑn] *n.* 马拉松赛跑

3. notoriously [no`tɔriəslɪ]
   adv. 恶名昭彰地

4. dunk [dʌŋk] *v.* 浸一下；浸泡
   Ben dunked his head in a bucket of water to cool off.

影视娱乐

时尚生活

政治财经

体坛文艺

Halfway through the race, he collapsed[5], and for 10 minutes he didn't move. But he managed to get up and not only finish the race, but shatter[6] the course record.

Scott says it was his mother, Lynn, who taught him how to persevere.[7] She died last March after living with multiple sclerosis[8] for 30 years.

So what propels[9] you to be able to do some of these things? Running the distances you do? A lot of people wouldn't even dream of it.

SCOTT JUREK, ULTRA-MARATHONER

I think for me it's that self-exploration,[10] that idea of there's something out there and the desire to see what my body, what my mind and down to what my spirit can do.

SANJAY GUPTA, CNN CORRESPONDENT

Were you always a runner? I mean, how did this start?

SCOTT JUREK, ULTRA-MARATHONER

For me, I actually used to hate running. I grew up hunting and fishing in northern Minnesota, and that really was where I got connected with the outdoors[11]. And I had got[ten] interested in running through Nordic ski racing and had to get ready for the . . . basically, the snow season by doing some running on the ski trails[12].

SANJAY GUPTA, CNN CORRESPONDENT

You obviously do this competitively. What's the furthest distance you've ever run?

他在比赛半途累倒在地上，长达 10 分钟一动不动。不过，他还是勉强爬了起来，不但完成比赛，还打破了比赛纪录。

斯科特说，是母亲琳恩教会了他如何坚忍不拔。他的母亲患多发性硬化症 30 年后，在去年 3 月逝世。

是什么促使你有办法做到这些事情？跑那么远的距离？这是许多人连做梦都不敢想的事情。

超级马拉松选手 斯科特·尤雷克

对我来说，我想是自我探索吧，我知道外面有个未知的世界，还有渴望知道自己的身体、心智、终究说来是精神，可以达到什么地步。

CNN 特派员 桑杰·古普塔

你一直都在进行跑步吗？我是说，你是怎么开始参与这种运动的？

超级马拉松选手 斯科特·尤雷克

其实我以前不喜欢跑步。我小时候经常在明尼苏达州北部打猎和钓鱼，也就是这样的经历让我喜爱野外。我后来是因为参加北欧滑雪比赛而对跑步产生兴趣，因为我必须先在滑雪道上跑步，为即将来临的雪季做准备。

CNN 特派员 桑杰·古普塔

你跑步的好胜心显然很强。你跑过最长的距离是多远？

---

down to
归结为；终归说来

down to 在这里是 come down to "归结为……（的问题）"的意思，文中是说超级马拉松终归说来是精神的历练。

· The choice of who gets the job is down to who is willing to work the hardest.
谁能获选得到这个职务，得看谁愿意付出最多努力。

down to 的其他常见词汇

down-to-earth
朴实的；务实的

· Vanessa is a down-to-earth person with an easy-going way about her.
瓦内莎是个务实的人，而且为人随和。

get down to business
开始处理正事；言归正传

· As soon as a plan is in place, we can get down to business.
等到计划就绪，我们就可以开始好好做事了。

5. collapse [kə`læps]
   v. 累倒；累垮

6. shatter [`ʃætə] v. 粉碎；破坏

7. persevere [ˌpəsə`vɪr]
   v. 坚持；不屈不挠

8. multiple sclerosis
   [`mʌltəpl] [sklə`rosəs]
   n. 多发性硬化症

9. propel [prə`pɛl] v. 推进；驱使

10. exploration [ˌɛksplə`reʃən]
    n. 探索；探险

11. outdoors [ˌaut`dɔrz]
    n. 野外；旷野（不可数）

12. trail [trel] n. 路径；路线

影视娱乐 时尚生活 政治财经 体坛文艺

SCOTT JUREK, ULTRA-MARATHONER

The furthest distance I've run is 165.7 miles in 24 hours.

SANJAY GUPTA, CNN CORRESPONDENT

So tell me how that works. Are you taking breaks or what are you doing?

SCOTT JUREK, ULTRA-MARATHONER

So the more time I take breaks . . . the clock is always going, so the idea is to continue running throughout[13] and as much as you can, 'cause you only get 24 hours. And the only times I did stop were to go to the bathroom, basically, and even eating is done on the run.

SANJAY GUPTA, CNN CORRESPONDENT

Have you heard about the medical aspects[14] of this? What have you been told?

SCOTT JUREK, ULTRA-MARATHONER

Well, I think it helps . . . I'm actually a physical therapist[15] and so know a little bit about the body. But you know, is it healthy to go that far in that amount of time? You know, it's hard to say, but the human body was built for endurance. If you look at our ancestors[16] and what they did . . . I mean, even think of my great grandparents and what they did for work out in the fields, and I think maybe our perception[17] of what is normal has changed over the years. And I like to always refer to what people used to do.

超级马拉松选手 斯科特·尤雷克

我跑过最长的距离，是在 24 小时内跑了 165.7 英里。

CNN 特派员 桑杰·古普塔

告诉我你是怎么做到的。你中途休息了吗？还是做了什么？

超级马拉松选手 斯科特·尤雷克

我休息的时间越多……时间不会等我，所以重点就是从头到尾持续地跑，尽自己所能尽量地跑，因为你只有 24 个小时。基本上，我会停下来的时候只是为了上厕所，连吃东西都是边跑边吃。

CNN 特派员 桑杰·古普塔

你有没有听说过医学方面的说法？有人跟你说过什么吗？

超级马拉松选手 斯科特·尤雷克

我觉得有帮助……其实我本身是物理治疗师，所以对人体稍有了解。不过，在那样的时间里跑那么远健康吗？很难说，可是人体天生就有忍耐力。看看我们的祖先及他们所做的事情……我是说，甚至看我曾祖父母在田里工作的情形。我认为我们对于何谓正常的看法多年以来可能已经有所改变。我总是喜欢参照人们从前做的事。

---

refer to

参考；参照

refer 可当及物动词或不及物动词，常与介词 to 连用，文中是"参考；求助于"的意思。

- Bob **refers to** the dictionary when trying to spell a difficult word.
  鲍伯想拼写难词的时候会参考词典。

refer to 的其他用法

refer to sb./sth.

提及；谈起

- Ellen often **refers to** her children in conversation.
  艾伦常常在谈话中提起她的小孩。

refer sb. to . . .

引导；转介（以便得到帮助）

- Joan **referred** her friend **to** a good family doctor.
  琼介绍她的朋友去看一名优秀的家庭医生。

refer sth. to . . .

送交；提交（处理、讨论等）

- The law firm **referred** the case **to** a lawyer with experience in settling corporate lawsuits.
  那家法律事务所把这个案子交给解决企业诉讼经验的律师处理。

---

13. **throughout** [θruˈaut]
    adv. 自始至终

14. **aspect** [ˈæsˌpɛkt] *n.* 方面；层面

15. **therapist** [ˈθærəpɪst]
    n. 治疗师；治疗专家

16. **ancestor** [ˈænˌsɛstə]
    n. 祖先；祖宗

17. **perception** [pəˈsɛpʃən]
    n. 见解；看法；感知

SANJAY GUPTA, CNN CORRESPONDENT

You talk about exploration and maybe to some extent exploring what the body can do, but at some point you made the decision to say, I'm gonna go from someone who didn't like to run to racing in the hardest, presumably,[18] running competitions in the world. Was there a moment when that happened for you and you said, "I can actually do this"?

SCOTT JUREK, ULTRA-MARATHONER

I think it was probably after my first 50-miler, after my first ultra-marathon. I'd run a marathon and then a month later decided to do this 50-mile race. A buddy of mine, Dusty Olson, said you've got to try this out.

And at 20 years old, most 20-year-olds aren't thinking about running 50 miles, but after I had completed that I said, of course, "Never again." But it was after a few hours, and I was like, "You know, yeah, I can . . . I think I can be pretty good at this."

SANJAY GUPTA, CNN CORRESPONDENT

Are you competing when you're out there? Are you competing against the other racers? Against yourself? Running away from something?

SCOTT JUREK, ULTRA-MARATHONER

I like to say I'm trying not to compete. I'm trying to work with my body. I'm not ~~compete~~ [competing] against myself. Obviously, there's a clock out there. And I do use the other racers in the competition to push my body to that edge because the competition really helps, you know, explore those boundaries[19]— you know, what am I capable of?

正常 *MP3-Track23* / 慢速 *MP3-Track53* ▮ *Going the Distance*

CNN 特派员 桑杰·古普塔

你提到了探索，在某种程度上可能也在探索人体能够做到什么地步。不过，你毕竟还是做了个决定，从原本不喜欢跑步，到参加堪称世界上最艰苦的跑步比赛。是不是有某个时间点让你突然改变心意，对自己说"我做得到"？

超级马拉松选手 斯科特·尤雷克

我想大概是在我参加了第一场 50 英里的比赛之后，在我的第一场超级马拉松赛之后。我当时跑完了一场马拉松，一个月后决定参加这场 50 英里的赛跑。我的一位朋友达斯廷·欧森说，你一定要跑 50 英里试试。

当时我才 20 岁。大多数 20 岁的年轻人通常不会想要跑 50 英里，所以我完成那场比赛之后，原本也是说，"再也不要了。"不过，才几个小时之后，我就不禁觉得："其实，我可以……我觉得我可以在这种运动中表现得不错。"

CNN 特派员 桑杰·古普塔

你在比赛的时候是在竞争吗？你是在和其他选手竞争？还是和自己竞争？或是想逃离什么？

超级马拉松选手 斯科特·尤雷克

我会说我尽量不要去竞争。我尽量和自己的身体协调合作，而不是和自己竞争。当然比赛会计时，而我确实会利用同一场比赛中的其他选手来敦促自己把体能发挥到极限，因为竞争确实有助于探索体能的极限，看我自己能做到什么程度。

to some extent 某种程度上

extent 是"程度；范围"的意思，to some extent 的意思是"在某种程度上；有部分"，要表示程度大小可以用 to a great/large/small extent，注意须加上冠词 a。

- To some extent, Terry has always been an entertainer.
  某种程度上来说，特里一直喜欢娱乐他人。
- To a great extent, Ted owes his success to hard work.
  泰德把他的成功绝大部分归功于努力勤奋。

18. presumably [prɪˈzuːməblɪ]
    adv. 想必是；推测是

19. boundary [ˈbaʊndərɪ]
    n. 界线；界限；边界

马拉松的分类

全程马拉松 traditional marathon
国际田径协会（IAAF）于 1921 年明确规定距离为 26 英里 385 码（42 公里 195 米）。

半程马拉松 half marathon
20 世纪 80 年代在民间开始兴起，距离为全程马拉松的一半，大约 13.1 英里（21 公里 97.5 公尺）。

超级马拉松 ultra-marathon
距离超过全程马拉松，计时赛常见的距离有 50 公里、100 公里、50 英里、100 英里等；计程赛常见的时间有 6 小时、12 小时、24 小时及两天以上的多日赛（multiday race）。通常每 5~10 公里就会设一个救护站（aid station），供选手补充食物、饮水或休息。

影视娱乐 时尚生活 政治财经 体坛文艺

King of the Mound[1]

Talk Asia Interview with Japanese Pitching Sensation Yu Darvish

图片提供：AP

MORGAN NEILL, TALK ASIA

Well, thank you very much for taking the time to talk to us today. I wanted to start by just delving a little bit into so much attention that you've gotten here. You've been called the best pitcher in Japan, which is the baseball craziest country I've ever seen. How do you manage to deal with all that pressure every day?

YU DARVISH, JAPANESE BASEBALL STAR

I don't really feel that much pressure. Instead, I'm just happy to play the game here. I have a pride in being a baseball player.

MORGAN NEILL, TALK ASIA

It's rare to see a pitcher who improves so steadily over time as you have. Your ERA[2] has dropped every

202

❷❹ CNN专访日本职业棒球投手——达比修有

名人小档案 ▼ 达比修有

达比修有（1986—）出生于大阪，父亲是伊朗人，母亲是日本人。目前效力于美国职业棒球得克萨斯骑兵队。由于日本国籍法规定"年满22岁时方须决定国籍"，所以达比修有在22岁前拥有双重国籍资格，年满岁数后则为了参加北京奥运棒球赛决定依日本国籍法规定只保留日本籍，放弃伊朗籍。达比修有擅长的球路包括快速球、变速球、滑球、切球、曲球、指叉球等，被日本媒体形容为恐怖的"多彩变化球"风格的投手。

Yu Darvish

Notes & Vocabulary

delve into
探索；探究

delve 在此当动词，意指"挖掘；探索；钻研"，通常会用动词短语 delve into (something) 来表示"探索、钻研、彻底搜索（某些记录、数据、事项等）"。

The investigator delved into the mystery of the missing jewels.

调查人员彻底调查珠宝失窃的谜团。

1. **mound** [maʊnd]
   n. 投手丘；土墩
2. **ERA** [ˈiˈɑrˈe]
   n. 投手平均自责失分率、防御率
   (= earned run average)

影视娱乐

时尚生活

政治财经

体坛文艺

《亚洲名人聊天室》摩根·尼尔

感谢您抽空接受我们的访谈。首先我想谈一下您受到高度关注的这件事。您被誉为全日本的最佳投手，而日本是我见过的对棒球最狂热的国家。您每天是如何面对那些压力的？

日本职业棒球明星 达比修有

我并不觉得真有那么大的压力，反而觉得我能在这里打球很开心。作为一个棒球运动员我感到骄傲。

《亚洲名人聊天室》摩根·尼尔

很少看到有哪个投手像您一样有如此稳定的

year, and you seem very focused on it. How do you set goals for yourself as a pitcher?

YU DARVISH, JAPANESE BASEBALL STAR

It might seem that I'm making steady[3] achievement, but no game is perfect. Still, that imperfection gives me my motivation to improve. I won't be satisfied unless I win all 25 games in a season. I think I can improve myself until I reach such perfection.

MORGAN NEILL, TALK ASIA

I've heard a lot of successful starting pitchers[4] say that the difference between a good pitcher and a great pitcher is as much mental as it is physical. How do you prepare yourself mentally before a start?

YU DARVISH, JAPANESE BASEBALL STAR

I always have the same mental state, even on the field. It is the same as when I am not pitching. I don't really get excited or nervous. It is important to remain calm all the time. The difference between a good pitcher and an excellent pitcher would be, well, a mere[5] good pitcher would get upset and too serious if he gets hit. But a great pitcher would stay calm and even think about getting the next batter out. That's the difference.

MORGAN NEILL, TALK ASIA

What drives you in baseball? What is it you love so much about this game?

YU DARVISH, JAPANESE BASEBALL STAR

You never know what will happen. You can see great plays and interesting games.

进步。您的投手防御率逐年下降，而您似乎对这点非常专注。作为一位投手，您如何为自己设定目标？

日本职业棒球明星　达比修有

我的成绩看起来是很稳定，但没有任何一场比赛是完美的。那种不完美给了我进步的动力。我不会感到满足的，除非我单季25场比赛全胜。我认为我可以进步达到那样的完美境界。

《亚洲名人聊天室》摩根·尼尔

我听过很多成功的先发投手说一名好投手跟一名伟大的投手之间的差别，在心理和生理上一样重要。您在先发出赛之前，心理上是如何做准备的？

日本职业棒球明星　达比修有

我永远都保持相同的心态，即便在场上也是如此。我不投球的时候也是一样。我不会感到兴奋或紧张。永远保持冷静是很重要的。一名好投手和一名优异的投手之间的差别……一个只能算是好投手的人在被打安打时会生气，会认为事态严重。但一名伟大的投手则会保持冷静，心里甚至想着如何让下一位击打者出局，差别就在于此。

《亚洲名人聊天室》摩根·尼尔

您打棒球的动力是什么？为什么这么热爱棒球呢？

日本职业棒球明星　达比修有

因为你永远不知道会发生什么事，你会看到很多优美和有趣的比赛。

Notes & Vocabulary

3. **steady** [ˈstɛdɪ]
adj. 稳定（发展）的；持续的
Ken is known for his steady approach to tackling problems.

4. **starting pitcher**
[ˈstɑrtɪŋ] [ˈpɪtʃɚ] *n.* 先发投手

5. **mere** [mɪr] *adj.* 仅仅；只不过
The movie star refused to talk to mere fans.

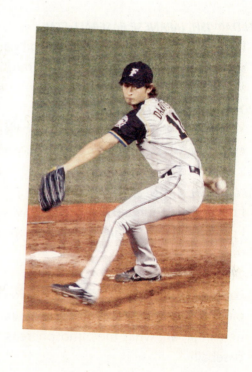

影视娱乐

时尚生活

政治财经

体坛文艺

MORGAN NEILL, TALK ASIA

Your father is Iranian, your mother is Japanese. What was it like for you growing up with that background here?

YU DARVISH, JAPANESE BASEBALL STAR

I grew up in a different environment from the typical[6] Japanese family. Compared to them, we had quite a different life, but my parents were a great influence, and I am very grateful for that.

MORGAN NEILL, TALK ASIA

I've heard you'd like to make baseball popular in Iran. First off[7], is that true, and secondly, how would you go about doing that?

YU DARVISH, JAPANESE BASEBALL STAR

I've organized games, sent baseball game kits and secured locations for practices in Iran.

MORGAN NEILL, TALK ASIA

Your father was a soccer player in college. Did you ever try and play soccer? Were you good?

YU DARVISH, JAPANESE BASEBALL STAR

I never even touched a soccer ball when I was small. I played only a little in my school gym class.

MORGAN NEILL, TALK ASIA

For people who don't come from big baseball playing countries, can you describe what it's like here in Japan, what the atmosphere is like around baseball?

《亚洲名人聊天室》摩根·尼尔

令尊是伊朗人，令堂则是日本人。这样的家庭背景让您在日本的成长是怎样的？

日本职业棒球明星 达比修有

我是在一个与一般日本家庭截然不同的环境中长大。与一般日本人相比，我们的生活非常与众不同，但我父母亲对我的影响很大，我对此非常感激。

《亚洲名人聊天室》摩根·尼尔

我听说您想将棒球推广到伊朗。首先，这是真的吗？其次，您要如何才能做到？

日本职业棒球明星 达比修有

我在伊朗办过比赛，寄棒球用具过去，并且找场地练球。

《亚洲名人聊天室》摩根·尼尔

令尊大学时是个足球运动员。您尝试过踢足球吗？身手如何？

日本职业棒球明星 达比修有

我小时候连足球都没摸过。我在学校体育课时玩过一点。

《亚洲名人聊天室》摩根·尼尔

对那些来自棒球运动不盛行的国家的人，您可否形容一下日本这里的情况，这里的棒球气氛如何？

---

compared to/with + N.
与……相比

compare 表示"比较；对照"的意思，之后可接介词 to 或 with，主要是将两件事情拿来相比，以便呈现出其差异之处。

- Compared to Graham, I don't make very much money.
  和格雷厄姆相比，我赚的钱不多。

相似用法

compare A with/to B
将 A 与 B 比较

- The investigator compared the handwriting on the envelope to the sample given by the suspect.
  调查人员把信封上的笔迹与嫌疑犯提供的笔迹样本比对。

compare A to B
将 A 比作 B；将 A 比喻为 B

- The coach compared the slow player to a turtle.
  教练把这名动作缓慢的选手比作慢乌龟。

6. typical [ˈtɪpɪkl̩]
   adj. 典型的；代表性的
   Justin is a typical teenager in that he loves music and hanging out with friends.

7. first off 首先；一开始
   First off, I want to thank you for inviting me to this event.

影视娱乐

时尚生活

政治财经

体坛文艺

YU DARVISH, JAPANESE BASEBALL STAR

Baseball is a game where you can never predict[8] what will happen next. With great players, the sport creates drama[9]. If you come to the stadium[10], you'll understand how exciting baseball is. I wish everyone could see a game in Japan.

MORGAN NEILL, TALK ASIA

And the fans, particularly I would say the fans of your team, are very enthusiastic[11], aren't they? Do you hear them while you're out there on the mound?

YU DARVISH, JAPANESE BASEBALL STAR

Fans support me no matter the situation—when I'm throwing well or totally battered[12]. It really helps me very much, and I believe all my teammates share this opinion

MORGAN NEILL, TALK ASIA

What's next for you? What do you still hope to achieve? You're very young as a baseball player. Where do you see yourself going in the future?

YU DARVISH, JAPANESE BASEBALL STAR

What I only think of now is the game I play next, and prepare myself for it. Therefore, for now, I don't have any particular future goals.

MORGAN NEILL, TALK ASIA

We've seen Ichiro, Matsui, Matsuzaka have great success playing in the United States. Could you see yourself doing the same some day?

日本职业棒球明星　达比修有

棒球是一种你永远无法预测接下来会发生什么事的运动。伟大的球员会让棒球比赛紧张刺激。你只要到球场里，就会了解棒球多么让人兴奋。我希望每个人都能在日本看一场棒球赛。

《亚洲名人聊天室》摩根·尼尔

那球迷呢？尤其是您所属球队的球迷，他们非常热情，不是吗？您在投手丘上的时候听得见他们的声音吗？

日本职业棒球明星　达比修有

无论场上情况如何球迷都支持我，无论我投得好或是完全被打败。球迷的支持对我的帮助很大，我相信我的队友都认同这点。

《亚洲名人聊天室》摩根·尼尔

您的下一步怎么走？您还想成就些什么？就一名棒球运动员而言，您还非常年轻。您认为自己未来会如何发展？

日本职业棒球明星　达比修有

我现在想的只有我的下一场比赛，然后准备好去比赛。所以，我现在对未来没有特定的目标。

《亚洲名人聊天室》摩根·尼尔

我们看到铃木一郎、松井、松坂在美国都打得非常好。有朝一日您是否也会走同样的路？

8. **predict** [prɪˋdɪkt]
   v. 预测；预知；预言
   The weather forecaster predicts rain for the weekend.

9. **drama** [ˋdrɑmə] *n.* 戏剧性；刺激

10. **stadium** [ˋstediəm]
    n. （有看台的）体育场；竞技场

11. **enthusiastic** [ɪnˏθuziˋæstɪk]
    adj. 热心的；热情
    The enthusiastic crowed cheered the home team.

12. **batter** [ˋbætə]
    v. 连续猛击；捣毁；磨损
    n. （棒球等的）击球手
    The poor economy battered many smaller companies.

达比修有的运动佳绩

❖ 甲子园锦标赛（Koshien Tournament）出赛 12 场、7 胜 2 败、防御率 1.47，曾投出无安打、无失分比赛（no-hitter）。

❖ 高中球速就达 150km/hr，美国大联盟数支球队前来邀请加入。

❖ 2004 年日本职业棒球太平洋联盟火腿队第一指名选入，签约金一亿日元。

❖ 2005 年继松坂大辅（1999 年）后以高中毕业新人的身份在职业棒球开幕战担任一军投手。

2009 年被 ESPN 誉为世界三大非大联盟投手之一。

影视娱乐

时尚生活

政治财经

体坛文艺

YU DARVISH, JAPANESE BASEBALL STAR

Ichiro, Matsui, and Matsuzaka, and all the other Japanese players are doing a great job in the States. They really encourage me to become a better player, but I don't particularly dream of playing in the major leagues or in the States right now.

MORGAN NEILL, TALK ASIA

For someone who says he's drawn to drama, you seem very even-tempered all the time. Are you like that in your life outside of baseball?

YU DARVISH, JAPANESE BASEBALL STAR

Yes, normally I'm very calm at all times.

MORGAN NEILL, TALK ASIA

What do you think you'd be doing if you weren't playing baseball?

YU DARVISH, JAPANESE BASEBALL STAR

I've never thought of that. I've never thought of becoming anything other than a baseball player.

日本职业棒球明星 达比修有

铃木一郎、松井、松坂和所有其他日本球员都在美国打得非常好。他们都激励着我成为一名更好的球员。但我现在并没有特别想要打大联盟比赛或去美国打球的想法。

《亚洲名人聊天室》摩根·尼尔

对一个自称喜欢戏剧表演的人而言，您的情绪起伏似乎不大。您不打棒球的时候也是这样吗？

日本职业棒球明星 达比修有

对，我一直都很冷静。

《亚洲名人聊天室》摩根·尼尔

假如您不是在打棒球，您认为自己会做什么？

日本职业棒球明星 达比修有

我从来没想过这点。除了当个棒球运动员，我从没想过自己会做其他事。

even-tempered

性情平和的；沉着的

形容词 tempered 意为"有……脾气的"，常与其他形容词组成复合形容词。类似的用法如下：

good-tempered 好脾气的

ill-tempered 坏脾气的

quick-tempered 暴躁易怒的

short-tempered 暴躁易怒的

- The **even-tempered** dog is perfect for a family with young children.
性情温和的狗最适合家里有小孩子的家庭饲养。

旅美日本球星

姓名生日	铃木一郎 Ichiro Suzuki 1973 年 10 月 22 日	松井秀喜 Matsui Hideki 1974 年 6 月 12 日	松坂大辅 Daisuke Matsuzaka 1980 年 9 月 13 日
原属球队	欧力士猛牛队 Orix Buffaloes 1992~2000	读卖巨人队 Yomiuri Giants 1993~2002	琦玉西武狮队 Saitama Seibu Lions 1998~2006
现任 MLB 球队	西雅图水手队 Seattle Mariners（2001~）	奥克兰运动家队 Oakland Athletics（2011~）	波士顿红袜队 Boston Red Sox（2007~）
投打守位	强打，外野手	强打，外野手	投手

影视娱乐

时尚生活

政治财经

体坛文艺

Battered[1] but Not Broken

Yao Ming Battles Back from Injury to Resurrect[2] His NBA Career

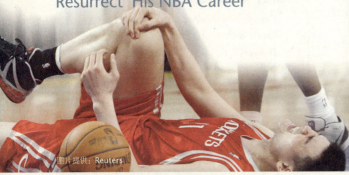

图片提供：Reuters

TERRY BADDOO, CNN ANCHOR

The Houston Rockets Chinese center Yao Ming will play no more than 24 minutes in each NBA game next season as he returns from injury. An NBA game lasts 48 minutes, so Yao will only play half of it. The team's athletic[3] trainer Keith Jones told the *Houston Chronicle* newspaper Thursday that the time limit would be applied[4] strictly, adding that the seven-feet-six-inch Yao would even skip lots of practice sessions[5] to limit the impact on his surgically repaired left foot. Ahead of his long-awaited[6] return, Yao spoke with Anjali Rao for the Talk Asia program.

正常MP3-Track25
慢速MP3-Track55

名人小档案 ▼ 姚明

具有小巨人、移动长城之称的姚明（1980—）来自上海，身高有 2.26 米，小学就开始打篮球，后来进入少年体校。1997 至 2002 年效力于 CBA 上海大鲨鱼队，之后转战 NBA 休斯敦火箭队，曾七度入选 NBA 明星赛。也曾三度代表中国参加亚洲篮球锦标赛，不仅带领中国拿下金牌，而且三次均拿下最有价值球员。2011 年 7 月 20 日，姚明正式宣布退役。

Yao Ming

Notes & Vocabulary

1. **battered** [ˈbætəd] *adj.* 受重创的
   The boxer was battered after his fight.

2. **resurrect** [ˌrɛzəˈrɛkt]
   v. 起死回生；使复活
   The singer released a new album to resurrect her career.

3. **athletic** [æθˈlɛtɪk]
   adj. 体育运动的
   Wilson is not very good at athletic activities.

4. **apply** [əˈplaɪ] *v.* 使用；应用
   The new regulations apply to all players in the league.

5. **session** [ˈsɛʃən] *n.* 一场；一节

6. **await** [əˈwet] *v.* 等候；等待
   Many fans turned out for the singer's long-awaited return to performing.

CNN 主播 泰瑞·巴杜

下个赛季，休斯敦火箭队的中国中锋姚明伤愈复出之后，在每一场 NBA 球赛的上场时间都不会超过 24 分钟。NBA 球赛一场是 48 分钟，所以姚明每次只能打半场。该队的运动伤害防护员凯斯·琼斯周四向《休斯敦纪事报》表示，这项时间限制将会严格执行，并且他指出 7 英尺 6 英寸高的姚明甚至会错过许多日常练习，以减少他术后恢复的左脚所受的冲击。在众人期待已久的复出前夕，姚明来到《亚洲名人聊天室》接受安姿丽访问。

影视娱乐

时尚生活

政治财经

体坛文艺

213

YAO MING, HOUSTON ROCKETS CENTER

Everything looks perfect on pictures, I mean those X-ray pictures, and ~~until~~ today, I'm walking on it well, full pressure on my foot already. But before I start to play the first real NBA game, I still have some [things] I need to [be] concern[ed] about.

ANJALI RAO, TALK ASIA

You know, many thought that your playing days were over when the injury happened. How did you feel when you heard people talking like that?

YAO MING, HOUSTON ROCKETS CENTER

Well, that ~~was~~ shocked me, of course. You know, you play this game almost 20 years, since you know ~~I'm~~ [I was] nine, and one day . . . well everybody know[s] that your career ~~will be~~ [is] going to end ~~at~~ some day. But just I'm not ready for that day yet, right? Maybe I'm 24 or 25, I watch . . . I know my body is kind of like going down every year. I know it's about time, but the day I know that I have a career-ending, threatening . . . that's almost the best time in my career. That's really difficult for me.

ANJALI RAO, TALK ASIA

Yeah, because you were sort of at a high when it happened.

YAO MING, HOUSTON ROCKETS CENTER

Uh-huh. It was about when I was going to reach my peak[7].

前休斯敦火箭队中锋 姚明

在照片上，我是说 X 光片，一切看起来都非常完美。一直到今天，我走起路来也都没有问题，已经把全身重量都压在脚上了。不过，在我真正上场比赛之前，还是有些事情必须注意。

《亚洲名人聊天室》安姿丽

当初你受伤的时候，很多人都认为你的篮球生涯已经结束了。你听到别人这么说，心里有什么感觉？

前休斯敦火箭队中锋 姚明

当然，我很震惊。你也知道，我打篮球已经将近 20 年，从 9 岁就开始打了。有一天……反正大家都知道职业生涯一定有一天会结束，只是我还没准备好那一天的到来，不是吗？也许在我 24 或 25 岁的时候，我看到……我知道我的身体好像年年走下坡路。我知道已经差不多是时候了，可是我知道自己的职业生涯可能即将结束的那一天，却几乎是我职业生涯中最风光的时刻。那对我来说真的很难接受。

《亚洲名人聊天室》安姿丽

是啊，因为事情发生的时候，你的状态正处于高峰。

前休斯敦火箭队中锋 姚明

的确。当时我才正要达到巅峰。

7. **peak** [pik] *n.* 顶峰；高峰

姚明伤病史

2005 年 12 月 左脚大脚趾慢性骨髓炎（osteomyelitis）手术治疗，停赛 21 场

osteomyelitis
骨髓炎是由细菌引起骨骼及骨髓组织的感染和发炎，需长时间使用抗生素治疗，或接受多次的手术治疗。

尽管错过 21 场比赛，姚明还是以最高票数入选了 2006 年度 NBA 全明星赛阵容。

2006 年 4 月 左脚骨折，休息 6 个月
　　　　　12 月 右膝受伤，停赛 34 场

2008 年 2 月 左膝发生应力性骨折（stress fracture），错过 2008 年季后赛

stress fracture
因日积月累、重复施加的压力而导致的疲劳性骨折，也称为"疲劳性骨折"（fatigue fracture）。

2009 年 5 月 脚踝扭伤，检查时发现左脚骨裂（hairline fracture），经讨论后决定接受手术治疗，2009 年至 2010 年赛季均未出赛

hairline fracture
骨裂属于较轻微骨折，骨头上出现细小裂缝。

影视娱乐

时尚生活

政治财经

体坛文艺

ANJALI RAO, TALK ASIA
Are you nervous about getting back on the court?

YAO MING, HOUSTON ROCKETS CENTER
Ah, yes. Now, before we decide[d] what [we] ~~are~~ [were] going to do on my foot, they ~~have~~ [had] different plan[s] come out about how to fix my foot—plan A, plan B and plan C. And we did a lot of researching on them, asking a lot of doctors. And we also asked a few players, either still playing NBA or retired, you know, how they feel after they had that same kind of surgery. You know, they give us . . . they give me a lot of good opinion[s], you know? It's really helpful at [in] the end. So we decide[d] [we're] going to . . . alright, we're going to do this, and we, we are going to see what happens.

ANJALI RAO, TALK ASIA
How tough was the rehabilitation[8] process?

YAO MING, HOUSTON ROCKETS CENTER
Like I just said, I need to be patient.

ANJALI RAO, TALK ASIA
Right.

YAO MING, HOUSTON ROCKETS CENTER
I need to be patient on this. You know, athletes, our attitude . . . our mentality[9] is always to try to be aggressive.[10] We want to be faster, quicker, stronger, and we don't want to waste any seconds. If we can do, like, a double in one day, why ~~we~~ wait ~~to~~ [until the] next day. But on the other side, you know, if

8. rehabilitation [ˌrihəbɪləˈteʃən]
   n. 康复治疗；康复
   The patient faces an agonizing rehabilitation.

9. mentality [mɛnˈtæləti]
   n. 心态；思想状况

10. aggressive [əˈgrɛsɪv]
    adj. 侵略的；有攻击性的
    Martin is an aggressive competitor.

《亚洲名人聊天室》安姿丽
你对于回到球场上会不会紧张？

前休斯敦火箭队中锋　姚明
会啊。在我们决定该怎么治疗我的脚之前，他们提出了许多不同的治疗方案——方案一、方案二、方案三。而且，我们也做了许多研究，问了许多医生。我们还问了几个球员，包括现役与退休的球员，问他们接受了同样的手术之后有什么感觉。他们给了我很多很好的意见，对我帮助良多。于是，我们决定要……要做这个，然后看看结果会怎么样。

《亚洲名人聊天室》安姿丽
康复过程有多困难？

前休斯敦火箭队中锋　姚明
就像我刚说的，我必须有耐心。

《亚洲名人聊天室》安姿丽
是。

前休斯敦火箭队中锋　姚明
我必须有耐心进行康复治疗。你知道，运动员，我们的态度……我们的心态就是随时保持积极心态。我们要更快、更敏捷、更强壮，绝不浪费任何一秒钟。我们如果可以在一天里做两倍的事情，又何必等到第二天。

影视娱乐

时尚生活

政治财经

体坛文艺

you want to take the best care of your body, you have to be patient. You have to slow down[11] at this case, in this case.

ANJALI RAO, TALK ASIA

But your whole career in the NBA has been plagued[12] by injuries, right? I mean you've missed at least 10 games every season since 2005, and that's led some to say that, you know, if it continues, sadly the Rockets might have to say goodbye to you. Do you feel like this season is make-or-break[13] for you?

YAO MING, HOUSTON ROCKETS CENTER

This coming season ~~in~~ [is] my key season. You know, I missed a whole year and I have a very serious injury history, and that would put me ~~on the~~ [at] risk. And also, ~~whoever~~ [whatever] team I play for, I think the team has a risk to take me, to keep me, also. That's . . . I mean that's the truth. We cannot get around that. So, next season I think the first goal I made is [to] play healthy through the season, of course, and then show people how good I can be. Hopefully, [I'll] still be as good as before.

正常*MP3-Track25* / 慢速*MP3-Track55* ▍ *Battered but Not Broken*

但另一方面，如果要好好照顾自己的身体，就必须有耐心。在这种情况下，就必须放慢脚步。

《亚洲名人聊天室》安姿丽

可是你在 NBA 的职业生涯一直不断到受伤病的困扰，对不对？我是说，自从 2005 年以来，每赛季至少缺席 10 场以上的比赛，所以有些人就说，这种情况如果继续下去，火箭队可能就必须和你说再见了。你觉得这一赛季会不会是你成败的关键？

前休斯敦火箭队中锋 姚明

接下来这个赛季是我的关键赛季。我已经错过了一整年，过去也有很严重的受伤历史，那让我面临很大的风险。此外，不论我为哪一队效力，那个球队签下我就必须承受风险，留下我也同样有风险。我是说，事实就是这样，这是无可回避的。所以，我为下一赛季设定的第一个目标，当然就是健康打完整个赛季，并且让大家知道我可以打得多好。希望我的身手能够和以前一样矫健。

---

put sb. at risk
让某人陷入危险

at risk 是指"处于危险的状态"或"承受着风险"，put sb. at risk 就表示"让某人陷入危险"，后面可用介词 of 加上危险的来源或事物。

- The airline's poor safety practices put passengers at risk.
  那家航空公司的安全演习做得不好，让旅客身处危险中。

risk 的其他常见词组

take/run a risk
冒险（做某事）
- If you don't take care of yourself, you run the risk of illness.
  如果你不好好照顾自己，就有生病的风险。

at the risk of doing sth.
冒着……的风险
- Bill is at risk of losing his job if he keeps missing work.
  比尔如果继续旷工，就有丢掉工作的危险。

get around
逃避；规避；欺瞒

get around 就像是绕道而行，所以也就规避了原本的冲突，通常是指"逃避某些规定"的意思。

- Alice can't get around the fact that she is not healthy enough to go back to work after her illness.
  艾丽丝无法逃避自己生病之后仍没康复到能回去上班的事实。

11. **slow down** 慢下来

12. **plague** [pleg] v. 折磨；使受煎熬

13. **make-or-break** [ˈmek ɔr ˈbrek] adj. 孤注一掷的

影视娱乐

时尚生活

政治财经

体坛文艺

Courting[1] Victory

Dreams Come True at the French Open for Chinese Champ Li Na

图片提供：Reuters

NATALIE ALLEN, CNN ANCHOR

China's Li Na is the winner of Saturday's French Open women's final, becoming the first Asian player to clinch[2] a grand-slam singles title[3]. The 29-year-old beat defending champ[4] Francesca Schiavone of Italy in a tiebreak[5]. Li now rises to fourth in world rankings. We get more now from CNN's Kate Giles.

LI NA, 2011 FRENCH OPEN WOMEN'S CHAMPION

Wow, of course it was exciting. You know, after I was lie [lay] down in [on] the clay court[6], I would think [thought], "Oh, this is the true, not only for

正常MP3-Track26
慢速MP3-Track56

名人小档案 ▼ 李娜

来自中国湖北的李娜（1982—），父亲曾是羽毛球选手，她6岁时也开始打羽毛球，教练发现她的臂力很强，因此建议转练网球。1997年李娜加入了中国国家网球队，2008年奥运会之后脱离国家队，转入自负盈亏的职业道路。她至今获得了5个WTA和19个ITF冠军头衔，是中国第一个单打世界排名前10的网球选手。截止2011年6月6日，她的WTA世界排名达到第4位，追平了伊达公子的亚洲选手最高网球单打排名纪录。2011年，李娜在澳大利亚公开赛获得大满贯亚军，并于法国公开赛获得大满贯冠军，成为第一位获得大满贯赛事单打冠军的亚洲网球选手。

Li Na

Notes & Vocabulary

1. **court** [kɔrt] *v.* 争取；招致
   Mandy courted disaster by not saving more money.

2. **clinch** [klɪntʃ] *v.* 成功取得；赢得
   The basketball team clinched a spot in the playoffs.

3. **title** [ˈtaɪtl]
   n. （体育比赛的）冠军

4. **defending champ**
   [dɪˈfɛndɪŋ] [tʃæmp]
   n. 卫冕冠军；上届冠军
   （champ = champion）

5. **tiebreak** [ˈtaɪˌbrek]
   n. 平分决胜局；抢七局

6. **clay court** [kle] [kɔrt]
   n. （网球）红土球场

CNN主播 娜塔莉·艾伦

中国的李娜是周六法国网球公开赛女单决赛的赢家，成为首位夺下大满贯赛单打冠军的亚洲选手。29岁的李娜在抢七局中击败卫冕冠军意大利选手斯齐亚沃尼。如今李娜的世界排名上升到了第四。本台记者凯特·吉尔斯带来进一步的报道。

2011年法国网球公开赛女单冠军 李娜

当然很令人兴奋。我躺在红土球场上以后，心想"这回是真的了，不是梦而已。"我知道现在这在中国是多大的新闻，因为我知道

WTA巡回赛总决赛

WTA巡回赛总决赛（The WTA Tour Championships），又被称为WTA年终总决赛，是国际女子网联在每年年末定期举行的一项国际顶尖女子网球赛事。其参赛者都是每年WTA巡回赛中名列前茅的选手。WTA年终总决赛通常被认为是继四大网球公开赛之后水平最高的女子网球赛事，在该项比赛中获得名次的选手也会获得仅次于大满贯赛事的WTA积分。因此这项赛事被视为每年网坛的压轴好戏。

影视娱乐

时尚生活

政治财经

体坛文艺

the [a] dream." And I know how big [the] news [is] now in China because I know how many people ~~was~~ [were] watching this match. But for me it was good. I mean, right now I just need to enjoy ~~for~~ [it with] the team, because, I mean, [in a] short time I couldn't go back [to] China and then come back ~~European~~ [to Europe] again for the Wimbledon. So I think if I ~~didn't~~ [don't] do well in the Wimbledon, maybe the people will forget me already.

KATE GILES, CNN ANCHOR/CORRESPONDENT
2011 has been a standout[7] year for the 29-year-old veteran. She reached the final of the Australian Open but fell short of winning. But in the months that have followed, she's changed her coach, she's improved on clay and she's developed the mental strength to back up her physical power.

LI NA, 2011 FRENCH OPEN WOMEN'S CHAMPION
I know it was a tough match, of course. I mean, she's [an] amazing clay court player. And I know if I come to the final set[8], [it's] not easy to win. So I just ~~tell~~ [told] myself, OK, hold 'em and stand up again. Try your best. I mean, if you win, you win; you lose, you lose. But I was happy; finally I can win the match.

KATE GILES, CNN ANCHOR/CORRESPONDENT
Li Na is paving the way for tennis in China. After this win in Paris, she should rise to world number four.

有很多人在看这场比赛。但对我来说，这真的很棒。我的意思是，现在我只需要和我的团队享受这一刻，因为短期内我无法回到中国，然后再回到欧洲打温布尔登网球赛。所以我觉得如果我在温布尔登表现不好，也许大家就会把我给忘了。

CNN 主播／特派员 凯特·吉尔斯

2011 年是这名 29 岁老将表现突出的一年。她在澳大利亚网球公开赛中打进决赛，但未能获胜。但在接下来几个月中，她换了教练，提升了在红土球场上的技术，并磨炼出可作为她体能后盾的意志力。

2011 年法国网球公开赛女单冠军 李娜

我当然知道这场比赛很难打。我是说，她是个了不起的红土球员。我知道如果我打进决赛，要打赢并不容易。所以我就告诉自己，撑住，再站起来，尽力而为。我的意思是，如果赢了就是赢了，输就是输了。不过我很高兴，终于能打赢这场比赛。

CNN 主播／特派员 凯特·吉尔斯

李娜正在为中国的网球运动铺路。她在巴黎赢得这场赛事后，她的排名应该可以升到世界第四。这创下了中国网球运动员的纪录。

---

fall short of
未达到

short of 本身有"少于；不足；不及"的意思，与动词 fall 搭配使用时，表示"未达到（预期、标准）"。

- The company fell short of this year's profit goal of $20 million.
  该公司未能达到本年度获利 2 000 万美元的目标。

pave the way for
为……铺路；做好准备

pave 当动词指"铺筑（路）"，pave the way 字面意思是"铺路"，延伸比喻"为……做好准备；提供……的条件"，后面可加 for 再接名词。

- Working in the newspaper office paved the way for the young man to become a reporter.
  在报社工作的经历为这位年轻人铺路，让他当上记者。

---

7. **standout** [ˈstændˌaut]
   n. 杰出的人（或事物）
   Jim is a standout student; he has the highest GPA in the school.

8. **set** [sɛt] n. （网球比赛的）盘

影视娱乐
时尚生活
政治财经
体坛文艺

223

That's a Chinese record. Li Na's success is big news back home. The Chinese sports minister flew to Paris to watch her play, and if an estimated[9] 65 million viewers tuned in to watch her semifinal[10] at Roland Garros, just imagine the figures[11] for her final. Her fans were some of the loudest and the proudest at Roland Garros.

FAMILY OF FANS
    Li Na!

FEMALE TENNIS FAN
    We hope so. It will be so good for the Chinese people.

MALE TENNIS FAN
    I think Li Na is facing a new kind of challenge today, but I think she's a really relaxed and she's in really good form.

KATE GILES, CNN ANCHOR/CORRESPONDENT
    Back at home she's front-page[12] material, and Li Na says if she could write the headline[13] herself, it would read, "Dreams come true."

李娜的成功在家乡是条大新闻。中国国家体育总局官员飞到巴黎看她比赛，如果估计有 6 500 万名观众收看了她在罗兰加洛斯球场的半决赛，想象一下她打决赛时的收视数字。她的球迷是罗兰加洛斯球场中最大声、最骄傲的一群。

球迷家族

李娜！

女网球迷

希望她能获胜。这对中国人来说太棒了。

男网球迷

我认为李娜今天面对了一种全新的挑战，但我认为她真的很放松，而且她的状态非常好。

CNN 主播／特派员 凯特·吉尔斯

回到家乡，她是头条新闻人物。李娜说，如果她可以自己写头条标题，标题会是"梦想成真"。

---

tune in

收听；收看

tune 在此当动词，指"（收音机、电视）调频道"，**tune in** 即表示"收听（收音机）；收看（电视节目）"，后面接 **to**，再加名词。

- Jeff tuned in to the latest inning of the baseball game.
  杰夫收看了那场棒球赛的最新战况。

tune in 其他用法

be tuned in (to sth.)

（对情况）了解；掌握

- The company just doesn't seem to be tuned in to customer needs.
  那家公司似乎不了解客户的需求。

---

9. **estimate** [ˈɛstəˌmet]
   v. 估计；估算
   City officials estimated the cost of the new stadium to be $500 million.

10. **semifinal** [ˈsɛmɪˈfaɪnl] *n.* 半决赛

11. **figure** [ˈfɪgjə] *n.* 数字

12. **front-page** [ˈfrʌntˈpedʒ]
    adj. （报纸）头版的
    The politician's alleged affair was front-page news.

13. **headline** [ˈhɛdˌlaɪn]
    n. 新闻头条；大字标题

影视娱乐

时尚生活

政治财经

体坛文艺

网球场 图解单词

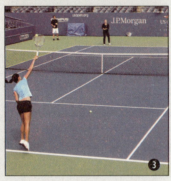

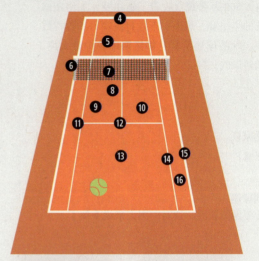

❶ clay court 红土球场
❷ grass court 草地球场
❸ hard court 硬地球场

❹ baseline 底线
❺ service line 发球线
❻ net post 网柱
❼ net 球网
❽ center service line 发球中线
❾ ad court (= advantage court) 左发球区
❿ deuce court [djus] 右发球区
⓫ side T 边 T 字区
⓬ T / middle T 中央 T 字区

⓭ backcourt 后场
⓮ singles sideline 单打边线
⓯ doubles sideline 双打边线
⓰ alley 单打边线与双打边线间的长条状区域
⓱ line judge 边线裁判
⓲ ball boy 球童
⓳ umpire [ˈʌmˌpaɪr] 主裁判

网球动作 图解单词

⑳ serve 发球
㉑ forehand 正（手）拍
㉒ backhand 反（手）拍
㉓ volley 截击
㉔ smash 扣球
㉕ ground stroke 底线抽球

计分板 图解单词

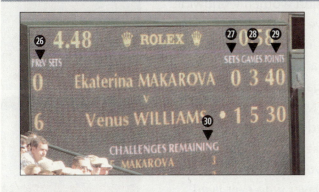

㉖ previous sets 前盘比数
㉗ sets 盘数
㉘ games 局数
㉙ points 分数
㉚ challenges remaining 申请回放（每盘各有三次机会）

比分说法	love 零分	forty 40 分	advantage 领先
	fifteen 15 分	deuce 平分	game 拿下赛点
	thirty 30 分		

影视娱乐　时尚生活　政治财经　体坛文艺

Her Toughest Opponent

How Tennis Champ Martina Navratilova Battled and Beat Cancer

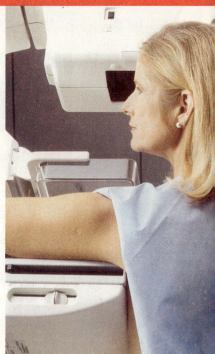

图片提供 :National Cancer Institute / Reuters

DR. SANJAY GUPTA, CNN CHIEF MEDICAL CORRESPONDENT
This year, more than 1.3 million women worldwide will hear the words "you have breast cancer"—four words that will change their lives forever. That single moment will become a turning point, the start of a tenacious[1] battle against a killer. The day she heard those four words, Martina Navratilova cried. A woman who defected[2] from Czechoslovakia at the age of 18, bravely blazed the trail for homosexual acceptance, a woman who many considered the best tennis player who ever lived, now braced for[3] the fight of her life.

Navratilova dominated the competition in the late '70s, '80s and early '90s. She won the Wimbledon singles title a record nine times. With 59 grand

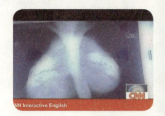

正常MP3-Track27
慢速MP3-Track57

名人小档案▼ 娜拉提洛娃

娜拉提洛娃（1956—）出生于当时的捷克斯洛伐克，8 岁开始参加网球比赛，17 岁正式成为职业网球选手，1975 年申请政治庇护移民至美国，2008 年取得捷克国籍。绰号"女金刚"的娜拉提洛娃在网坛缔造了辉煌纪录，共夺得 18 个大满贯女单冠军，长达 332 周稳坐世界球后之位，纵横单双打赛事。娜拉提洛娃曾在 1991 年出版传记，并在传记中公开她的同性恋性向。2010 年 2 月被检查出患乳腺癌初期，她将此称之为"人生中最难缠的对手"，并用坚毅、积极的态度面对治疗。

Martina Navratilova

CNN 首席医学特派员 桑杰·古普塔博士

今年，世界各地超过 130 万名女性将听到这句话，"你得了乳腺癌"——这几个字将彻底改变她们的人生。听到这句话的那一刻将成为一个转折点，是和这个致命疾病斗争的起点。娜拉提洛娃听到这句话的那天哭了起来。她 18 岁时离开祖国捷克斯洛伐克，为争取社会接纳同性恋勇敢开路，而且被许多人认为是史上最优秀的网球选手，现在却必须准备为自己的生命奋战。

娜拉提洛娃在 20 世纪 70 年代晚期、80 年代与 90 年代初期称霸球场，创下九度赢得温布尔登单打冠军的纪录。她拿下 59 座大满

Notes & Vocabulary

blaze the trail
开拓道路

blaze 当动词指"火焰熊熊燃烧"，**blaze the trail** 的字面意思是"烧出一条小路"，表示拓荒，也就是"做开路先锋"的意思，类似中文"披荆斩棘"。

- Jackie Robinson blazed a trail for African American athletes in major sports leagues.
  杰基·鲁宾逊是非裔美籍运动员跻身运动大联盟的开路先锋。

1. **tenacious** [təˋneʃəs]
   adj. 顽强的；坚忍不拔的
   Connie is a tenacious worker who never gives up.

2. **defect** [dɪˋfɛkt] *v.* 背叛；叛变
   Several athletes defected from North Korea during the sporting event.

3. **brace for** 做准备
   Employees at the company braced for bad news after the financial audit.

影视娱乐

时尚生活

政治财经

体坛文艺

slam tennis titles, she has more titles than any other man or woman.

MARTINA NAVRATILOVA, TENNIS CHAMPION

Well, I had a mammogram[4] in January and they said I need to come back for a closer look. In February, I went back and they magnified[5] it. They said, "well, there's a cluster. Probably do a biopsy[6] just to be sure." First I went to Denver to get the biopsy on a Tuesday and they said, "Ah, it looks pretty good. Should be nothing." Wednesday, my doctor Mindy, who is a very good friend of mine, calls me and says, "Are you sitting down?" And I'm like, "Uh, why?" She said, "Well, it came back positive."

DR. SANJAY GUPTA, CNN CHIEF MEDICAL CORRESPONDENT

Navratilova was struck with the most common type of non-invasive[7] breast cancer. Intraductal cancer[8] is also known as ductal carcinoma in situ, often referred to as[9] DCIS for short. The word "carcinoma" means it begins in the skin or tissue, like breast tissue. This cancer starts inside the milk ducts[10]. In Navratilova's case, the news is encouraging, because the cancer is isolated and had not spread to the surrounding[11] tissue. But like more than a million women worldwide, the diagnosis[12] came as a shock. She didn't feel sick at all. She was the picture of health and fitness. On March 15, Navratilova, surrounded by her support team traveled to the U.S. state of Colorado for the first stage of her treatment—a lumpectomy[13].

A lumpectomy is a surgical procedure to remove the lump along with some of the tissue that surrounds the area. It's a breast preserving surgery, far less

贯冠军，是所有男女网球选手中拥有最多冠军头衔的选手。

网球名将 娜拉提洛娃

一月的时候我做了乳房 X 光片，结果他们说我必须回院进一步检查。二月时，我回到医院，他们把影像放大说，"这里有个肿块，也许做个切片确认一下。"某个星期二我先到丹弗做切片，他们说，"啊，看起来很好，应该没什么。"星期三，我的医生明迪也是我很好的朋友，打了电话给我，说："你现在坐着吗？"我说，"嗯，为什么这么问？"她说，"检验结果是阳性。"

CNN 首席医学特派员 桑杰·古普塔博士

娜拉提洛娃患的是最常见的一种非侵袭性乳腺癌。管内癌又称为乳管原位癌，通常简称"DCIS"。乳管原位癌里的"carcinoma"一词意指这个疾病从于皮肤或组织开始发展，例如乳房组织。DCIS 则是从乳腺内开始。在娜拉提洛娃的病例中，有个令人振奋的消息，因为癌细胞是单独的，没有扩散到周围的组织。不过，和世界各地的 100 多万名女性一样，诊断结果还是让人震惊。她丝毫不觉得身体不舒服，她就是身强体健的形象。3 月 15 日，在支持团队的陪伴下，娜拉提洛娃前往美国科罗拉多州接受第一阶段的治疗——乳房肿瘤切除。

乳房肿瘤切除是一种外科手术，目的在于切除肿瘤和周围的部分组织。这是一种乳房保留手术，比起切除大量乳房组织的乳房切除

4. **mammogram** [ˈmæməˌɡræm] *n.*
   乳房 X 线照片

5. **magnify** [ˈmæɡnəˌfaɪ]
   v. 放大
   The scientist magnified the tiny insect with a microscope.

6. **biopsy** [ˈbaɪˌɑpsɪ]
   n. 切片检查

7. **non-invasive** [ˌnɑnɪnˈvesɪv]
   adj. 非侵入性的
   The doctor used a non-invasive procedure to cure the patient.

8. **intraductal cancer** [ˌɪntrəˈdʌktəl] [ˈkænsə]
   n. 导管内癌

9. **refer to A as B** 把 A 称为 B
   Only tourists and outsiders refer to San Francisco as "Frisco."

10. **milk duct** [mɪlk] [dʌkt]
    n. 乳管；乳腺

11. **surrounding** [səˈraʊndɪŋ]
    adj. 周围的；周遭的
    While staying in Napa County, Donald and Susan spent days exploring the surrounding countryside.

12. **diagnosis** [ˌdaɪɪɡˈnosəs]
    n. 诊断；诊断结果

13. **lumpectomy** [ˌlʌmˈpɛktəmɪ]
    n. 乳房肿瘤切除（术）

radical[14] than a mastectomy[15] in which a lot of breast tissue is removed. The surgery typically takes between 15 and 40 minutes, and scarring is minimal[16], but the lumpectomy is only one step on the journey to become cancer free.

The next stage of Navratilova's treatment, radiation, will begin on May 12. Radiation therapy, also called radiotherapy, is a highly targeted, effective way to destroy microscopic[17] tumors that may have escaped surgery. In Navratilova's case, she will receive radiation therapy four to five times a week for six weeks.

One side effect of radiation therapy is exhaustion[18] caused as the body works to repair damage to healthy cells. Typically fatigue[19] occurs in the later weeks of treatment.

MARTINA NAVRATILOVA, TENNIS CHAMPION
My worst day by far of the six weeks was Friday of the fourth week, which was the day off. I think we played Thursday and then we played Saturday, and Friday I went to hit and I was so tired I lasted about 15 minutes. I had to stop. I had no energy. And I thought . . . and it gets worse, usually.

IWONKA KUCZYNSKA, COACH
She was in pain. She was very tired and I felt like she maybe [might] pass out[20] or something like this. I was very scared for her.

MARTINA NAVRATILOVA, TENNIS CHAMPION
Yeah, it was nice to win. I played better at the second set. I was really tired in the first set—wasn't

术温和得多。这种手术通常需要 15~40 分钟，留下的疤痕也很小，但乳房肿瘤切除术只是摆脱癌症的第一步。

娜拉提洛娃下一个阶段的治疗是利用放射治疗，将于 5 月 12 日开始。放射线治疗又称为放射治疗，是一种高度精准又有效的方法，能够摧毁手术没有切除的极小肿瘤。娜拉提洛娃将接受为期 6 周的放射治疗，每周 4~5 次。

放射治疗有一个副作用，就是人体为了修补健康细胞受到的损坏会造成疲劳。疲惫的感觉通常会在治疗后期出现。

网球名将 娜拉提洛娃
在那 6 周当中，我最惨的一天是第 4 周的星期五，那天没有比赛。我们周四和周六都有比赛，周五练了球，可是我觉得好累，撑了大概 15 分钟。我得停下来，根本没有体力。然后我想……通常情况还会更糟。

教练 伊汪卡·库钦斯卡
她很痛苦。她非常疲惫，我以为她可能会昏倒或什么的。我为她感到很害怕。

网球名将 娜拉提洛娃
是啊，赢球的感觉很好。我在第二盘的表现比较好。我在第一盘真的很累，连球都看不

14. radical [ˈrædɪkəl]
adj. 激进的；极端的
The specialist is considering a radical procedure to replace the burn victim's damaged tissue.

15. mastectomy [mæˈstɛktəmɪ]
n. 乳房切除手术

16. minimal [ˈmɪnəməl]
adj. 极小的；最小的
It took minimal effort for Josie to complete the puzzle.

17. microscopic [ˌmaɪkrəˈskɑpɪk]
adj. 极小的；微小的
Many dangerous diseases are caused by microscopic organisms.

18. exhaustion [ɪɡˈzɔstʃən]
n. 筋疲力尽；疲惫不堪

19. fatigue [fəˈtig] *n.* 疲劳；劳累

20. pass out 昏倒
Several runners passed out from heat stroke.

简单的乳房自我检查方式

女性应该了解自己乳房的情况，并定期做乳房自我检查。检查的方式为站在大镜子前，双手下垂然后高举，注意两侧乳房是否对称、表面是否有不正常凹陷、皮肤是否有橘皮样变化、乳晕周围是否有类似湿疹的病灶。并轻捏乳房看是否有红色或是咖啡色的分泌物。然后在乳房上涂抹肥皂，利用指尖和指腹依照一定方向绕着乳晕滑动，检查是否有不正常硬块。一旦发现乳房有异状，应该立即到医院就诊，避免延误治疗良机。尤其是 40 岁以上的女性更应该特别注意。

影视娱乐

时尚生活

政治财经

体坛文艺

seeing the ball. Then I warmed up, so to speak, and played better, and Jana played well.

DR. SANJAY GUPTA, CNN CHIEF MEDICAL CORRESPONDENT
June 16, the day Martina Navratilova had looked forward to for a while, the day of her last radiation treatment.

Like all women who have been diagnosed with cancer, she will see her doctor regularly for follow-ups[21] to ensure there is no recurrence[22]. She'll also have a mammogram every six months.

MARTINA NAVRATILOVA, TENNIS CHAMPION
I think a lot of people still thought that I had . . . you know, there was still much more serious surgery and then chemo[23] and all this and it was "just radiation," just radiation, so I really feel like I escaped, you know, the big C[24]. It's a very scary word, but I learned a lot and, you know, I hope I don't have to go through something like that for a long time, but if it happens again, I'll be ready.

ductal carcinoma in situ 乳管原位癌

乳房切除

乳房肿瘤切除

放射线治疗

乳管原位癌（简称 DCIS）是最有可能经由定期乳房 X 光检查（mammogram）与临床诊断及早发现的乳癌。一般病人没有明显症状，通常是乳房有小硬块（lump）或乳头出现分泌物（discharge），不过有八成乳管原位癌病患都是经由 X 光检查出来。

治疗方法包含乳房肿瘤切除（lumpectomy）加放射治疗（radiation therapy）、乳房切除术（mastectomy）及荷尔蒙疗法（hormonal therapy）。若不予以治疗，在首次诊断后的平均 10 年内，约有 30% 的病例会发展成侵袭性（invasive）乳腺癌。

正常 *MP3-Track27* / 慢速 *MP3-Track57* | *Her Toughest Opponent*

到。后来我算是已经完成热身运动，所以打得比较好。杰娜也打得很好。

CNN 首席医学特派员 桑杰·古普塔博士

6 月 16 日是娜拉提洛娃期待已久的日子，也就是她接受最后一次放射治疗的日子。

如同所有诊断出癌症的女性，她也将定期复诊追踪，确保病症没有复发。她也会每 6 个月做一次乳房 X 光检查。

网球名将 娜拉提洛娃

我想许多人仍以为我做了很多大手术和化疗等等，但我做的"只是放射治疗"，只是放射治疗。所以，我真的觉得自己逃过癌症的魔掌。癌是个很可怕的字眼，但我学到了很多，也希望再也不必经历这样的事。不过，如果再次复发，我也已经做好准备了。

so to speak
可以说是；可谓
此短语通常是句子中的插入语，用来表示那样的说法也许不太适当或不太准确，不过意思大概如此。

· Todd considers himself an expert, so to speak, on current events.
关于时事，托德自诩为所谓的专家。

21. **follow-up** [ˈfɑloˌʌp]
   n. 后续行动；后续事物
22. **recurrence** [rɪˈkɜːəns]
   n. 复发
23. **chemo** [ˈkimo] n. 化疗
24. **big C** [bɪg] [sɪ]
   n. 癌症（指 cancer）

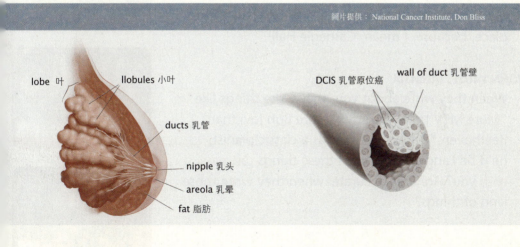

图片提供：National Cancer Institute, Don Bliss

lobe 叶 | llobules 小叶 | ducts 乳管 | nipple 乳头 | areola 乳晕 | fat 脂肪 | DCIS 乳管原位癌 | wall of duct 乳管壁

Unconventional[1] Maestro[2]

CNN Interview with the Remarkable[3] Chinese Pianist Lang Lang

图片提供：Reuters

LANG LANG, PIANIST

It's quite important, actually, to have a proper rehearsal right before the concert tonight. I played my first concert at Carnegie when I was 18 years old, and, from that point on, I fell in love with this place, because, I mean, Carnegie Hall!

JOHN VAUSE, TALKASIA

When they write about you, they write things like "More MTV than Mozart," "More Bon Jovi than Beethoven," "If Jerry Lewis was a classic pianist, he'd be Lang Lang." Do all these things rest easy with you? Are they accurate[4] when they write those kind of things?

正常MP3·Track28
慢速MP3·Track58

名人小档案 ▼ 郎朗

郎朗（1982—　）出生于中国辽宁省沈阳市的一个音乐世家。幼年时期便展露出音乐天赋，年仅9岁便进入中央音乐学院学习。11岁获得德国青年钢琴家比赛冠军。13岁荣获日本柴可夫斯基国际青年音乐家比赛冠军并与莫斯科爱乐乐团演奏肖邦的第二钢琴协奏曲，NHK电视台进行了实况转播。14岁进入美国费城的科提斯音乐学院，随格拉夫曼学习。17岁在芝加哥的拉文尼亚音乐节上代替因病请假的安德烈·瓦兹（André Watts）演奏，自此一鸣惊人，声名大噪。

Lang Lang

钢琴家 郎朗

在今晚的演奏会之前，其实有必要进行一次正式的预演。我18岁的时候在卡内基音乐厅（注）举行了第一场演奏会，从此就爱上了这个地方。我是说，这里是卡内基音乐厅！

《亚洲名人聊天室》约翰·沃斯

评论家写到你的时候，常会这样描述，"比莫扎特还要具备MTV的特质"，"比贝多芬更具备邦·乔维的特质"，"杰瑞·刘易斯如果弹钢琴，一定就像郎朗一样"。你同意这些评论吗？这样的说法正不正确呢？

Notes & Vocabulary

rest easy (with)
放心；不担心
rest easy 原本意思是"放心；不担心"，常用句型是人 + rest easy + 事情。文中的意思较接近 sit well "可以被接受的"，也就是记者问郎朗外界的评论是否可以接受。

· Donna rested easy knowing that her assets were safe in a stable bank.
唐娜知道她的财产安然存放在可靠的银行里，觉得很放心。

其他与 rest 连用的短语

rest assured (that)
尽管放心
· You can rest assured that your secret is safe with me.
你可以尽管放心，我会保守你的秘密。

rest on/upon
依赖；以……为依据
· Personal happiness rests upon an individual's outlook on life.
一个人的快乐在于对人生的态度。

1. unconventional [ˌʌnkən'vɛnʃən]
   adj. 不依惯例的

2. maestro ['maɪstro] n. 大音乐家

3. remarkable [rɪ'mɑrkəbḷ]
   adj. 非凡的；卓越的

4. accurate ['ækjərət]
   adj. 准确的；精准的

注
卡内基音乐厅是在 1819 年由慈善家（philanthropist）安德鲁·卡内基（Andrew Carnegie）出资，威廉·波奈特·杜斯尔（William Burnet Tuthill）设计，具有意大利文艺复兴（Italian Renaissance）时期的建筑风格。卡内基音乐厅位于纽约曼哈顿中城区，是美国著名的古典与流行音乐表演场地。每一季度约有 250 个表演场次。

影视娱乐

时尚生活

政治财经

体坛文艺

LANG LANG, PIANIST

I don't think so. I mean, first of all[5], that it's nice to hear something, you know, fresh or something different than the normal image of a classical musician. But I am playing Beethoven, and I am playing Mozart.

JOHN VAUSE, TALKASIA

Well, but why would they write that kind of thing? Why do you think they have this image of you?

LANG LANG, PIANIST

I don't really know, but maybe I don't play like what they normally expect.

JOHN VAUSE, TALKASIA

Can you explain what happens to you when you get up on stage, when you perform?

LANG LANG, PIANIST

Yeah, actually, that process is the best part of being a pianist, which is when I'm walk[ing] on the stage, it'll feel kind of [like] a time machine. ~~That~~ It is a very short walk, but it's so important. You need to have that walk to bring~~s~~ ~~to~~ you ~~to the~~ next to the piano, and, when you sit down there, you start thinking about the piece you're gonna play. And then, when you start, your finger . . . you know, when your fingers start touching the keys, the journey starts.

JOHN VAUSE, TALKASIA

So everything comes alive.

钢琴家 郎朗

我觉得不正确。首先，能够听到新鲜的说法，不同于古典音乐家的寻常形象，当然很不错。不过，我弹的是贝多芬，是莫扎特。

> 5. **first of all** 首先
> First of all, coffee is delicious.
> Second, it wakes you up.

《亚洲名人聊天室》约翰·沃斯

他们为什么会这么写？你觉得他们为什么会对你产生这种印象？

钢琴家 郎朗

我不知道，也许是因为我的演奏与他们一般的预期不一样吧。

《亚洲名人聊天室》约翰·沃斯

你能不能谈谈自己站在舞台时的感觉，当你开始表演时的感觉？

钢琴家 郎朗

好，实际上，登上舞台是作为钢琴家最棒的部分，走上台的时候，我觉得有点像是搭乘时光机。虽然只是短短的一段距离，却非常重要。你必须走过这段距离，才能到钢琴旁边。坐下来之后，就开始思考接下来要弹的曲目。然后，你的手指放在琴键上，旅程就开始了。

《亚洲名人聊天室》约翰·沃斯

这时一切就都活了过来。

郎朗的音乐经历

11 岁获第四届德国青少年国际钢琴比赛第一名，并获杰出艺术成就奖。

13 岁获第二届柴可夫斯基国际青年音乐家比赛第一名。

14 岁考入著名的美国科蒂斯音乐学院，师从著名钢琴大师格拉夫曼。

17 岁在芝加哥的拉文尼亚音乐节上代替因病请假的安德烈·瓦兹（André Watts），演奏了柴可夫斯基第一钢琴协奏曲，获得满堂彩。

17 岁获伯恩斯坦艺术成就大奖。

24 岁于德国慕尼黑奥林匹克体育场参与世界杯开幕演出。

影视娱乐 时尚生活 政治财经 体坛文艺

LANG LANG, PIANIST
　Yeah.

JOHN VAUSE, TALKASIA
　Are you aware of the audience at the same time?

LANG LANG, PIANIST
　No. No, I don't [I'm not]. I know there's some . . .
　you know, I know there're people listen[ing], who
　listen to you, sitting there.

JOHN VAUSE, TALKASIA
　But it's a blur[6].

LANG LANG, PIANIST
　Yeah. But you don't really know, you know, you
　don't really feel that they are there. But you do feel
　there's a connection between music and yourself
　and the listener.

JOHN VAUSE, TALKASIA
　Last year, you performed at the Grammies.

LANG LANG, PIANIST
　Last year was the 50th anniversary of the Grammies,
　and I had a [the] great privilege to play with
　the great jazz legend Herbie Hancock—that was
　amazing.

JOHN VAUSE, TALKASIA
　Another sort of nontraditional[7] route[8], if you like—
　performing at the Grammies. I think this year, *People*
　magazine's Sexiest Man Alive, I think you were
　number ten. This is not the route that a classical
　pianist normally takes, is it?

钢琴家 郎朗

没错。

《亚洲名人聊天室》约翰·沃斯

你这时候也会意识到观众的存在吗？

钢琴家 郎朗

不会，不会。我知道有人在听，那些人坐在台下听你演奏。

《亚洲名人聊天室》约翰·沃斯

但只是一团模糊。

钢琴家 郎朗

没错。其实你不会真的感觉到他们在台下，但你可以感觉到音乐和你自己还有听众之间的联结。

《亚洲名人聊天室》约翰·沃斯

去年，你在格莱美奖颁奖典礼上演出。

钢琴家 郎朗

去年是格莱美奖 50 周年，我非常荣幸能够和伟大的爵士传奇乐手赫比·汉考克一同演出——那是很棒的经历。

《亚洲名人聊天室》约翰·沃斯

在格莱美颁奖典礼上演出——如果你接受这种说法，这又是一条不太传统的路线。在今年《人物》杂志选出的"年度最性感男人"当中，你好像是第 10 名。这也不是古典钢琴家通常会走的路，对不对？

---

be/become aware of sth.

意识到

aware of sth. 表示"注意到或意识到某件事情"，相当于 conscious of sth.，前面常接 be 动词或 become。

· Halfway through his class, the professor became aware of the fact that he was boring his students.

课上到一半，教授发现他让他的学生感到无聊。

相关用法

wake up to sth.

开始意识到某事的发生

· Allen woke up to the fact that one of his employees was stealing from him.

艾伦终于发现他的一名员工一直在偷他的钱。

---

6. **blur** [blɜ] *n.* 模糊不清的事物
   The bird flew by so fast that all I could see was a blur.

7. **nontraditional** [ˌnɑntrəˈdɪʃən]
   adj. 非传统的
   Dan and Barb wanted a nontraditional wedding that would be held in a bar.

8. **route** [rut / raʊt]
   n. 路线；途径
   The hikers used a map to determine their route back to camp.

影视娱乐

时尚生活

政治财经

体坛文艺

LANG LANG, PIANIST

Yeah, it's not. I mean even when I heard about this "sexiest man alive" interview, you know, they said, and they're gonna do [an] interview with you and stuff. For what? For the Sexiest Man Alive this year. And I was like "Oops! That's pretty cool!" And . . .

JOHN VAUSE, TALKASIA

It was you, and Hugh Jackman, and Daniel Craig, and yeah . . .

LANG LANG, PIANIST

Brad Pitt—I mean, all those great stars. Yeah, it was quite a cool project, actually.

JOHN VAUSE, TALKASIA

When you were 14, you moved to the States?

LANG LANG, PIANIST

Yeah, so, when I was 14, I went to America, and I went to [the] Curtis Institute in Philadelphia. And I remember the first lesson I came to Gary Graffman, my teacher, and I said to him, "Mr. Graffman, I'd like to go into every competitions; I'd like to win all the competitions," you know. And so, and he look[ed] at me. He said, "I mean, this is not the right way for you to think about musically. You're too competitive! You know, you need to calm down[9] and to think about music, not think about [being] number one!"

钢琴家 郎朗

是啊，的确不是。他们说要做"年度最性感男人"的访问的时候，他们说他们要跟你做个访谈什么的。我说为什么呢？他们说是为了今年年度最性感男人这件事。我只觉得："哇！这挺酷的！"然后……

《亚洲名人聊天室》约翰·沃斯

入选的有你，还有休·杰克曼和丹尼尔·克雷格，还有……

钢琴家 郎朗

布拉德·皮特——都是大明星。那确实还挺酷的。

《亚洲名人聊天室》约翰·沃斯

你是在 14 岁的时候搬到美国的吗？

钢琴家 郎朗

是啊，我 14 岁的时候到了美国，就读费城的科蒂斯音乐学院。我还记得我上的第一堂课，老师是盖瑞·格拉夫曼，我当时对他说，"格拉夫曼老师，我想参加所有比赛，我想赢得所有的比赛。"结果他看着我，说，"这不是看待音乐的正确方式。你太好胜了！你要冷静下来，好好思考音乐，而不是只想着要当第一名！"

---

competitive

好胜的；好斗

competitive 为"好胜的；好斗的"之意，常用短语 be competitive with 是指"与……竞争"，也就是"具有竞争力"的意思。

- Stewart is a competitive sales rep.
  斯图尔特是一个竞争心强的业务代表。
- Tim is competitive with his sister.
  提姆与他的姐姐一同较劲。

【同义词】
- aggressive
- combative

9. **calm down** 冷静下来
   The teacher told the excited students to calm down and take their seats.

音乐老顽童格拉夫曼

郎朗的老师盖瑞·格拉夫曼（Gary Graffman）于 1928 年出生，是当今仅存的 20 世纪钢琴大师，在音乐教育方面的贡献非常深远。格拉夫曼自己也是音乐神童，3 岁学钢琴，7 岁就破格进入科蒂斯音乐学院，第一次登台就与奥曼第（Eugene Ormandy）合作，也曾拜塞金（Rudolf Serkin）、霍洛维兹（Vladimir Horowitz）为师，其间所接触的音乐大师都是古典音乐名人堂中的不朽人物。格拉夫曼从 1986 年接掌科蒂斯音乐学院，到 2006 年卸下院长职务，至今仍在该校任教。在这 20 多年间，格拉夫曼教出许多杰出的钢琴家。

影视娱乐

时尚生活

政治财经

体坛文艺

I said, "But this is probably American style, but it's [I'm] Chinese, we like to be, everything, number one." I said, "If you'd like to be a famous pianist, without competition how could you become famous?" He said, "You know, think about it: If you're good, somebody who's having a fever, you know, one day, and then they need to have a last-minute replacement, then, here you comes out, steal the show, then you will become famous.

JOHN VAUSE, TALKASIA
That's exactly what happened.

LANG LANG, PIANIST
That's what exactly happened in Chicago for me. I mean, he's totally right.

JOHN VAUSE, TALKASIA
If this all ended tomorrow, would you be happy with everything you've achieved[10]?

LANG LANG, PIANIST
No.

JOHN VAUSE, TALKASIA
Would you be happy?

LANG LANG, PIANIST
No, no, no. I mean . . .

JOHN VAUSE, TALKASIA
There's more you want to do.

我说，"这也许是美国人的观念，但我是中国人，我们什么都想拿第一。"我说，"你如果想当有名的钢琴家，不参加比赛怎么会出名呢？"他说，"想想看：只要你有实力，说不定哪天有人发烧，临时必须找人代替上场，这时候你就可以把握机会，抢尽风头，从此你就会一鸣惊人了。"

steal the show
抢风头

steal the show 的字面意思是"偷走了表演"，指配角因为表现太突出，让原本的主角大为失色，抢走全场的注意力，引申为"抢风头"的意思。

- Andy stole the show at the party last night.
  安迪在昨晚的聚会上抢尽风头。

10. **achieve** [əˋtʃiv] *v.* 完成；实现
    Taking vitamins with a sensible diet can help one achieve good health.

《亚洲名人聊天室》约翰·沃斯
结果真的就是这样。

钢琴家 郎朗
结果我在芝加哥遇到的情况确实就是这样。他说的一点也没错。

《亚洲名人聊天室》约翰·沃斯
如果你的人生明天结束，你对自己的成就会觉得满意吗？

钢琴家 郎朗
不会。

《亚洲名人聊天室》约翰·沃斯
你会满意吗？

钢琴家 郎朗
不会，不会。我是说……

《亚洲名人聊天室》约翰·沃斯
你还有更多想做的事。

郎朗创造的"第一"纪录

第一位在美国白宫举办独奏会的中国钢琴家，并被美国前总统小布什当场称赞为"世界和平的使者"。

第一位在北京人民大会堂举办独奏会的钢琴家。

第一位在天安门广场演奏钢琴协奏曲《黄河》，并由中国中央电视台向全世界转播演奏实况的钢琴家。

第一位担任联合国儿童和平基金会"国际亲善大使"的钢琴家，也是历来最年轻的。

第一位进入卡内基音乐厅董事会的中国人，也是其历史上最年轻的董事，并名列"当代最伟大的艺术家"。

第一位获得格莱美古典音乐最佳演奏奖提名、并在颁奖典礼上演奏的中国人。

影视娱乐

时尚生活

政治财经

体坛文艺

LANG LANG, PIANIST

There's so much more I want to do. I don't want to end just like this tomorrow. I mean, there's . . . I'm only 26. There's so many years ahead yet.

JOHN VAUSE, TALKASIA

But do you think about the next 10 years, or the next 20 years?

LANG LANG, PIANIST

Yeah, of course.

JOHN VAUSE, TALKASIA

Are you planning that? I mean, where will you be in 10 years time?

LANG LANG, PIANIST

I don't really plan 10 years, 20 years, but I do plan five years.

JOHN VAUSE, TALKASIA

What, well, five years, what's the . . . what's the plan?

LANG LANG, PIANIST

Cut down the concerts and to really develop the education programs around the globe—selective[11] cities. And I['d] really like to inspire more kids, learning piano and to love what we do—make music.

正常*MP3-Track28* / 慢速*MP3-Track58* ┃ *Unconventional Maestro*

钢琴家 郎朗

我还有许许多多想做的事。我不想明天就这样结束。我是说……我才 26 岁，未来还有很长的路。

《亚洲名人聊天室》约翰·沃斯

可是你会想到未来 10 年或 20 年的事情吗？

钢琴家 郎朗

当然会。

《亚洲名人聊天室》约翰·沃斯

你已经在计划了吗？我是说，你 10 年后会怎么样？

钢琴家 郎朗

我不会预先计划 10 年、20 年后的事情，但我确实会做 5 年计划。

《亚洲名人聊天室》约翰·沃斯

那么，你的 5 年计划是什么？

钢琴家 郎朗

减少演奏会，在全球各地的特定城市推广教育方案。我真的很想启发更多孩子学钢琴，并且爱上我们的工作——制造音乐。

---

cut down
减少……的量

cut down 是 "消减；删减；减量" 的意思，后面常用介词 on 加上事物。

- Steve cut down on fats in his diet.
  史蒂夫减少他饮食中的油脂含量。

11. **selective** [sə`lɛktɪv]
    adj. 有选择性的；挑拣的
    My brother said he forgot my birthday because of his selective memory.

影视娱乐

时尚生活

政治财经

体坛文艺

Piano Prodigy[1]

Young Virtuoso[2] Marc Yu
Wrestles[3] with "Little Mozart"
Label and Promising Future

图片提供：Chloe Hui Yu / Jenine Baines

CNN ANCHOR

Well, you know, he is barely tall enough for his feet
to reach the pedals of his piano, but nine-year-old
Marc Yu is already a veteran of the concert halls. His
musical talent singled him out as something out of
the ordinary at the tender[4] age of two, and earned
him comparisons to another child prodigy, Mozart.
Well, we caught up with Marc Yu after he made his
debut at the Royal Albert Hall in London and asked
him for his thoughts on music and his future.

MARC YU, MUSICAL PRODIGY

I can remember how I started to play. I was at a
friend's party when I was about two-and-a-half and
I heard some children singing "Mary Had a Little

正常MP3-Track29
慢速MP3-Track59

名人小档案▼ 余峻承

余峻承（1999—）来自中国澳门特别行政区，是古典乐界知名的音乐神童。3岁就开始弹奏贝多芬的名曲，8岁时就已多次与交响乐团合奏。2005年时他成为最年轻的戴维森学者（Davidson Fellows）获奖者，2007年他为国家地理频道拍摄《天才儿童（Brain Child）》专辑，2008年受中国钢琴家郎朗邀请，于伦敦皇家阿尔伯特音乐厅（Royal Albert Hall）表演，并于2009年与郎朗于纽约卡内基音乐厅（Carnegie Hall）演出。

Marc Yu

CNN 主播

你知道吗？他的个子很小，双脚勉强才能踩到钢琴的踏板，但是9岁的余峻承已经是音乐厅里的老手了。他的音乐天分让他在年仅两岁时便已显得与众不同，并被人拿来和另一名神童——莫扎特做比较。我们在余峻承在伦敦皇家阿尔伯特音乐厅首演后和他碰了面，并且问他对于音乐和他的未来的看法。

音乐神童 余峻承

我还记得当初是怎么开始弹琴的。我两岁半那年在朋友的聚会上听到有小孩子在唱"玛丽有只小绵羊"，于是我就跳到钢琴边弹出

Notes & Vocabulary

single out
使突出；特别挑出

single 当动词是"（单独）挑出；选出"的意思，通常与 **out** 连用，文中是指因优秀而"突出"，有时也表示故意专找某人的麻烦。

· Jack **singled out** Stephanie to lead the sales team to Hong Kong.
杰克特别挑了斯蒂芬妮带领销售团队赴香港。

近义词

distinguish from
从……中区别出；杰出

· Many male birds **distinguish** themselves **from** females with their more colorful plumage.
许多雄鸟的羽毛色彩较鲜艳，与雌鸟显得不同。

out of the ordinary
不寻常的

out of 在这里指"在某界限之上、之外"，**ordinary** 当名词指"平常、一般的状态"，这个短语表示"超乎寻常"、"不同凡响"的意思。

· Investigators searched for anything **out of the ordinary** at the crime scene.
调查员在犯罪现场寻找任何不寻常的事物。

1. **prodigy** [ˈprɑdədʒɪ]
   n. 天才；奇才

2. **virtuoso** [ˌvɛtʃuˈoso]
   n. 音乐好手（演唱或演奏）

3. **wrestle** [ˈrɛsl]
   v. 苦恼；努力应对

4. **tender** [ˈtɛndə]
   adj. 稚嫩的；脆弱的

Lamb," so I jumped on the piano and played out "Mary Had a Little Lamb." But I can remember very well when I was three making my concert debut on the piano playing a G Major sonatina[5] by Beethoven. "Mary Had a Little Lamb" is, of course, a nursery rhyme[6], but you've got to start somewhere.

My job is to interpret[7] the meaning of the piece[8] to the audience. That is actually my job. And Beethoven wants the artist to do that, so I don't think it's that hard for me.

Being called "Little Mozart" is flattering[9]. But it might be a little bit silly because Mozart was a great composer[10]. His mind automatically composed melodies. But my goal is to become a virtuoso, and Mozart was just a good pianist. He wasn't a grand virtuoso, like Franz Liszt.

My goal isn't really to become a composer, but what people really mean by that is saying that Mozart is the general model for children who are amazing musicians, and my playing is brilliant for a child, so I usually take it as a compliment[11].

古典音乐曲式小词典

symphony [ˈsɪmfənɪ] 交响曲

suite [swit] 组曲

march [mɑrtʃ] 进行曲

concerto [kənˈtʃɛrˌto] 协奏曲

sonata [səˈnɑtə] 奏鸣曲

sonatina [ˌsɑnəˈtinə] 小奏鸣曲

serenade [ˌsɛrəˈned] 小夜曲

etude [ˈeˌtud] 练习曲

正常*MP3-Track29* / 慢速*MP3-Track59* | *Piano Prodigy*

"玛丽有只小绵羊"。可是我记得很清楚，3岁那年我举行第一次钢琴音乐会的时候，弹的是贝多芬的 G 大调小奏鸣曲。当然，"玛丽有只小绵羊"是一首儿歌，但是你总要有个开始吧。

我应该要做的是向观众诠释那首曲子的意义。那其实是我的工作，贝多芬要钢琴师做到那一点，所以我不觉得那点很难做到。

说我是"小莫扎特"是一种恭维，但是这样说有点傻，因为莫扎特是个伟大的作曲家。他的心里会自动谱出旋律，但是我的目标是成为一名钢琴大师，莫扎特只是个不错的钢琴师，他并非钢琴大师，这点和李斯特不一样。

我的目标并非成为一名作曲家，但是大家会这么说的意思其实是，莫扎特是那些了不起的儿童音乐家的共同典范，而我的演奏就一个小孩而言算是很棒的，所以我通常都把它当成是一种赞美。

---

what sb. mean by . . .

某人说（做）……的意思是

此语用来表示"某人说或做……的意思是……"，by 后面加上名词或动名词，表示所说的话或做的事。文中的 that 是指前面提到他人称余峻承"小莫扎特"。

- Ruth wondered what her mother meant by telling her to expect a surprise when she got home.
  鲁思在想妈妈跟她说回家时会有惊喜是指什么。

---

5. **sonatina** [ˌsɑnəˈtinə]
   n. 小奏鸣曲

6. **nursery rhyme** [ˈnɜsrɪ] [ˈraɪm]
   n. 儿歌；童谣

7. **interpret** [ɪnˈtɜprət] *v.* 诠释

8. **piece** [pis]
   n. （艺术）作品；曲；篇

9. **flattering** [ˈflætərɪŋ]
   adj. 奉承的；阿谀的

10. **composer** [kəmˈpozə]
    n. 作曲家

11. **compliment** [ˈkɑmpləmənt]
    n. 恭维；赞美

---

rhapsody [ˈræpsədɪ] 狂想曲

ballade [bəˈled] 叙事曲

minuet [ˌmɪnjəˈwɛt] 小步舞曲

scherzo [ˈskɛrtso] 谐谑曲

impromptu [ɪmˈprɑmptju] 即兴曲

divertimento [dɪˌvətəˈmɛnto] 套曲

fantasy [ˈfæntəsɪ] 幻想曲

影视娱乐

时尚生活

政治财经

体坛文艺

附录：美式英语与英式英语和澳大利亚英语的差别

世界上有不少国家以英语为母语，但因地域不同，口音也有所差异，甚至在同一个国家，不同的地区、不同社会阶层都会带有不同口音。这里我们就美语、英式英语和澳大利亚英语中最常见的差异作出说明。

一、英式发音

虽然英音及美音间有一些差异，但也有大致的规则可循。美语是含卷舌音的语言，即 [r] 音会完整发出来。而英国人会把 bigger 去除卷舌音，意思就是词尾的 r 通常不发出来，或者是会弱化成非重音的元音 [ə]，即 bigger 读成 [ˈbɪɡə]、near 读成 [nɪə]、artist 读成 [ˈɑtɪst]，而美国人则读成 [ˈbɪɡər]、[nɪr] 及 [ˈɑrtɪst]。

这两种音调的发音，词尾音常会发得不一样，词尾为 y 的词就是一例。标准英语发音会把词尾 y 发成 [ɪ]，而美语发音则会发成 [i]。例如：英国人读 quickly 会读成 [ˈkwɪklɪ]，但美国人读成 [ˈkwɪkli]。请注意 KK 音标系统对词尾 y 用的音标是用英式发音 [ɪ]，而不是美式发音 [i]。

标准英音与美音之间另一个区别是元音 a 的发音区别。通常，美国人会发 [æ]，而英国人会发 [ɔ] 或 [æ]。例如，美国人把 can 读成 [kæn]，而英国人读成 [kɑn]。但也不是全部如此，例如 pasta 这个词，美国人读成 [ˈpɑstə]，而英国人则读成 [ˈpæstə]。

这里有一段来自英国的饭店前台人员与美国人 Tom 之间的对话，您可仔细听听两种发音的区别。(请听 MP3 Track60）

F.D.: Globetrotters Hotel front desk. May I help you?

Tom: Yes, I'd like to know why there is a man standing in my bedroom.

F.D.: There's a man standing in your bedroom?

Tom: Yes, he seems like a nice man, but he's staring at me very strangely.

F.D.: What does he look like?

Tom: He is tall and thin. He has gray hair on the sides of his head and on top . . . nothing.

F.D.: Is he smiling?

Tom: No, he's just quietly standing there, doing and saying nothing. It seems so strange.

F.D.: What's he wearing?

Tom: A bathrobe. He looks like he's been using my shower.

F.D.: Using your shower? That's unusual.

Tom: I know. I also think it's pretty strange. That's why I called you.

F.D.: Shall I call the police?

Tom: Maybe you'd better. I don't think he should just stand there all night with nothing to do. He'll get bored, and I don't think I can sleep well with him watching me like that.

F.D.: I'll call the police. What's your room number?

Tom: It's 1004.

F.D.: 1004? Let's see. So you are Mr. Johnson?

Tom: No, this is Tom Smith.

F.D.: Are you sure Mr. Smith? I have a Mr. Johnson registered at that room number.

Tom: Yeah, I'm sure my name is Mr. Smith—Tom Smith.

F.D.: Mr. Smith, your room number is 1006. You're looking at Mr. Johnson. You're in his room!

Tom: Oh . . . Thanks, good–bye.

二、澳大利亚英语

澳大利亚英语源于英国伦敦的伦敦（Cockney）腔，如果大家看过电影《窈窕淑女》（*My Fair Lady*）就会有印象，典型澳大利亚发音中有两个元音与一般英音及美音明显不同，一是 [e] 发成 [ai] 而且拉长；一是 [o] 发成 [ɔi] 而且拉长。而词尾及词中的 r 跟其他的英音相同，通常不会读出来。

例如：

emergency, car, sir, heart, prefer, hurt 中的 r 不卷舌。

male, pain 的音近似 [ai]。

side, fine 的音近似 [a]，又带一点 [ɔ] 音，比美音的 [ai] 短。

car, heart 的音比美音 [ɑ] 更长。

bad, allergy 的音比美音 [æ] 扁，近似 [ɛ]。

technician 的音比美音的 [ɛ] 更扁。

shock, hospital, doctor 的音介于 [ɑ] 与 [ɔ] 之间。

这里，虽用 KK 音标来说明澳大利亚英语的特色，但实际上并非能完全用 KK 音标标出，在此只是供读者参考。请仔细听下列这一段澳大利亚人 Sam 与美国人 Tom 之间的对话，以了解这两种发音间的差别。（请听 MP3 Track61）。

Sam: We have an emergency! We have a young male, approximately 25 years old, who has been hit by a car.

Tom: I've been hit by a car?

Sam: Just lie still. Don't move. The subject is bleeding from his side and is in .

Tom: I'm bleeding? Where's the blood? Oh, there it is.

Sam: Please Sir, stay here until the ambulance arrives to take you to the hospital.

Tom: Who are you?

Sam: I am an EMT, Emergency Medical Technician. I saw the accident and I called it in to the hospital.

Radio: This is the Sydney Hospital. Does the subject have insurance?

Sam: Do you have insurance?

Tom: Yes, I have insurance.

Sam: He has insurance. Have you ever had a heart attack or have a history of heart disease?

Tom: No, and no history of heart disease. Am I going to be OK?

Sam: You're going to be fine.

　　对学习者来说，没有哪一种发音才是正确或错误的，可以参考的只有某一地区的标准发音而已（如标准英语、标准美语）。因此，如果您想多了解不同地区口音的异同，您可以利用自己的听力材料，多听各种不同的英语媒体，从中发现其中的区别。

Notes

....

....

....

....

....

....

....

....

....

....

....

....

....